Four Fine Gentlemen

Four Fine Gentlemen

Hester Chapman

University of Nebraska Press

Lincoln and London

Publishers on the Plains

Copyright © 1977 by the estate of Hester Chapman

Printed in Great Britain

First published in the United States of America
by the University of Nebraska Press, Lincoln, Nebraska 68588

Library of Congress Catalog Card Number 77-20589
ISBN 0-8032-1401-4

Contents

Illustrations

Preface

The lives of these seventeenth-century patricians seem to form a pattern underlying a comparatively short period—slightly less than a century—of English history. The first of them, Anthony Ashley Cooper, Earl of Shaftesbury, was born five years after Shakespeare's death; the last, Charles Talbot, Duke of Shrewsbury, died a year before the publication of *Robinson Crusoe*. The careers of all four are connected; and their characters are in strong, almost violent contrast with one another.

Shaftesbury was a political revolutionary and innovator, whose genius brought him from eminence to infamy and disgrace. When Sir William Temple's diplomatic achievements gave place to private life, his charm and humour were enhanced, both by leisure and by the protean nature of his hobbies and gifts. Sir John Reresby, a sharp-witted, Church-and-King Yorkshire squire, became the spectator and recorder of high drama under Charles II and James II. The haunted, over-sensitive, accomplished Duke of Shrewsbury, abjuring power and influence, sank into a neurotic condition unique in an age to which he was utterly unsuited.

From these men's fragmentary memoirs and their diaries and letters, it is possible to catch glimpses and hear the voices of their most celebrated contemporaries—kings, queens, ambassadors and statesmen. Not only so; as privileged persons, they dealt familiarly with a cross-section of the common people of England, France and the Low Countries. They were as much at their ease in taverns or coffee-houses as in courts and palaces: as ready to face acclaim or abuse in national assemblies as at the gatherings of the merchant classes. Hobnobbing with the great, they were equally unconstrained in the company of spies, prostitutes and broken men. A brief reconsideration of this quartet might therefore pass as entertainment—a breathing-space in the more strenuous pursuit of historical knowledge.

Anthony Ashley Cooper
1st Earl of Shaftesbury
(1621—1683)

Also, I heard the voice of the Lord, saying,
Whom shall I send, and who will go for us?
Then said I, Here am I: send me.

Isaiah, vi, 8

Anthony Ashley Cooper, 1st Earl of Shaftesbury
after J. Greenhill

In the summer of 1610 Sir Anthony Ashley, then in his sixtieth
year, gave up his post as Clerk of the Council to James I, and
retired to his manor of Wimborne St Giles in the county of Dorset. Formerly an Elizabethan sea-captain, he could look back on
an adventurous and profitable career; he had served under the
Earl of Essex at the siege of Cadiz, and accompanied Sir Francis
Drake on his Portuguese expedition, thereafter submitting to a
charge of peculation, for which he was sentenced to imprisonment in the Fleet. This slight setback in no way affected his status
as a wealthy and respected landowner whose talents and interests
had made him something of a celebrity, not only because of his
naval exploits, but as the translator from the Latin of *The Mariners'
Mirror*, for many generations the handbook of those concerned
with charting the Atlantic and the Mediterranean. His fame was
also associated with a more lasting achievement; his introduction
of cabbages into England. Having grown this then exotic
vegetable with success, he set about improving his property; he
built almshouses, restored the parish church, and so added to his
land that it spread to the borders of Hampshire on one side and
those of Wiltshire on the other.

He was a widower; and now began to look out for a suitable
husband for his only child and heiress, Anne, a diminutive and
somewhat characterless girl in her late teens. His choice eventually
fell on Sir John Cooper of Rockbourne, whose lands included
properties in Hampshire, Staffordshire, Derbyshire and Middlesex, and whose only fault was his taste for gambling; in every other
way he fulfilled Sir Anthony's requirements. In 1616 the young
couple were married and set up house with Sir Anthony, who,
corresponding rather sycophantically with Sir Robert Cecil,
seems to have angled for a peerage and a place at Court for his
son-in-law.

These schemes came to nothing; nor did Anne Cooper at once
produce the heir desired by her father. Several children died in
infancy; and it was not until 22nd July 1621 that she gave birth

to a boy who was to become, first, a Royalist captain, then a Parliamentarian general, then a Royalist again, and, finally, Chancellor of the Exchequer, Privy Councillor to Charles II, Baron Ashley, Earl of Shaftesbury and Lord Chancellor of England.

His grandfather, continuing to direct the Coopers' affairs, decided that he should be baptized as Anthony Ashley; he selected his wet-nurse, a tanner's wife, and his godparents, two of whom, Henry Hastings and Lady Norton, were to be major influences in his youth. There was one disappointment. This longed for and treasured grandchild was, like his mother, undersized and inclined to delicacy.

He grew up in a setting that combined picturesque shabbiness and orderly planning with all the splendours of untamed nature. The ancient house looked out over formal grounds. Encircling the hollow in which they lay was the forest, richly coloured from spring to autumn, and in winter lowering, a little sinister. St Giles, cut off from the village, almshouses and church by the heavy luxuriance of oak and ash, seemed more remote than was really the case; it had a certain mystery, as of an enchanted dwelling in a medieval legend. Its influence seems to have created a sense of power. A clever and sensitive child would feel himself a person of some importance in such surroundings; and as his infancy came to an end, old Sir Anthony's heir, the hope of his house, at the same time indulged and stimulated, appears to have entered into dreams of greatness that eventually became reality. This tendency was increased by the fact that the Coopers were very rich; even Sir John's gambling made but slight inroads on their wealth. And Sir Anthony had always been an excellent administrator; his gift for financial organization was inherited by his grandson.

As soon as the child was born, Sir Anthony sent for a German astrologer and physician, Dr Olivian, 'greatly skilled', Shaftesbury recalls, 'and very learned in nativities'. He foretold 'great things' for him, some of which, as the Doctor did not fail to point out, came to pass before the subject of them reached maturity.

Very early in life, at about the same time that young Anthony came under the jurisdiction of his first tutor, a strict Puritan ('Youth,' said his grandfather, when engaging this gentleman, 'cannot have too deep a dye of religion'), he began to assess his elders. His mother, although 'modest and virtuous', was negligible, his father 'very lovely and graceful in face and person . . . and of an easy and affable nature'. But his grandfather was magnificent —'of a large mind in all his actions . . . scarce paralleled in his age', wise, courageous, and never tired of his grandson's company. 'He grew every day more and more fond of me,' Shaftesbury says. The old man delighted in little Anthony's chatter. Fifty years later, Shaftesbury remembered himself as 'a prating boy, and very observant' of the head of his house.

In 1626 Sir Anthony, now over seventy, decided to strengthen his position by marrying an heiress. His choice fell on a widow of nineteen, Mrs Philippa Sheldon, a relation of James I's and Charles I's egregious and detested favourite, George Villiers, first Duke of Buckingham, from whom, according to Shaftesbury, 'he expected great preferment' for himself and his son-in-law. Again, nothing came of this plan, and Sir Anthony occupied himself with the education of the child who would inherit the greater part of his fortune, and whose second tutor, Dr Guerdon, made a parade of piety. However—'business and conversation in the world,' said his employer, 'will wear it to a just consideration.' Meanwhile, the pupil soon perceived that Dr Guerdon was 'a great lover of money' and inclined to hypocrisy—'but he served well enough for what he was designed for, being formal, and not vicious'.

In January 1628 Sir Anthony died, and six months later Lady Cooper, who had given birth to another boy, George, and a daughter, Philippa, followed him to the grave. Sir John Cooper then married a City heiress, the widowed Lady Morrison; he died in March 1631, leaving his children with a stepmother and a stepgrandmother. And so Anthony Ashley Cooper, now in his tenth year, became an orphan. He may have mourned his grandfather; he did not miss his parents. He was already, and rather alarmingly, self-sufficient; and he believed that he could look forward to a successful future, as long as it was based on the support of the Protestant religion. For Dr Guerdon had convinced him that the danger of Roman Catholicism still threatened his country, and that he was destined to be one of those who must combat the invasion of popery. Then, and for the next generation, an enforced return to the old faith continued to be a nightmare in the imaginations of the majority of English people.

Sir John Cooper had appointed his brother-in-law, Edward Tooker, and Sir Daniel Norton, the husband of Anthony's godmother, as his children's guardians; and for the next four years they lived with the Nortons at Southwick in Hampshire, or in their London house in Fleet Street. The young baronet was now in a very difficult position; for his father's debts amounted to some £35,000, and his estates, passing, as was then the custom in the case of a minor, into the hands of the Court of Wards, were in danger of exploitation, either by Charles I or by his courtiers, who might get leave from the King to buy them cheap and sell them at a profit. Prolonged litigation began between his guardians on the one side and his great-uncle, Sir Francis Ashley, Sir William Button and old Mr Tregonwell ('one that never knew generosity or kindness but for himself', Shaftesbury recalled) on the other. Of these three predators, Sir Francis was the most dangerous, for he was the King's Serjeant-at-Law and a close friend of the Attorney of the Court of Wards.

Sir Daniel Norton not only informed Anthony of the progress of his case, but encouraged him to attend the hearings. Finally, he allowed him personally to plead his cause with the Attorney-General, which he did so eloquently that that official announced, 'I will defend it, though I lose my place.' At the last hearing, presided over by the Master of the Wards, Sir Francis Ashley spoke with equal brilliance; and Anthony's heart sank when the Master remarked, 'Sir Francis, you have spoken like a good uncle.' The Attorney-General then replied, it seemed without effect, while Anthony's guardians resigned themselves to defeat. The boy, seeing his case as desperate, appealed to God as his great-uncle got up to conclude. Sir Francis began—and fell, 'his mouth,' Shaftesbury says, 'drawn down to his ear, was carried out of the Court, and never spoke more'.

The effect of this response to his prayer on a lad of fourteen— who had been taught to feel God's hand in all his doings—cannot be overestimated. Henceforth, many of his speeches and letters, and even, sometimes, his everyday talk, embodied a conviction of being in the right, whatever the issue. In fact, he could not be wrong, because he was directly guided by his Puritan Deity. The magic potion of those divine commands inspired and supported his tergiversations, his changes of policy, his contempt for those who withstood him, his defiance in the face of danger.

He had been shown the way—one with many deviations, some of which led to power and greatness—and he must follow it. His prescience, his sudden desertions of the losing for the winning side, before either party realized what the future held, although instinctive, were generally attributed by him to the instructions of the God who had struck down his wicked uncle in the moment of victory. The Court of Wards was Shaftesbury's road to Damascus. St Paul himself was not more fanatically dedicated to his cause than the boy who was to achieve distinction as a soldier and a statesman, and who finally became the apostle of revolution, violence and terror. His sense of rightness grew into a habit that was to sustain him when his orthodoxy yielded to free-thinking.

When Sir Daniel Norton died in 1638, Anthony went to live with the Tookers at Salisbury, every now and then going over to St Giles, where he had his own horses and hounds; so he began to take his place in local society. Soon after his sixteenth birthday he went up to Oxford, attended by two servants and a tutor; there, within a few weeks, he became a celebrity.

By this time he had overcome his disadvantages; for his indifferent health and lack of height generated what would now be described as a compensatory determination to excel, enhanced by an ingenuity that increased with success. As he could not begin to compete in the displays of athleticism and brute strength in which many of his fellow students delighted, he set about discovering their weaknesses. One of these was overexpenditure; he therefore collected a group of supporters by giving or lending money to those in difficulties, and so became their leader and adviser. The watering down of the college beer was one of the students' grievances; and when they consulted him, he proposed that they should all remove their names from the buttery books —with the result that the authorities, seeing their profits disappear, 'struck sail,' as he puts it, 'and articled with us never to alter the size of our beer.'

Anthony followed up this minor triumph by organizing an attack on the ancient and odious tradition described by the seniors as 'tucking' the freshmen. This was a form of initiation. The older boys, having summoned their juniors, one by one, first scraped their faces from the lips to the chin, and then forced them to drink a beer-glass of salt water, taking care that the wound should be soaked in the mixture. Anthony convened a party of

'stout and very strong' freshmen—'giant-like boys' —who stood
ready for the signal agreed to, that of his boxing the first bully's
ears. The freshmen then fell on, so belabouring the seniors that
they had to make terms. When the Master came upon the scene,
he supported the freshmen, which caused, says Shaftesbury,
'the utter abolition . . . of that foolish custom'.

This way of dealing with those he could never have defeated
alone was to characterize Ashley Cooper's whole career. His
habit of moving into a position of strength became subtler, but
did not otherwise vary; the resultant power carried him from one
triumph to another for nearly forty years.

He left Exeter College in 1638 in order to study law at Lincoln's
Inn. Now it was time that he should be suitably married. His
guardian advised him to approach the Lord Keeper Coventry.
Of the Lord Keeper's four daughters, Anthony preferred the
eldest, Margaret; they were exactly of an age—seventeen—and
his admiration for her increased with his visits to her parents, who
received him eagerly; for they knew that Dr Olivian had advised
him to ally himself with another family.

Anthony was so much taken with Margaret Coventry that his
usual aplomb deserted him. Chatting and jesting with her sisters,
he found himself unable to pay her the attentions expected of a
suitor; and so her parents came to the conclusion that he did not
want her. Eventually, they asked him which of their girls he
favoured, and, 'that being cleared', he says, 'all matters went
successfully on'. They were married in February 1639, and set up
house with her parents in Canonbury. A little later they moved into
St Giles, where Anthony fell more than ever in love with this
'lovely, beautiful, fair woman', who combined the Christian
virtues with 'wit and wisdom beyond any I ever knew, yet the
most sweet, affectionate, observant wife in the world . . . exceed-
ing all in anything she undertook'.

This happiness had one flaw: his increasingly poor health; for
few days passed without very severe pain in his left side. He
endured it stoically—'for I hated pitying, and loved merry company'. In the evenings, he entertained his guests with his skill in
palmistry and fortune-telling, being secretly primed by his valet,
who found out from the other servants various personal
details and family intrigues that his master would then present
as the result of his own powers of divination. This harmless

cheating was to take another and rather sinister form in his later years.

Shaftesbury's most enjoyable memory of his early manhood was of his godfather, Mr Henry Hastings, 'son, brother and uncle to the Earls of Huntingdon', and a perfect example of the old school –that school which has never been young. This gentleman's clothes—'always green cloth, and never all worth when new £5': his pets—the spaniels and cats that prowled about his trencher at meals: his library, of two books, the Bible and Foxe's *Acts and Monuments*: his 'old green hats with their crowns thrust in so as to hold ten or a dozen eggs': and the pulpit in his chapel, stuffed with venison pasties and apple tarts—all these were unforgettable. A bachelor, he took his pleasure with his tenants' wives, always speaking kindly to their husbands, whom he entertained with beef puddings and small beer. Impressed and amused by this democratic concupiscence, his godson made it his business too to be agreeable to everyone who did not stand in his way, while envying the old gentleman's magnificent physique (he died in his hundredth year) and his ability to hunt at the age of eighty. All his life, Shaftesbury was inspired by Mr Hastings' abstemiousness, his care for detail, his gaiety, simplicity and genial contempt for the conventions. He himself, elegant, sophisticated and witty, yet maintained, when occasion required, the blunt forthrightness and independence of mind that had characterized his godfather.

From 1639 till 1642 Ashley Cooper's existence was busy and peaceful, one of country pursuits and domestic contentment. His neighbours sought him out, delighting in his company; his wife adored him; his financial worries were at an end. So he found time to exercise his charm as an entertaining, rather unusual host and friend. He was also, secretly, ambitious. He desired a more brilliantly lit stage, a higher sphere for talents he now knew to be far above average. The opportunity for their display came suddenly. He used it as became his temperament and background—deliberately, and with an eye to the future.

2

In 1640 Ashley Cooper, then in his nineteenth year, tried and failed for election as a Member of Parliament; but this did not affect his resolve to enter a scene in which Pym and Hampden were now famous, and London was becoming the centre of revolution. He left St Giles to stay with his younger brother-in-law in Worcestershire, hoping to stand for election in that district; here again, his efforts were unrewarded. His opportunity came when he and Thomas Coventry were invited by the burgesses of Tewkesbury to a hunt, followed by a dinner. Their hosts were of the Puritan-Protestant persuasion, therefore much concerned about what they considered the 'popish' tendency of the Court party, and deeply suspicious of Queen Henrietta Maria's influence —although they may not have known that she had already appealed to the Pope for men and money to subdue the 'rebels' in Parliament. One of the guests was old Sir Harry Spiller, 'a crafty, perverse, rich man in power, as being of the Queen's Privy Council, a bitter enemy of . . . the Puritans, as rather inclined to the Popish way'. This gentleman, sitting opposite Cooper, took it upon himself to rally and then to insult the Tewkesbury burgesses about the quality of their entertainment. He was at once challenged, mocked, and finally defeated by Cooper, who achieved 'a perfect victory' over him. The delighted townsmen asked their youthful defender to represent them in the Short Parliament, which was dissolved by Charles I in May of the same year.

Cooper was not elected for the Long Parliament, and took no share in public affairs till the outbreak of the Civil War in 1642, when the King raised his standard at Nottingham. Here he joined the Royalists as a spectator. A year later he organized a regiment of foot and a troop of horse for Charles I at his own expense. But having come to the conclusion that war must and could be avoided, he decided to approach the King with a view to arranging an agreement. With characteristic self-assurance the twenty-one-year-old peacemaker began, 'I think I could put an end to the war, if Your Majesty pleased.' Desired to proceed, he proposed to act as intermediary between the Roundhead leaders and those of the Cavaliers, truthfully adding that both sides were already weary of the struggle, and that a free Parliament 'should do what more remained to be done for the settlement of the nation'. 'You are a young man, and say great things,' the King coldly replied, and dismissed him. Under the jurisdiction of Charles's German nephew, Prince Maurice, and the Marquess of Hertford, Cooper continued to support the Royalists; but the King's rebuff resulted in his looking on their efforts with a critical eye.

When Dorchester, Weymouth and Portland surrendered to the King, the Royalist troops disobeyed orders and sacked all three cities, upon which 'some pretty hot words' passed between Cooper and Prince Maurice. The younger man was then given the governorship of Weymouth; having held this post for a year, he was removed from it and made Sheriff of Dorset instead. This deprivation, followed by an inadequate consolation prize, Charles I's refusal to listen to his advice, and the news that the King had not only made peace with the Irish Catholics, but was about to enlist them, convinced Cooper that he must change sides. 'The King's aim,' he says . . . 'was destructive to religion and the state.' He therefore 'cast himself on God . . . and privately came away to the Parliament . . . resolving to follow the dictates of a good conscience'. This step entailed the loss of his estates: but that must be put up with, in view of the fact that he was—as in the case of his great-uncle's attempts on his inheritance—divinely favoured. His sacrifice having been accepted by Parliament, he and his wife remained in London till July 1644, when he was commanded to return to Dorset as 'field marshal' of a Roundhead brigade, in order to take Wareham from the Royalists. When that town surrendered, he was made commander-in-chief of the Parliamentary forces in Dorset, and his estates were restored. He then decided to attack a key stronghold, that of Abbotsbury manor and church, garrisoned by Sir John Strangways for the King.

The ensuing siege was fiercely prolonged. When Sir John refused to surrender, Cooper's men, led by himself, succeeded in entering the church and capturing those inside it. Again, he called on Strangways to yield: and when Sir John 'disdained to answer . . . we fell on', and, after a six hours' struggle, 'it pleased God at last to give us the place'. When the Royalists asked for quarter, Ashley Cooper replied that the rules of war made that impossible, took Strangways and his brother prisoner, and set fire to the manor house, which was burnt to the ground. He then overcame the strongholds of Sturminster Newton and Shaftesbury, moving on to relieve Taunton in December 1644. So it became increasingly clear that God was still directing him; but as his health had broken down, he summoned his wife to join him at Tonbridge, where he drank the waters. He then returned to civil life, the administration of his estates, and his duties as High Sheriff of Wiltshire and Justice of the Peace for that county and Dorset. His military career was over—and also, all hope for the success of the Royalist cause.

This period of withdrawal would have provided great happiness for both the Coopers, had it not been for his indifferent health and her inability to produce an heir. She had had several miscarriages; and in the autumn of 1647 gave birth to a dead girl. Her husband's devotion to her was shadowed by anxiety, which took the form of sending her to try various cures (all ineffectual) while his admiration for her talents—in 'housewifery, preserving, works with the needle, cookery' —increased. 'Her wit and judgement,' he adds, 'were expressed in all things.' They were often parted; for his duties made it necessary for him to sit on a number of committees and to attend courts of justice in Salisbury, Dorchester and Blandford. There, obtaining reprieves for some, he gave sentences of death, burning in the hand and the pillory, for others. These sessions alternated with meetings on the bowling green, dinners for his neighbours, an occasional day's hunting and visits to London.

So he had no share in the final defeat of the Royalist forces, the Scots' sale of Charles I to Parliament, and the disputes between the different parties in the Commons. The struggle for mastery by Presbyterians, Independents and Levellers, the triumph of Cromwell's New Model army, that army's purge of the House in 1648, the consolidation of Cromwell's authority, his decision to try the King for murder and high treason, the establishment of a Republic—all these events formed the background of Cooper's existence. By degrees, their impact convinced him of the need for national freedom; that became the cause he maintained throughout his days of power. Yet his conception of it was anomalous. He saw England's liberation from anachronistic tyranny in terms of the mass, impersonally. Individuals must therefore sometimes be sacrificed. It was expedient that men, and women too, should be spied on, hunted down and suffer death for the people, a people led by himself—and God, naturally. That such aims presupposed another kind of tyranny—perhaps a worse one—was not considered by Ashley Cooper, then or later. Nor could he have foreseen that his methods would drive them into increasingly belligerent opposition to whatever government, monarchist, republican or military, prevailed. That ambition had become the mainspring of all his actions was rationalized by his picture of himself as a patriot dedicated to a cause which might change its outward form, while remaining basically inviolable.

He now sought re-election before arming himself for the struggle; but his having fought for the Royalists barred his entry to Parliament. His gallantry and competence as their general did not promote his joining Cromwell's government in any capacity. He seems to have been content with his local duties, to the point indeed of disregarding the upheavals in the Rump Parliament. Yet its proclamation of 4th January 1649 became his political slogan. It ran 'that the people are, under God, the original of all just power; that the Commons of England . . . being chosen by and representing the people, have the supreme power in this nation; that whatsoever is enacted . . . by the Commons in Parliament assembled, hath the force of law . . . although the consent of the King or the House of Peers be not had thereunto'.

On 20th January the trial of Charles I began; sentence of death was passed on the 27th. On the 29th Ashley Cooper left St Giles for London, reaching Bagshot on the 30th—the day of the execution—where he stayed the night, arriving at his house in Lincoln's Inn Fields on the 31st. He made no written comment on an event described by many as the most horrible crime since the Crucifixion ('women miscarried, men fell into melancholy, some with consternations expired') but all his life he waged war—sometimes deviously and always ruthlessly—on the principles set out by the King in his speech from the scaffold.

'For the people, [Charles said] truly I desire their liberty and freedom as much as anybody whatsoever. But I must tell you, their liberty consists in having government . . . *It is not their*

having a share in the government; that is nothing appertaining to them. A
subject and a sovereign are clear different things.'

Some years later, Cooper came to the conclusion that he himself
—with a few others of his own choosing—must decide what the
people's share in the government should be. Meanwhile, he
resigned himself to private life. This was not difficult, for he was
fully occupied with local business, and hopeful that his wife's
fourth pregnancy would result in an heir; she was within six
weeks of her time and apparently in good health.

On 10th July they were at St Giles, and about to sit down to
supper, when she had a stroke. Put to bed, she seemed to recover,
looked up, spoke and kissed her husband: she reassured him—her
head ached, but that was all—and then had another stroke, followed by several more. So the night passed. At noon the next
day she died.

His grief broke out in an agony of praise. That lost and lovely
creature was 'far beyond any woman'. Their nine years' marriage
had been perfect—so it seemed in recollection—and existence
without her was unendurable. As he had no children, and nothing
but his duties to live for, he decided to marry again. On 25th
April 1650 he became the husband of the seventeen-year-old
Lady Frances Cecil, sister of the Earl of Exeter, a staunch but
still wealthy Royalist. In 1651 she bore a son, who died in
infancy. In the following year she gave birth to another Anthony
Ashley, who lived to inherit his father's titles and continued his
line.

Cooper then set about rebuilding St Giles. The rather ram-
shackle Elizabethan structure was replaced by an elegant but
unpretentious mansion in the Palladian style of red brick with
stone facings; and here, as if he were already prepared for re-entry
into public life, he received a summons from Cromwell, who had
dissolved the Rump Parliament, and was about to begin his campaign of administrative reform. It was therefore announced that
'Sir Anthony Ashley Cooper baronet be ... pardoned of all
delinquency', and elected to sit on the Council of State. He soon
became the friend and collaborator of the Lord Protector,
achieved increasing influence in the short-lived 'Barebone' Parliament, and negotiated peace with the Dutch emissaries after
Monk's victory over Van Tromp. In the summer of 1652 his wife
died; but he was now too busy to consider a third marriage—he

ceased to keep a diary—and the rumours of his offering his hand
to one of Cromwell's daughters were unfounded.

In August 1654 he became President of the Council. One of
his duties was that of tracking down Royalist conspiracies; and in
an interview with a Dorsetshire suspect, who sent an account of
Cooper's methods to the exiled Charles II, his technique is seen as
approaching its apotheosis. He began his examination in the
manner afterwards described by his enemies as wheedling. He
and the prisoner, Colonel Robert Phelips, were old acquaintances,
and had often hunted and played bowls together. So Cooper,
having greeted the Colonel as a friend, asked for the names of the
other plotters. These being denied him, he gently observed,
'Truly, I pity you; you will cast yourself away by standing upon
these punctilios of honour.' This oblique threat had no effect;
eventually Phelips succeeded in convincing Cooper that he had
had no share in any conspiracy, and was released.

Cromwell's victories at Dunbar and Worcester and his successful war with Spain prevented anarchy, but did nothing to subdue
his enemies in Parliament. In this conflict, Ashley Cooper became
one of his most valuable, albeit temporary, allies. Elected in the
new Parliament, his combination of humour and invective made
him a formidable adversary of the militant, Republican party, who
refused to sign the declaration of loyalty to the Protector. Cromwell rejected the offer, urged on him by Cooper, that he should
be proclaimed King; so the two men parted, while Cooper,
retiring from the Council, joined the Opposition, apparently on
the grounds that Cromwell had submitted to the militants, and
was about to divide up the country into districts ruled by the
major-generals, a dictatorship his former ally tried to defeat.
When Cooper's reputation as an anti-Cromwellian reached the
exiled Royalists in February 1655, Charles II wrote offering him
a pardon and a place in the government in return for his furthering
a restoration. 'Your experience tells you,' the King added, 'how
unsettled all things must be till I am restored to that which belongs
to me . . . and you are master of too good a fortune not to desire
this security.'

But Cooper had decided on another period of waiting, and
ignored this approach, while considering a private alliance with
the Cavaliers. His choice fell on Lady Margaret Spencer, the
twenty-eight-year-old niece of Lord Southampton, and sister of

the Earl of Sunderland who had been killed fighting for Charles
I. She came to him with a dowry of £4,000, and was a devoted
wife. This connection with two leading Royalist families brought
her husband under suspicion of treachery to the government; but
he remained firmly neutral till January 1656, when he was again
elected as Member for Wiltshire. Cromwell, seeing him as a political enemy, excluded him from sitting, but received him as a friend;
he used to say, not quite seriously, that he knew no one so difficult
to manage as 'the little man with three names', and allowed him
to sit in January 1658 as a member of the Opposition. Cooper
took the opportunity to speak against the establishment of a new
House of Lords, which he did with great force and wit. Cromwell
dissolved this Parliament in February, ruling (as Charles I had)
without one till his death in September, when he was succeeded
by his son Richard.

The nineteen months that elapsed between the Protector's
death and the Restoration plunged the English people, of whatever persuasion, into confusion and anxiety. The public state of
mind is best described by a ballad circulated before the execution
of Charles I.

> Now thanks to the Powers below
> We have even done our do,
> The Mitre is down, and so is the Crown,
> And with them the Coronet too . . .
> Then let's have King Charles, says George,
> Nay, we'll have his son, says Hugh,
> Nay, then let's have none, says jabbering Joan,
> Nay, we'll all be kings, says Prue.

Of the few who kept their heads, and continued to speak with
precision and point, the most notable was Ashley Cooper—though
he had nothing but contempt for the Georges, Prues and jabber-
ing Joans whose rights he proclaimed. His plea for national
liberty and free Parliament was perfectly sincere; yet it might be
compared to the skilful unrolling of a length of shot silk, which
so changes its colours under different lights as to bewilder and
dazzle those mistrusting him, though it allures the parties hoping
for his support. After the downfall of Richard Cromwell's government, his power was enhanced by the return of the Rump (or

anti-monarchical) Parliament in 1659. Meanwhile, he refused to join in any plot organized by the exiled Royalists, who were sending over emissaries to General Monk, that seemingly incorruptible Parliamentarian. Cooper also allied himself with the General, and with his wife, an extremely forceful lady, who had been a laundress and was known as Dirty Bess. In December Monk wrote asking Charles II to trust him, adding that as soon as he received His Majesty's leave, he would go to London to await his instructions. 'I shall own you in everything you shall act for God's glory and the good of my people,' the King replied.

Meanwhile, Cooper had been twice arrested and examined on suspicion of Royalist activities, and on each occasion was able to prove his innocence; but his Republican enemies continued to watch him. Although they did not know that he, Sir Arthur Hazelrig and Colonel Morley were in secret communication with Monk's commissioners about the restoration of the Rump Parliament, they decided to arrest him again, this time at his house in Covent Garden. They sent to find out if he was there; their messenger, meeting him as he arrived home engaged him in conversation, and then left. Guessing, Cooper later recalled, 'that the business was but a pretence', he watched the man turn the corner of the street, and then took refuge with his barber, who lived opposite. From there, he saw the officer return with a party of musketeers to search the house. They ran their swords into the hangings and broke open the chests, but only succeeded in frightening Lady Cooper, while her husband slipped away to a hiding-place in the City, whence he emerged to appeal for the restoration of the Rump Parliament, which he described as the only one capable of making 'the sword subservient to the civil interest'.

When the Rump reassembled a new Council of State was decreed, and on 7th January 1660 Cooper took his seat, nineteen years after his first election. The Council, of which he was again a member, were then asked to renounce Charles II. Cooper, with a number of others, refused to do so; still he held aloof from the exiled Royalists, thus driving Charles's chief adviser and minister, Sir Edward Hyde, later Lord Clarendon, to despair. 'I cannot understand why he should be so mad, when he is related through his wife to one of the most worthy persons in the kingdom,' wrote the Chancellor to Lord Mordaunt, who was approaching Monk on the King's behalf.

When the General arrived from Scotland, Sir Arthur Hazelrig
asked Cooper to command the army against him; he refused,
because he had given his word to Monk 'to be his friend, and
therefore could not break it'. But no one knew—even Cooper
did not know—what Monk's intentions were. The Rump Parliament was counting on his and his troops' support; the Council
of the City of London wanted him to bring about an entirely free,
enlarged, anti-Rump Parliament, one which would readmit the
Presbyterian Members excluded by Oliver Cromwell; the majority
of these men were monarchists, and supported by the London
citizens, who were now clamouring for the Restoration of their
Black Boy; for that saturnine, inscrutable, old-young man had
become a national hero.

Still everything depended on General Monk; and his remarks
epitomize the variation in public feeling. During his march from
Scotland he had said, 'May my right hand rot off, if I have the
least design for [the King].' A month later, he told a Royalist
agent that he would consider a Restoration. Dining with another,
he drew his host aside, 'took a lusty glass of wine', said, 'Here's
a health to my Black Boy!' and drank it down. In the following
week he announced, 'I have no design for Charles Stuart.' Finally,
he refused to answer any questions, while remaining in touch
with a number of Royalists. To one, he said, 'I conjure you to
secrecy, upon peril of your life. I intend to send you to the King
—but I am resolved not to give him anything in writing.'

On 11th February Ashley Cooper, having reconciled Monk
with the City authorities, returned from the Guildhall in his coach,
to be surrounded by people shouting, 'Down with the Rumps!'
in a threatening manner. Smiling, he leant out and said, 'What,
gentlemen, not *one* good piece in a rump?' and was cheered for
what they took—rightly, as it happened—to be a change of policy.
With Mrs Monk—'my lady', as he always called her—and her
brother Thomas Clarges, he then set himself to persuade the
General to restore the Presbyterian members, and dissolve the
Rump. Arguing with him from suppertime till three in the morning, they at last succeeded, and this group was summoned to meet
Monk at Whitehall. Ashley Cooper, accompanying them, was
confronted by Sir Arthur Hazelrig. 'As soon as he ... saw so
considerable a number of the old, secluded Members,' Cooper
recalled, 'he went pale with passion.' Walking up to his former

ally, he shouted, 'This is your doing—and it shall cost blood!'
'Your own, if you please,' Cooper replied. 'I shall not be secured,'
and the next day escorted the seventy-three restored Members to
their places. So Parliament became fully representational; and
again, Cooper was approached by Charles II. Still he waited, till
Charles's Declaration from Breda—promising those who had
fought against his father 'amnesty and liberty', and also consultation with Parliament on all national issues—reached England,
together with another letter to Cooper from the King, at the
beginning of April. But it was not until the first week in May that
he gave Charles his promise of support, and then he did so on
the instructions of Parliament.

In fact, according to his own standards—and, presumably, the
advice of the Almighty—Ashley Cooper's behaviour had been
perfectly consistent. The people of England, having demanded
monarchy, must not be denied. He had remained neutral until he
was certain that that was what they desired. He had simply waited
for them—and Monk—to make up their minds.

On 8th May Charles II was proclaimed King of England 'by
inherent birthright and lawful and undoubted succession'. Cooper
and the other eleven members of the Council were then instructed
to leave for Holland with Parliament's humble request to His
Majesty to return to his loving people. He received them at The
Hague.

And so these two great duellists, whose fight for political
supremacy was to last for more than twenty years, met in courteous formality—but not face to face; for the top of Ashley's head
was barely level with the ends of the King's cravat. Neither, then,
knew how dangerously well, in all else, they were matched.
Neither trusted the other. Yet in this moment of triumph for both,
each was already aware of the other's skill, in dialectic, in manipulation, in calculated inactivity—and in ruthless cunning.

3

The backgrounds, temperaments and schemes of Charles II and Anthony Ashley Cooper so contrasted with, while occasionally complementing, each other, as to provide one of the strangest and most dramatic relationships in English history. In 1660 both had reached the height of their powers, with a fair knowledge of what is vaguely termed the world. Since his twelfth year the King's world had been one of frustration, bitter hardship and physical danger. Bred up in the most luxurious Court in Europe by reverently affectionate tutors and loving parents, he had then faced what appeared to be perdurable ruin and loss for the next fourteen years. Shabby, penurious, hungry, sponging, stubbornly hopeful and desperately courageous, he had had to deal with the petty wranglings and ineffable stupidity of his family, the contemptuous and uncertain patronage of his so-called allies, and the treachery of a number of his followers. These ordeals had not affected his strength of purpose; nor had they destroyed his ability to delight and allure those he used in the ceaseless struggle to regain his rights. But long before he stepped ashore to kneel and give thanks to God on Dover sands, he had lost all faith in human integrity, and—it was just as well, in view of what awaited him—could afford to discount, while gracefully acknowledging, the wild acclaim, the vociferous raptures of his subjects. His cynicism, founded on contempt and disillusion, had given him patience, heartless good humour and unfailing perspicacity—with an iron determination never again, no matter what the cost, to return to the nightmare of exile.

While Charles was submitting to this treadmill, Ashley Cooper, equally brilliant, subtle and resolute, had lived in wealth and ease, moving from one success to another, gaining ground, financially and politically, through marriages, friendships, acquisition of property and carefully regulated expenditure. There was another, even more vital difference. The King, now in his thirty-first year—he entered London on 29th May, his birthday—had a superb physique and seldom knew the loss of a night's sleep.

Cooper, nine years his senior, was frail, afflicted, an indomitable wisp of a man, often in pain and sometimes facing the possibility that he might break down altogether, and so have to leave the arena which he was entering with the intention first to excel and then to dominate. But perhaps the deepest difference between the two men was that of birth. Cooper, an aristocrat, a privileged patrician, could trace his descent as far back as the fourteenth century. He was 'pure' English, rooted in his own country. He only twice, and then very briefly, set foot on the continent. Charles II, of Italian, French, Danish and Scottish blood, was in fact a foreigner, not only by descent, but through his years of enforced adaptation to the customs and manners of Germany, Spain, France, the Low Countries, and—worst of any—the savage squalors of his northern kingdom. He had sold himself, lied, prevaricated, and offered to abjure his religion (all in vain) on several occasions. Ashley Cooper trusted rather in the Deity than in his Presbyterianism. He wore his beliefs as lightly as his master did; that became a shared characteristic. Another was their gift of persuading, seducing and if necessary deceiving those who opposed them. Both were attractive, amusing, accomplished, and so quick-witted as sometimes to bewilder their simpler-minded associates. Charles's advantage lay in the gracious informality of his address, and in his genial bestowal of trivial kindnesses. He was considered 'debonair, easy of access', according to more than one contemporary. Cooper had to work a little harder, and risk a certain frankness, as he did when he described his motives to his former brother-in-law, Sir Henry Coventry. Acknowledging Charles's wish for his services, he explained that after Cromwell had deceived him, he 'never had other opinion but that the King would come in, nor other desire that he should'. He had therefore 'hindered any government to settle . . . as far as he could [be] instrumental in it'; hence the need for his apparent neutrality. This account, although necessarily disingenuous, was not untruthful.

A contrast of rather less importance was that of family life. Charles II began his reign burdened by his widowed sister Mary of Orange, two brothers, James of York and Henry of Gloucester, and visits from his mother and his younger sister, Henrietta Anne. He was fond of, and felt himself responsible for, all of them; but they added to his difficulties. Ten years later, only

James was still alive; and his doltish obstinacy taxed his brother's patience beyond bearing. Ashley Cooper's brother and sister, George and Philippa, were both married, it seems satisfactorily, and had retired to the country; neither took advantage of his position, and he had little or nothing to do with them. His marriage was happy, but his son by Frances Cecil was delicate, slightly deformed and mentally negligible; he had no children by his third wife.

He now had to justify his Parliamentary activities; he did this by services of which he alone was capable. Seventeen years later, when he had been imprisoned in the Tower for attempting to overthrow the régime, he reminded the King that although he had had 'a principal hand' in his Restoration, he had never betrayed, 'as Your Majesty knows, the party or councils I was of . . . I observed', he went on, 'the leaders . . . both laity and clergy, ready and forward to deliver up the rights and liberties of the people'—and so he had again changed sides. But this reconversion gave him the reputation—one that has endured—of an unscrupulous careerist; while those who had suffered the miseries of exile naturally resented his achieving a political status he had not earned through deprivation. Hyde did not then share this feeling. He considered Cooper to be not only valuable but sincere, and stood up for him, while distrusting certain other members of the King's immediate circle. So the two men began by co-operating—they had first met in 1643—in spite of the fact that the Chancellor found Ashley Cooper 'of a slippery humour', and thought that he should have worked for the King's recall instead of waiting for it to happen.

Cooper's establishment in the Restoration government was marred by an accident which temporarily affected his health. On his way to The Hague his coach overturned, and he was severely bruised in the side; but he was able—he may have forced himself —to precede the King, so as to receive him at Blackheath at the head of his regiment. A few days later he became a Privy Councillor, through Monk's recommendation, and Charles's principal adviser on all administrative details. The King's and Hyde's lack of experience in such matters resulted in Cooper's attendance at their consultations, and he soon became indispensable.

He worked under the Earl of Southampton, his wife's uncle, now Lord Treasurer, and his position was not, ostensibly, one of great importance; but as Southampton was elderly, feeble and unsuited to his duties, Cooper became responsible for many of them. With others of the thirty Privy Councillors, of whom twelve had been Parliamentarians, he was on some forty committees, and eventually had to deal with finance, the Caribbean plantations—where he himself had property—and the religious and legal settlements arising out of the reorganization of the kingdom. He rose to every requirement with zest, ingenuity and a knowledge of detail that enabled him to speak in the Commons with unfailing effect. It was at this point that the Chancellor recorded his admiration of Cooper's oratory; he noted that the younger man's eloquence was enhanced by a subtly gentle delivery; the bitterest sarcasms, and the most damning condemnations, the most fervent appeals were rather insinuated than driven home; his command of language was only equalled by the quiet force of a speaker as sure of himself as of his audience's attention.

He had need of all his gifts and of all his trust in divine guidance when the question of the regicides arose. These men, with whom he had on certain occasions allied himself—while having nothing to do with the condemnation of Charles I—had been excepted from the amnesty of Breda, and were now to be tried. A commission, of which Ashley Cooper, with other ex-Parliamentarians, was one, sat in judgement on them, after much disagreement in the Commons about their punishment. He urged the majority should be imprisoned and fined, and this plea was partially granted; finally, only twelve were sentenced to death: while Charles II, sitting in council over the penultimate decision, scribbled a note to Hyde which ran, 'I confess I am weary of hanging. Let it sleep.'

For the rest of his life, and for centuries to come, Ashley Cooper was arraigned of mercilessness, treachery and the most detestable form of time-serving. It was said then, as it still is, that he should have refused to sit on the commission which condemned his former allies to the hideous death of the seventeenth century. He would indeed have made a noble (although useless) gesture, if he had disobeyed the King's command, retired to the country and left the political scene for ever. The fact that he, as a former Parliamentarian, was not alone in sentencing the regicides, and that his absence would not have affected their fate, has been, and will no doubt continue to be, ignored, as were his successful efforts to save the lives of several others. Hazelrig, for instance,

2

escaped death through his influence, and was sent to the Tower, because, Cooper pointed out, he was not of sufficient importance to suffer the extreme penalty. Yet it could not be forgotten that, discussing the position of the regicides in the event of a Restoration, he had said to Colonel Hutchinson, 'Not a hair of their heads, nor a penny of any man's estate shall be touched for what has passed.' Now that promise came under the heading of the 'punctilios of honour' against which he had warned his Cavalier acquaintance six years earlier.

In fact, Cooper was merely following the custom of the age and of his contemporaries, in carrying out the orders he had sworn to obey when he became a Privy Councillor. But as his later career made him one of the most famous figures in European politics, this, his first important act in the new Government, was to be recalled in horror and loathing. The genius of a great poet saw to it that he should be remembered, not as a servant of the state, but as the false Achitophel, the prototype of a murderer, a traitor, and the degraded slave of greed and ambition. Certainly, Cooper was no Brutus; nor did he stand for the combination of Iago and Richard III with which his detractors have associated him.

Shortly after his return Charles II received a number of deputies whose members desired to express their loyalty by presenting him with addresses of homage and thanksgiving. One of these, from the Dorsetshire nobility, was headed by Sir John Strangways. With the Privy Councillor who had taken him prisoner and destroyed his manor-house in 1644, he knelt before the King, aware that while he had lost nearly everything he possessed, the man beside him, coolly waiting for royal favour, had obtained it without sacrifice, and was now a Government official. Their new master did not outwardly differentiate between the Cavalier and the ex-Parliamentarian; nor did he then trouble to assess the hostility of the Anglican aristocrat for the Presbyterian politician. Both could be used; and while disregading the claims of the one (Strangways received no compensation) he was preparing to disappoint the hopes of the other; for he and Hyde had decided to restore the use of the Prayer-Book. Ashley Cooper seems to have accepted this policy; he took no share in the discussions about it, merely repeating his desire for toleration, and adding that the time had not yet come for a permanent religious settlement.

He then sat on the committee which attainted four dead men—Cromwell, Ireton, Bradshaw and Pride; their bodies were disinterred, hanged at Tyburn and re-buried on the site of what is now Connaught Square. Such barbarity may have struck him as pointless and absurd; but he was already conscious of its importance in the eyes of the populace whose hero he became when he rose to defy the monarchy he now served. With the Chancellor, recently created Earl of Clarendon, Ashley Cooper was the hardest working member of the King's ministry. As Samuel Pepys noted, two years later, he was 'a man of great business—yet of pleasure and drolling too'. Only so could he maintain his position and influence, balancing between the long-winded, outdated conscientiousness of Clarendon and the wild frivolities of George Villiers, second Duke of Buckingham.

This nobleman, succeeding his murdered father in 1628, was now in his thirty-fifth year; he had played his hand as King's Ward, runaway student, fighting Cavalier, shady exile and treacherous intriguer with a recklessness that yet brought him triumph in the face of apparent disaster. He was fascinating, witty, beautiful and talented—his best play, *The Rehearsal*, shows an amazing mastery of farce—and sustained a taste for what would now be called left-wing politics, which at this time he took care to conceal. The King chose to ignore Buckingham's betrayal and desertion of the Royalist cause—they had been brought up together and had much in common—and he became the star of the Restoration Court, together with his cousin, Charles's mistress, Barbara Castlemaine. That handsome shrew, whose insolence was only equalled by her stupidity and greed, did not influence the King—none of his mistresses did—but both Buckingham and Ashley Cooper, soon to be allies, were under the impression that they could work on their master through her; in this, as in so much else, Charles deceived those nearest him: for he followed a partially secret policy of great skill and suppleness, while giving the impression of a frank, casual, pleasure-loving, kindly soul, who asked no more, as he used to say, than that every man in the kingdom should sit under his own vine and fig-tree. One of Charles's mistakes was his belief that, having once deceived Ashley Cooper, he could continue to do so. He was to pay a high price for this error.

Another intimate, Sir Charles Berkeley, a rather dull man, was the close friend of the Duke of York, who had recently been forced into a shotgun marriage with Anne Hyde, Lord Clarendon's daughter. Berkeley was useless, idle, and only a little more corrupt than Sir Henry Bennet, later Lord Arlington. Bennet and Lady Castlemaine were Catholics. She practised her religion openly; Bennet could not afford to do so. The King, whose official faith was, as it were, geared to the Church of England ('I do not wish,' he said once, 'to be the Head of Nothing') had long been drawn towards Catholicism; if he had any sincere religious convictions, which is doubtful, they were of that persuasion. This was another aspect of his character which remained unsuspected by Ashley Cooper till some years after the Restoration.

In April 1661 Cooper became Baron Ashley of Wimborne St Giles and Chancellor of the Exchequer. This post, combined with that of Under-Treasurer to Southampton, gave rise to charges of accepting bribes, on the assumption that everyone thus employed added to his income in this way. He could have amassed a large fortune; he did not do so because he was already a rich man, who had no taste for display, as is shown by his rebuilding St Giles on a comparatively modest scale. Pepys, reporting on his accounts and methods, described them as satisfactory, and found Ashley himself 'a very ready [i.e. open to enquiry] quiet and diligent person'. This self-created impression was not so much the result of highmindedness as of common sense.

In these first years of his administration, Ashley made it his business to allay the King's suspicions of his loyalty by supporting Charles's efforts for toleration of religious dissent, whether Catholic or Presbyterian, while Clarendon, a High Anglican, withstood them, as did Parliament. So Ashley became affiliated with the group headed by Digby (now Earl of Bristol), Lady Castlemaine and Arlington that aimed at bringing down the Chancellor. Ashley did not then know that the King, while supporting Clarendon, had planned to abandon his faith, such as it was, for Catholicism. His advocation of religious tolerance was part of a scheme that failed. In 1662 he began a correspondence with the Vatican, in which he offered to alter the rubric so that it would conform to that of Rome; this having been effected, he would then announce his own conversion. By 1663 the plan had to be abandoned, partly because the King had begun to take in the national loathing and fear of the old faith, and also because the Pope shrank from the violent reaction of the English Parliament and its effect on Charles's Catholic subjects. His fourteen years' absence and the willing acceptance of his Catholic bride—Catherine of Braganza was the greatest heiress in Europe—misled him; he still hoped, some time or other, to achieve the conversion which would be the basis of an autocracy ordered on continental lines; for this seemed to him the only way to rule a turbulent people. Charles's intentions were confided to James of York and his Catholic ministers, who kept his secret, but did little or nothing to forward his plans, while Ashley spoke in the House of Lords of His Majesty's 'unshakeable firmness in [the Protestant] religion'.

Two thousand Presbyterian ministers, refusing to conform, lost their benefices. The greater part of the dissenting laity, Ashley among them, adopted the Anglican faith. At this point, possibly at one of Barbara Castlemaine's famous supper-parties, the lady sitting next to the little Lord, as Charles called him, asked him what his religion was. 'Madam, wise men are but of one religion.' 'Which is that?' 'Madam, wise men never tell,' he replied, and the riposte was well received by a circle whose beliefs, with the exception of Clarendon's, were subordinated to the accumulation of riches and power.

Partly on these grounds, the Privy Council were at one with Parliament in their anxiety about the increasing prosperity of the United Provinces, whose activities threatened their supremacy in trade and their private fortunes. War was desired by the majority; the King, Clarendon and Southampton, fearful of the expense, were against it, but agreed to demand redress from their Dutch rivals. When this attempt at a peaceful settlement failed, naval action began in February 1665, and Ashley was appointed Treasurer of Prizes.

This produced a furious protest from Clarendon. He was convinced that Ashley would profit dishonestly by the office, and refused to seal the order. 'Your Majesty may be abominably cozened,' he said, adding that Southampton would be thereby passed over and insulted. Charles told Ashley to see the Chancellor privately. He did so, and an argument ensued, in which Clarendon was defeated. As Ashley's salary had been raised to £1,500 a year, he had no need, and did not attempt, to divert the Prize moneys to his own use. He knew that he would have been

impeached if he had done so; for his accounts were regularly
inspected, and he was responsible to Charles for all disbursements.

With so much business on his hands—and even more anxiety,
for the national finances were not only inadequate, but in a state
of chaos—Ashley had to remain in London, and was unable to
attend to family affairs. Lady Ashley kept him informed of such
matters from Wimborne St Giles, the most urgent being that of
her thirteen-year-old stepson's tendency to make himself ill by
over-eating. Her husband reassured her as best he could: but he
himself was worried about the boy's health. 'My Dearest,' he
wrote ... 'You gave the child the best that could be, but his
extreme wilful disorders taken in eating always gives me great
fears until he be removed to a place of other discipline,' thus
referring to the plans for his son's entry to the University. After
giving her instructions about household arrangements and his
grant of lands in Carolina, he ended his letter to 'that treasure
God has given me in so faithful and affectionate a wife, to whom
I vow myself a most sincere and truly affectionate husband,
Ashley.'

Without this support it would have been difficult for him to
carry the burden of administration, while sustaining the carefree
sociability required of a courtier. As in his youth, Ashley still
'loved merry company', and his policy of being on good terms
with everybody urged him to renew his friendship with Clarendon,
and even to achieve a working relationship with Lauderdale, now
Secretary of State for Scotland, whose dirty habits and rough
manners seem to have disgusted everyone but the King. Meanwhile, the war swung between triumph and disaster, at appalling
cost. Rejoicings at the victories of 1665 were halted by the sudden
influx of the plague, which drove the Court from London and
established Parliament in Oxford. Here, Ashley met the man
who became his closest friend: John Locke, not yet famous as
a philosopher and mathematician, but already known as an
innovator in medicine. Ashley consulted him about the increasing
attacks of pain in his side—these were apt to bring on jaundice
and fits of nausea—and was so impressed by the results of Locke's
advice as to depend on him as on no one else.

In September of this year he left Oxford for Wimborne St
Giles where he and Lady Ashley entertained Charles II, Queen
Catherine and their Court; the visit was useful—for the King's

distrust of Ashley had recently been heightened, perhaps by Clarendon's criticisms—but exhausting; for Ashley was combining the prosecution of the war with efforts to lessen Parliament's attacks on the Dissenters.

Returning to Oxford in November, he wrote in great distress to Lady Ashley as 'My dearest Dear' of the 'sad news of your being ill', enclosing a list of medicaments, and concluding, 'It very much adds to my affliction that 'tis not possible for me to come to you this week ... The Lord in mercy preserve my Dear and restore your health, is the most hearty and humble prayer of, my Dearest, your most truly affectionate husband.' Another worry was his son's inability to distinguish himself in any way; young Ashley Cooper became the despair of his Oxford tutors for the next three years. He was frail, ungainly, stupid and charmless.

His father spent the early part of 1666 resting at St Giles or taking the waters. In June the Fire of London enforced his return to work, and further complicated the economic problems with which he had to deal. Officially, Ashley discounted the story that Papists, throwing 'fireballs', had caused the destruction of half the city; he may have realized how useful it would be in later years.

Meanwhile, Clarendon continued to impugn his integrity, finding a new grievance in Ashley's censure of the importation of Irish cattle; this was fiercely supported by the landowners, on the grounds that to import cheap meat from Ireland (and from Catholics too!) would ruin the farmers. Any question relating to beef, that semi-sacred commodity, whether imported on the hoof or salted down and sold by the barrel, convulsed the English people. The bill prohibiting the sale of both kinds was urged by Ashley and Buckingham, now working together for the first time, and opposed by the Duke of Ormonde as Viceroy of Ireland, his fiery eldest son Lord Ossory, and Clarendon. By the autumn, feelings had risen so high in both Houses that Ashley's oratory, growing more violent with each session, caused an explosion from Ossory, who exclaimed, 'Such language can only come from one who was of Oliver Cromwell's Council!' Ashley replied, 'Your lordship must give me reparation—or I will take it my own way.' A duel between a vigorous young man and a middle-aged invalid could have but one end; the

Speaker described Ossory's remark as out of order, and told him to apologize, which he did.

This incident drew attention, not only to Ashley's political past, but to the fact that both he and Buckingham were out of favour with the King, who had always supported Ormonde, one of his most faithful followers in adversity, against his enemies, and was beginning to suspect the other two noblemen's loyalty. Charles knew Buckingham to be politically unreliable and dismissed him from Court and from the Privy Council in the following year. As allies, he and Ashley formed a potentially dangerous combination; for the little Lord was beginning to assert himself, as he did when disagreeing with one of his former brothers-in-law, Sir William Coventry, about the distribution of the Prize moneys. 'He did snuff,' Pepys records, 'and talk as high to him as to any ordinary seaman.' Sir William took the outburst quietly, and gave in; Clarendon did not, when Ashley contradicted him at Council meetings.

When peace was signed in July 1667, this hostility did not affect Ashley's attempts to shield Clarendon from his enemies at Court and in Parliament. The Lord Chancellor had become a scapegoat for every disaster—the Dutch invasion of Sheerness, the sale of Dunkirk, increasing financial chaos—and when he was in danger of impeachment for high treason, a motion successfully opposed by Ashley in the House of Lords. Charles advised Clarendon to retire, and when he refused, dismissed him. Having done all he could for the Chancellor, who fled to France, Ashley went to St Giles for three weeks, returning to realize the uncertainty of the King's favour, and the possibility, as he later put it, of himself ending his career as 'another traveller to Montpellier'. Yet he was now more than ever indispensable.

In the following summer his health broke down completely, and he appeared to be dying. All treatments failed. Then John Locke, who had been living in his household for the past year, was consulted, and after discussions with Ashley's London physician, Dr Sydenham, faced his patient with an ultimatum. The suppurating hyatid cyst on the liver, which had now burst, must be operated on, or he would die. Ashley had never feared death; but he settled for the horrors of surgery. Locke proposed to insert a tube in the wound to draw off the poison during the course of this dangerous and cruel operation. Ashley agreed, submitting to the ordeal on 12th June 1668. Six weeks later, he was nearing convalescence—and then another decision had to be made. Should the tube be removed, or remain where it was, open, for further drainage? Calmly, Ashley summoned Locke and two other doctors, to whom he put the following questions—'Whether I may travel in a coach, ride on horseback, boat, or use any other such exercise safely, with a tube of this length?' Locke thought that he could; and the famous silver pipe remained in Ashley's body until he died, fifteen years later.

4

Temporarily restored to health, Ashley spent the greater part of his time at Exeter House, his Strand mansion, acquired in 1667. While maintaining a certain state, he and Lady Ashley lived unostentatiously; their household amounted to no more than thirty-six persons, of whom the most notable was Ashley's secretary, Thomas Stringer. This gentleman, Ashley's first biographer, idolized his master. With John Locke who, equally devoted, had his own rooms and his laboratory, here at St Giles, Stringer was treated rather as a friend than as an employee; both men rejoiced in Ashley's informality, gaiety and wit, while sharing his political views.

They were responsible for his library, a rather formidable array of books on law, philosophy, science, history, theology and agriculture. Some years after Ashley's death, Locke recalled his ability to 'see through the design of a work . . . which he ran over with vast rapidity', and his 'naturally gay' temperament. 'He himself,' the philosopher added, 'was always easy, he loved that others should be so . . . being a great enemy to constraint.' Ashley's private hobbies were confined to his country life— architecture, interior decoration, garden-planning and the breeding of horses. In all these matters his knowledge was expert and detailed. He found time for everything, making notes of what psalms should be read at family prayers, and recording the effects of wind and weather on his orchards and flower-beds. He was not much interested in the arts, and seldom went to the theatre. Entertaining, discussion and an occasional game of cards were his principal relaxations.

As a result of Clarendon's fall, he was now the most influential member of the King's unofficial Cabinet Council, or Cabal, whose names—Clifford, Arlington, Buckingham, Ashley and Lauderdale—revived the use of a word not then associated with corruption. Of these, Clifford and Arlington were secret Catholics, Lauderdale was an ex-Presbyterian, Buckingham an agnostic, and Ashley an Anglican convert, who still had no knowledge of Charles's plans for public and private reconciliation with the old faith. On 25th January 1669 the King summoned James of York, who with his wife had just become a Catholic, to confer with three others of that persuasion—Arundell of Wardour, Clifford and Arlington—as to how best to proceed in the announcement of his own conversion and the establishment of Catholicism in England. All agreed that Louis XIV should be approached, and emissaries were sent to him and to the Pope. So the negotiations which resulted in the Dover Treaty of 1670 began, while Ashley continued to urge toleration for Dissenters on the King. Charles agreed with him on this point, suggesting toleration for Catholics as well, to which Ashley replied that this was inadvisable. Catholics, he explained, in a pamphlet he wrote with Locke, 'are less apt to be pitied than others', because of the cruelty 'of their own principles and practices'. Ashley added that the increasing immigration of Dissenters was having a bad effect on trade; this, with colonial expansion, was his special concern. In the same cause, he urged war on the Dutch, with or without the French alliance.

Ashley's policy now seems inconsistent. In fact, his attitude towards 'popery' became atavistic. It was partly the result of his early training and partly derived from what might be called racial memory, enhanced by fear of a Catholic invasion. Only eighty years had passed since that holocaust had been miraculously averted; it still had a nightmare power over most men's minds, and was conjoined with Foxe's records of Queen Mary's reign, the Gunpowder Plot and the activities of the Inquisition.

Ashley shared the general suspicion, spreading rapidly at this time, that England was in danger from a Catholic rebellion. It had nothing to do with his efforts to restore the national prosperity, and was based rather on emotion than reason. For Charles II's Catholic subjects were in a diminishing minority; a very few, feeling themselves unjustly treated, threatened retaliation; their numbers shrank as their belligerence increased. Hostility against many loyal, peaceable and patriotic Catholic families was increased because the laws against recusancy were negligently applied, and sometimes ignored altogether.

In September 1669 Ashley succeeded in arranging his son's marriage to Lady Dorothy Manners, a Rutland heiress. Locke escorted the youth to Belvoir Castle, and was responsible for his courtship and the presentation of two jewels to his bride; his father's letters give the impression that young Ashley could not be relied upon to approach her without supervision. The marriage pleased everyone—even Lady Dorothy, who became devoted to her father-in-law, corresponding with him regularly. She fulfilled all his hopes by giving birth to a son, who was to become famous as the author of *Characteristics of Men, Manners, Opinions and Times*, which appeared in the first decade of the eighteenth century.

In the eight months that elapsed between his son's marriage and the signing of the secret Treaty in May 1670 Ashley was busier than ever before; he had no suspicion that the festivities in Dover and London celebrating the visit of the King's sister Henrietta Anne, now Duchess of Orléans and Louis XIV's emissary, concealed the ratification of an agreement between her brother and brother-in-law of which the terms have been either vilified or excused by a number of historians.

In return for a sum of £150,000 Charles promised to declare himself a Catholic, and bring about—it was not specified how or when—the conversion to that faith of the English people. In the event of their resistance, French troops would be landed to put down any rebellion of 'unquiet spirits'. The Anglo-French war against the Dutch Republic was to be subsidized by Louis at £225,000 a year, and a number of Dutch islands handed over to England. Clifford, Arlington and the French Ambassador Colbert de Croissy signed this treaty, on behalf of the two Kings; it was concealed from Buckingham, Lauderdale and Ashley. The only matter of dispute was about which should come first, Charles's conversion, or the attack on the Dutch. Charles postponed the first—in his own mind, it seems, indefinitely—for he now knew what the effect of such an announcement on Parliament, people and ministers would be. But the national need for money was so desperate that he decided to promise what he had no intention, then, of performing. He has been praised by his defenders for his resourcefulness and successful deception of Louis, who continued to believe that one day, perhaps quite soon, he would declare his Catholicism. That in doing so he would be breaking his coronation oath did not of course concern his good brother and cousin.

It was later arranged with Ashley and the other members of the

Cabal that the English navy should attack the United Provinces by sea and the French armies by land. He himself, looking on the Dutch as England's most dangerous rival in trade, took longer than the other two duped ministers to assent to this plan; finally, he began preparations for the war with his usual energy. Disliking a French alliance, he regarded it as a temporary measure which would lapse at the end of the struggle.

Charles II then completed his schemes by setting up his *Traité Simulé;* this was confined to the agreements about the war, while omitting the conversion clauses, and signed by all the members of the Cabal. Ashley and Buckingham insisted on the additional acquisition of the islands of Woorne and Goree as the price of English cooperation. Louis's subsidy proved inadequate; the task of supplementing it by moneys raised at home fell on Ashley; and during the whole of 1671 he and Clifford wrestled with the complications of this problem.

Breaking the alliance between his country and the United Provinces did not trouble Ashley. England's circumstances made war a necessity, and he urged its support in a number of speeches. Clifford then hit on a plan which is still associated with Ashley's name—the Stop of the Exchequer. The Treasury's payments to the bankers, and thus to the principal merchants and their clients, were suspended in order, so Clifford declared, to avert national bankruptcy. The resultant outcry was fierce and prolonged. In a short, forceful memorandum under five heads, Ashley pointed out the useless folly of this proceeding to the King—and was ignored. Eventually, Charles agreed to a settlement which partially satisfied the bankers; but both they and many other contemporaries blamed Ashley for a measure he had done his best to invalidate, and for which Clifford and the King were responsible.

Charles II prorogued Parliament from 1671 to 1673; on 2nd March 1672 he issued his Declaration of Indulgence for Dissenters and Catholics, thus breaking his promise (embodied in the Treaty of Breda) to consult the Houses on all national issues. In the same month war was declared on the Dutch. In April, Ashley, now President of the Council of Trade and Plantations, was made Earl of Shaftesbury and Baron Cooper of Pawlett, and in November Lord High Chancellor of England. While appreciating his genius for administration, the King trusted him less than ever;

but he hoped that when Parliament met again he would find a protector from its hostility in one so honoured; also, that the increasing popularity of 'our Earl', as Stringer calls him, might thereby be diminished.

To a certain extent Charles's hopes were realized. When Shaftesbury drove out from Exeter House in his state coach, with his gentlemen and footmen walking on either side, these progresses were considered ostentatious; and his appearance on the Woolsack 'in an ash-coloured gown, silver lace and full-ribboned pantaloons' was harshly criticized by those he had surpassed. It was at this time that he sat for his portrait to Greenhill in the great blond periwig that, rather grotesquely, added to his height, and inaugurated a fashion that lasted for the next twenty years. In fact, he was now not only eminent but conspicuous. This new aspect made him the butt of the pamphleteers and wits, giving rise to a number of anecdotes that became part of his legend and were published several years later, together with his nicknames, for two of which the King himself was responsible. Charles referred to his Chancellor as 'Little Sincerity' and 'Lord Shiftesbury'. Some courtiers called him 'Count Tapski', while others maintained that the remedy of the silver tube was part of a cure for venereal disease. So Shaftesbury's reputation presently became that of a lecher; he 'ran', it was believed, to the brothels five nights out of seven. A favourite story was that of the King's comment when Shaftesbury entered the Council Chamber preceded by a page carrying the emblems of his office. 'Here comes the greatest whoremaster in England,' Charles is supposed to have said, to which his Lord Chancellor replied, 'Of a subject, Sire.' Both these unauthenticated remarks, recorded twenty years later, are almost certainly apocryphal. Another story describes one of Shaftesbury's superannuated employees ('an old knight') being sent to entertain his ladies of pleasure with cheesecakes and wine in Hyde Park until his master was ready for them. The accusation of lechery cannot of course be disproved: but the evidence is rather suspect. No amount of work would have prevented Shaftesbury visiting the whorehouses, if he had so desired; but it is noticeable that Pepys, who became one of his bitterest adversaries and was the first to record such activities, made no mention of this habit in his correspondence, then or later.

On the same grounds, Shaftesbury was thought to have been

caricatured in some eight or nine plays, the best known being Otway's *Venice Preserved*, which was not put on till 1681. It was then assumed, as it still is, that he had inspired the character of Antonio in the highly comical obscenities of the 'Nicky Nacky' flagellation scenes. It may have been so; but here again, there is no proof that this was the author's intention.

Constant intercourse with harlots would not have been possible in the first period of the war, when Shaftesbury was visiting the dockyards and ports by day, returning to deal with Council meetings and correspondence in the evenings; and as he was summoned to wait on the King two or three times a week, besides appearing at receptions and supper-parties, he would have had little or no leisure for the pleasures of the alcove. He escaped to St Giles when he could, as is shown by his correspondence with gardeners and stewards. Meanwhile, the pressure of public and private business increased with every month, and with his command of that pressure he became fiercely ambitious; he seems to have felt that he was on the way to become the most powerful figure in the state. And then, suddenly, his dislike of Catholicism was heightened by his discovery—apparently through Arlington—of the conversion clauses in the Dover Treaty.

Shaftesbury's reaction to this betrayal was shown by his attacks on the policy of what came to be known as the Court Party. His only recorded comment—'a black cloud is gathering over England' —was made to Stringer. He had never been easy-going; now he became fanatical, to be attacked, in his turn, as 'the fairy fiend that haunts both Houses'. In 1673, aware of what lay behind the Declaration of Indulgence, he ceased to support it. What would now be described as a cold war began between him and Charles II. Shaftesbury's rage at being deceived was concealed by courteous suavity towards, and subservient flattery of, the King: he praised his master's adherence to the Church of England in most of his speeches, because he did not wish Charles to know that he had discovered his secret. And the King was equally bland, equally false, equally resolute. His principal advantage lay in the royal prerogative, but he could not use it as often or as arbitrarily as he wished. In some ways, his position was more precarious than that of his Lord Chancellor: but he was surer of himself and of his power, in spite of the fact that Shaftesbury's hatred of the old faith was shared, and indeed surpassed, by the majority of the

English people. Charles constantly avowing his support of Protestantism and of his subjects' liberty, counted, rightly, on his French cousin's financing his schemes; for Louis's ambassadors continued to assure their master that a Catholic revolution was imminent. Rumours of this assurance added to anti-Catholic feeling in both Houses, and reached the general public, thus creating a desire for violent action; while Shaftesbury was told by Buckingham, still his chief ally, that the King had been seen praying in his wife's chapel at Somerset House. The Duke was apt to say anything that came into his head, according to his mood; and Charles was far too clever to advertise his apostasy in this manner, quite apart from the fact that he was basically irreligious. York, on the other hand, disliked concealing his beliefs, and did not long continue to do so. Now a widower, he was determined to marry a Catholic, and in 1673 he set in hand negotiations for an alliance with Princess Mary Beatrice of Modena. Meanwhile, Charles's declarations of loyalty to the Church of England became quite masterly; one of his best was made soon after he wrote to inform the Queen of Spain of his Catholicism.

At about this time the King began to question his own wisdom in promoting Shaftesbury. 'What do you think,' he asked Ormonde, 'of my giving him the seals?' 'Your Majesty has doubtless acted very prudently in so doing,' the Duke replied, 'if you know how to get them from him again.' Charles took this warning to heart, while still depending on his Lord Chancellor's advice; as he did in the matter of two Dutch agents, Zas and Arton, who in January 1673 arrived with letters to Shaftesbury, suggesting that he should influence the King to make peace with the Dutch, thus splitting the Cabal and inaugurating an anti-French policy. Examined, they were found to be spies. Lauderdale said they should be tortured and hanged. Shaftesbury's advice was typical of the tactics he used when he became known as King of London. He said, 'Show him [Zas] the rack, tell him of it, but do not execute it,' with the result that both men were sent to the Tower, to be released a year later.

In the following month Charles told the Houses that he intended to enforce his Declaration of Indulgence, and Shaftesbury added to this statement with his famous *Delenda est Carthago* speech. Just as Rome decided to bring down the government of Carthage, he told the Lords, 'the King may well say to you, "Tis *your* war." '

He went on, 'If you permit the sea, our British wife, to be ravished [by the Dutch] an eternal mark of infamy will stick upon us.' After a long debate, the Houses agreed that £1,260,000 should be raised, but voted against the Declaration of Indulgence, on the grounds that Popery was increasing—in high places especially— and also that to accept the Declaration would be to overstress the royal prerogative. 'We are confident of him [Charles],' it was observed, 'but we know not what the succession may be.'

For this question had become paramount. After eleven years, Queen Catherine was still childless. The Catholicism of the heir-presumptive was a *secret de polichinelle*, and his replacement by his ten-year-old daughter Mary, who was being educated in the Anglican faith, could not, at that time, be considered. This situation increased the panic, which reached its climax five years later. According to Shaftesbury and Buckingham, the solution lay in Charles's following the example of Henry VIII and divorcing the Queen in order to beget a Protestant successor. The King refused to do this, or to forbid his brother's marriage with the Italian Princess; and as he was surrounded by Catholics and allied to a Catholic monarch, his protestations of loyalty to the Church of England did not allay the suspicions of the Houses. In fact, his position was one of appalling difficulty. Louis's successful invasion of Dutch territory had not been followed by victories at sea (the battle of Sole Bay was a draw) and Charles's nephew, William of Orange, now the national hero, had suggested peace with England, rightly guessing that his uncle's funds were running out. On 8th March 1673 Charles cancelled the Declaration of Indulgence in return for the money needed to continue the war.

A fortnight later, Parliament followed up this triumph by passing the Test Act, which eliminated all Catholics from positions in the forces and the civil service, with the result that York, compelled to withdraw into private life, no longer attempted to conceal his change of faith. So it seemed that Charles's foreign policy had been defeated by the combination of William's defiance of Louis XIV, Parliament's insistence on religious conformity— and Shaftesbury's abandonment of the war; for in June he was urging Charles to make peace.

When the Houses met in October the members' attention was drawn to the Speaker's chair. On it was a rosary, and underneath a huge wooden sabot, displaying the lilies of France on one side and the English lion and unicorn on the other. So the secret of the Dover Treaty had been revealed. There is no evidence that Shaftesbury was responsible for this dramatic protest. Stringer, his most faithful disciple, would have recorded it if he had been.

Danby then replaced Clifford as Lord Treasurer and allied himself with James, who sent for Shaftesbury and called him a madman. He also implored Charles to 'make an example' of the Lord Chancellor by dismissing him from all his offices. On 9th November Shaftesbury was ordered to relinquish the seals, which he did with a smile, remarking, 'It is only laying down my gown and putting on my sword.' This summing-up of his situation was a threat; for he was now the leader of a large, anti-Catholic, anti-French majority in the Lords, and therefore, as Charles realized, a powerful and dangerous adversary.

It was essential to bring him over to the Court Party. The newly appointed French Ambassador, Ruvigny, came to wait on him with an offer of £10,000, a dukedom in England and 'what command he pleased' in France, on condition that he supported Louis's alliance with Charles. Shaftesbury received the envoy with enigmatic courtesy; he was believed to be considering the offer, which he then refused. When Charles sent for him, to be met with another refusal, the interview was conducted as between equals, although with surface amiability.

The fascination exercised by Charles II over nearly all who had to do with him may sometimes have been felt by Shaftesbury; but he had long been aware that the King's friendly ways, his wit and his informality concealed a ruthlessness equal to his own. So it was that when Charles accepted his refusal with apparent equanimity, and went on to say, as he had many times before, that he 'would never forsake the Protestant interest', but that he was about to prorogue Parliament till January 1674, Shaftesbury replied, 'Sire, those who have prevailed upon you to prorogue the Parliament will not stop there. They are such busy fools as will hasten your destruction.' He added that he could no longer serve His Majesty in the Lords, because 'You are gone into a party contrary to the interest I have contended for,' and after the usual interchange of courtesies, took his leave. Joining Stringer in his coach, Shaftesbury remarked, 'The nation is near its ruin,' adding that this was due to the King's addiction to 'Popery, and the exorcism of its priests'.

On 9th January 1674 Shaftesbury addressed the Lords in a
rabble-rousing speech, urging that all Catholics should be compelled to leave London. He had been informed that some 16,000
persons of that persuasion were resolved to strike a desperate
blow. No one, he said, could be sure of his life while such people
were 'in liberty at the gates of the City', and that a massacre
would follow if nothing was done to prevent it. His oratory
moved both Houses to propose further anti-Catholic measures
—but whether Shaftesbury himself really believed in the horrific
situation he had described is extremely doubtful; he did think,
not unreasonably, and with the majority of the English
people, that the country was in danger of being colonized by
France.

On 24th February 1674 peace was signed with the United
Provinces, and Charles, advised by Danby, prorogued Parliament
until the following November. Shaftesbury was then dragged
into a plot against Samuel Pepys, now Secretary of the Admiralty
and Member of Parliament for Castle Rising, on the grounds
that the Earl had once spoken of seeing an altar and a crucifix
in the Secretary's house. Shaftesbury refused to testify, he had
no definite recollection of those emblems of Popery, he said,
and so Pepys was cleared. As he and Shaftesbury left the Committee of Elections responsible for the charge, the Earl genially
remarked, 'Mr Pepys, next time we meet, we will remember
the Pope!', but the Secretary, enraged, refused to be conciliated,
and desired Shaftesbury to exculpate him, categorically, in the
Lords. Shaftesbury ignored this demand and retired to St Giles
in order to deal with the question of his two grandsons' education.

Shaftesbury had recently become aware that the elder of
these boys, now in his fourth year, was exceptionally intelligent,
as was his brother. Their training could not therefore be left
to such a ninny as their father; and so he decided that he himself
would become their guardian, and appoint others to succeed
him if he died before the children came of age. In order to secure
the arrangement, he required his son to sign a deed to this
effect, which Ashley seems to have done without objection,
heedless of any protest from his wife. Perhaps she made none;
for, quite apart from the fact that her father-in-law ruled the
household, she admired and loved him. So the pattern of Shaftesbury's own childhood was repeated. The third Earl justified

this step by becoming one of the most distinguished men of his age; his *Characteristics* are part of our literature.

Shaftesbury returned to London to lead the protests about the retention of a standing army, in particular about the regiments hired out to the French. It was feared that the King might strengthen the powers of his Catholic subjects by the use of these forces, and so cause another civil war. The fact that the powers of the English Catholics were almost non-existent was not considered, either by Shaftesbury or by those nobles who now formed, under his jurisdiction, the Country, as opposed to the Court Party; the latter was headed by Danby, Lauderdale and Arlington. Shaftesbury's group, of which the principal members were Buckingham, Russell, Holles, Halifax (Shaftesbury's nephew by marriage), Wharton and Salisbury, then put forward a bill excluding all Catholics from the succession, which was thrown out. In May Charles II retaliated by dismissing Shaftesbury from the Privy Council; he described him as *fourbe et fripon* to the French Ambassador. Shaftesbury returned from St Giles to be offered the post of Vicar-General; this entailed the reform of Church affairs, and was part of a plan to win him over to the Court Party. He refused what he described as 'a great office with a strange name', adding, 'I am ashamed I was thought so easy a fool by them [who] should know me better.' He presently set in hand a movement for the dissolution of Parliament; for it had become clear that a general election would bring the increasingly formidable and popular Country Party into power, thus defeating Danby's authority.

Little or no immediate progress was made with this plan, for in April 1675 Shaftesbury decided to withstand Danby and Lauderdale, now the leading ministers of the Court Party, on their introduction of the Test Bill. This made it a crime 'upon any pretence whatsoever' to take up arms against the King, or—and this was what the Country Party were determined to defeat—to alter the form of government in Church or State. In a long speech containing many historical instances, Shaftesbury outlined the fatal consequences of such a law, adding, 'How must we again be priest-ridden, when the Church shall, by Act of Parliament, and your oaths, be thus separate, and set above the civil power? This does indeed set the mitre above the Crown!' Halifax then spoke against the taking of oaths in general. 'If all the town was sworn not to rob,' he said, 'no man would sleep with open doors, or without locking up his plate.' Shaftesbury pointed out that in some cases resistance to monarchical power was justifiable, concluding, 'Kings are but men—and compassed with more temptation than others.'

These and other arguments were dismissed during debates that continued till 12th May, when Shaftesbury observed that as religious belief could never become static he would be glad to know what, exactly, was meant by the Protestant religion. This Socratic enquiry was of course a trap, into which the Lord Keeper, Finch, immediately fell. With heavy sarcasm, he urged that 'it might not be told in Gath, nor published in the streets of Askelon, that a Lord of such eminence and ability should not know what was meant by the Protestant religion'. Shaftesbury waited, unmoved. The Bishop of Winchester then solemnly informed him that 'the Protestant religion was comprehended in the Thirty-Nine Articles, the Catechism, the Homilies and the Canons'.

This reply was what Shaftesbury had been hoping for; in a brilliant speech, of detailed and cooteric learning, he analysed the discrepancies in the Articles (comparing the seventeenth with the eighteenth, and both these with the nineteenth and twentieth) giving dates, citing the Popish and unrevised origins of the Canons, urging the need for the improvement of the Catechism and the Homilies—and thus utterly routing the enraged bishops on their own ground. When one of them was heard to say, 'I wonder when he will have done preaching,' Shaftesbury turned upon him and replied, 'When I am made a bishop, my lord'—and a murmur of approbation rose from both sides of the House.

The Bill was then amended; but Danby voted down the amendment. Next day, Buckingham mocked the Court Party for their 'eloquent and well placed nonsense', and the Bill was held up. Charles, still financed by Louis XIV, was able to prorogue Parliament until October 1675, in a speech in which he referred to 'the ill designs of our enemies'. On 25th June the King ordered Shaftesbury to leave London.

Two months later, during a visit to a Dorsetshire neighbour, Shaftesbury was set upon by Lord Digby, Bristol's son, who, drawing his sword, was held back by their host. Digby shouted,

'You are against the King, and for seditions and factions, and for a Commonwealth, and I will prove it—and by God, we will have your head at next Parliament!' Shaftesbury promptly brought an action for slander against the young man, who was ordered to pay damages of £1,000.

As soon as Parliament was about to meet again, Shaftesbury and Locke wrote and circulated an anonymous pamphlet entitled *Letter from a Person of Quality to a Friend in the Country*, priced at 1/-, in which Danby was accused of trying to establish absolutism through military force. The Lords ordered it to be burnt by the common hangman, with the result that the price rose to 20/- and its circulation spread to the coffee-houses, which Danby attempted, vainly, to close.

In February 1676 Charles II 'advised' Shaftesbury to leave for the country. His Secretary of State having delivered this message, the Earl replied, with his humble duty, that His Majesty had been misinformed about his subversive activities and that private business kept him in London. In October he sold Exeter House, moving to Thanet House in Aldersgate, thus strengthening his connections with the City. He had been silenced by the prorogation of Parliament—it was not to meet till February 1677—but through pamphlets and private conferences his plans for putting forward its dissolution were now complete. On 15th February he, Buckingham, Wharton and Salisbury rose to declare that, by a statute of Edward III, Parliament, having been so long prorogued, had ceased, legally, to exist and should therefore be dissolved. This, Shaftesbury's first great political error, came very near to destroying both his cause and his career.

It had not been possible to make this a surprise attack; nor was the Country Party united behind it. Undeterred, the four peers decided to press on, drawing attention to their solidarity and firmness of purpose by dressing alike in magnificent suits of turquoise blue; this colour was especially becoming to the superbly elegant Buckingham, who, as highest in rank, rose to inaugurate their declaration as soon as the Commons had withdrawn, leaving the Lords in possession of the House. When he concluded, his speech was described as a breach of privilege. Shaftesbury then got up to support him, with further quotations from the statute of Edward III and references to

Magna Carta, speaking, according to Andrew Marvell, 'with extraordinary vigour'. He was followed by Salisbury and Wharton, and a discussion lasting some five hours ensued, to be resumed next day, when all four rebels were arraigned of contempt and required to kneel and ask pardon of the House, while withdrawing their statements. Salisbury, Wharton and Shaftesbury refused; characteristically, Buckingham did not appear till some hours later. Then, having been arrested by Black Rod and brought to the Bar, he excused himself by saying that he had had to go to his lodgings in Whitehall on account of servant trouble. 'You very well know,' he explained, 'what exact economy I keep in my family. I only went home to set my house in order.' But he would not take back anything he had said. The Lords, having committed the rebels to imprisonment during the King's pleasure, then asked them if they had anything to say.

This, the set question, was what Shaftesbury and his companions had been eagerly awaiting. One after another, they solemnly desired their Lordships' leave to take their own cooks with them to the Tower—the implication being that if they did not, orders would be given to poison them; a calculated insult to the royal authority, as represented by those who had sentenced them. This riposte broke up the composure of the House; it was greeted with laughter and angry exclamations, and the request was granted. Charles, who attended this debate, and was standing by the fireplace, remained impassive.

Shaftesbury then asked another favour, that of driving in his own coach from Thanet House to the Tower, as his state of health did not permit his being taken there by water. His plan was to progress towards what he represented as his martyrdom through the streets of the City, thus provoking demonstrations—bonfires, even—on his behalf. This also was allowed him: but no demonstrations took place.

The Lieutenant of the Tower was then instructed to separate the prisoners. Salisbury, Wharton and Buckingham were allowed visitors; Shaftesbury's son and three noblemen of the Country Party were refused admittance. Lady Shaftesbury, his cook and eight servants attended him. She sometimes spent the nights in the Tower, returning at intervals to Thanet House.

Shaftesbury assumed that with the next prorogation of Parliament his sentence must automatically lapse, and that he would be released. But Charles II held a trump card. In April 1677 he did not prorogue, but adjourned the Houses till May. They were then adjourned again till December. So Danby's command of Parliament and the temporary defeat of the Country Party were effected almost without opposition.

5

Shaftesbury was in his fifty-seventh year when he entered the Tower, and his health had deteriorated. Yet mentally he had never been more alert, more determined, not only to obtain his freedom, but to continue his campaign against the party which threatened to curtail, if not to destroy, the liberties of the English people. A fierce resolve to dominate went hand in hand with the pursuit of this cause, and increased with the continuation of his exile from the political scene; at this time it did not occur to him that the King and Danby would keep him out of action for more than a few weeks.

The conditions of his imprisonment were liberal. His rank and eminence entitled him to a suite of rooms and leave to walk on the leads or in the gardens. His visitors included Stringer, four stewards, a solicitor, a physician, a surgeon and an apothecary. He was allowed books and writing materials, and his correspondence on all private affairs was voluminous and uncensored. Through the gazettes he kept in touch with everything that was going on, at home and abroad; he followed the French campaign against the Dutch—it had become alarmingly triumphant—through maps sent in by Stringer, who also passed on his directions for the care of his properties in Dorsetshire, Carolina and the Caribbean. Shaftesbury remembered to order a popular Latin grammar for his six-year-old grandson, issued detailed instructions for the planting of cider apples at St Giles ('the Redstreak, the Black Apple, the Sour Pippin, the Bramsbury Crab, the Grouting') and made out lists of influential men in the Church, the forces and ministries all over Europe, which became a private *Who's Who* for future use. Against each name he wrote either V (vile) or W (worthy), sometimes doubling or trebling these letters, according to his opinion of the person concerned.

Meanwhile Danby, aware that he could not keep his great enemy in prison indefinitely, hurried on with his ostensibly anti-Catholic policy (while accepting bribes from Louis XIV), building up the navy, regulating the national finances, and supporting the general desire for the war with France, which Charles, as Louis's pensioner, was determined to avoid.

Still hoping to effect Shaftesbury's separation from the Country Party, Danby sent a mutual friend, Edmund Warcup, to Lady Shaftesbury; he told her that if her husband 'would well assure for his faithful loyalty and inviolable service to the King and the Lord Treasurer' (Danby himself), that minister would be able to arrange Shaftesbury's release. Lady Shaftesbury's reply was courteously firm. Her lord, she said, had been 'much injured', and would 'stand upon his honour'. Once free, he might consider treating—on his own terms: but he would not be parted from his friends.

At Easter the four prisoners pleaded for liberation from 'the dirty and stinking air' of the Tower, and were denied; in May, the substitution of another adjournment for the prorogation of Parliament made it clear that their imprisonment would be a long one. Meanwhile, the Lords' prejudice against, and fear of, Shaftesbury were emphasized by Buckingham's being given two days' and Salisbury three weeks' leave of absence; Shaftesbury asked in vain for temporary release.

In June, believing that he could go over the head of Parliament's and Charles's decision, he applied for a writ of *habeas corpus* at the King's Bench Bar. Here he told the judges, 'I am not so inconsiderable a person, but what you do in my case must be law for every man in England,'—only to be sent back to the Tower. It then dawned on him that what Charles and Danby required was, not an appeal to justice, but cringing submission, and an acknowledgement that he had insulted the Lords. As Shaftesbury would not then consider this abasement, the number of his visitors was reduced, and he was further exacerbated by the release of Wharton, Salisbury and Buckingham.

The preferential treatment of the Duke was especially hard to bear. Shaftesbury had often spoken of him as 'giddy-pated and inconstant', and the criticism had of course been repeated. Now, hearing a coach drive up, and leaning from the window to see his former ally about to step into it, he called out, 'What, my lord, are you leaving us so soon?', to which Buckingham replied, 'Ay, my lord. You know that we giddy-pated fellows never stay long in one place'—and drove away, to be received at Whitehall.

Lady Shaftesbury then asked Charles to release her husband on the grounds of health. (In fact, his physique had been much improved by the enforced inactivity, and the King must have known this.) Charles received her kindly, but said that if the Tower did not suit Shaftesbury, he might be moved to another prison; there could be no question of his being set free: and the Earl decided to remain where he was. In July Lord Stafford, a Catholic and a friend of York's, was admitted, and told the prisoner that his freedom could be effected through the heir-presumptive —on certain conditions. Shaftesbury replied, 'I suppose I apprehend your lordship. You would have the Duke write a new creed for me, yet would do worse, if it were in his power. He would have my head,' he went on, 'but I shall yet wear it, in despite of him—and live, perhaps, to come betwixt him and his great hopes.'

This defiance, these threats of excluding James from the succession (a solution already considered by the Country Party), were repeated to the King; and Shaftesbury remained in prison. By December he was desperate, and made another approach to Charles, in which he reminded him of his past services. But that was not enough. In January 1678 he wrote again, more humbly, and was again denied. In February he decided utterly to humiliate himself, both to Charles and to the Lords, by acknowledging that he had been 'ill advised' and 'casting himself at their Lordships' feet'.

On the 26th of that month he was freed, and next day took his place in the House. His year's imprisonment had made him a martyr-hero in the eyes of those supporters of the Opposition who suspected Charles, detested Danby and York, and desired war with France. So once more Shaftesbury led and invigorated the Country Party. Louis XIV, determined to prevent England's declaring war, was now bribing this group to bring about the dissolution of Parliament before both Houses enforced hostilities on the King. Russell, Buckingham, Colonel Algernon Sidney (a new recruit) and other noblemen took these bribes. Shaftesbury refused them.

He was less interested in the promotion of the war than in the problem of the succession. When Charles, whose eight sons were illegitimate, died, he would be succeeded by York; the Duke's children by Mary Beatrice would be brought up as

Catholics; and the Duke himself had never troubled to conceal what form of government he meant to use. He must therefore be set aside—but not, Shaftesbury considered, in favour of his eldest and fervently Protestant daughter Mary (his child by his first wife), whose marriage to her cousin, William of Orange, had been arranged by Charles and Danby in the autumn of 1677. Shaftesbury knew nothing of William's aims or character; he saw him as his uncles' ally, and discounted both his Calvinism and his resistance to the might of Louis XIV.

The alternative to James's exclusion was Charles's divorce. Meanwhile, the national loathing and dread of Catholicism—and thus of the Duke himself—must be brought to boiling-point through oratory, however crude, in both Houses, and pamphleteering. The latter was memorably produced by Andrew Marvell, who wrote, 'Popery is such a thing as cannot . . . be called a religion; nor is it to be mentioned with the civility which is . . . decent to be used.' One of Shaftesbury's anonymous hack writers followed this with 'Imagine you see your father, or your mother, tied to a stake in the midst of flames, when . . . they scream and cry out to God, for whose cause they die.' In the Commons, a member argued, 'Lay Popery flat—and there's an end of arbitrary government'—while Chief Justice Scroggs observed that Catholics 'have no natural sense nor natural consciences . . . They are wicked and cruel'. Finally, to gatherings at John's coffee-house and in his own home, Shaftesbury decribed York as 'heady, violent and bloody', and told the Lords, in James's presence, that the danger did not come from Catholics—or even Jesuits—living quietly in the country, but 'from great personages that live in this city', glancing towards the Duke as he concluded.

In February, when peace was signed between France and the United Provinces, Shaftesbury pointed out that the terms were entirely in Louis's favour, thus further denigrating Danby's policy. He then retired to the country till Parliament reassembled in October.

He seems not to have been immediately aware that, three months earlier, a new, dramatically evil, grotesquely hideous adherent to his cause had emerged from the lowest depths of London's underworld, and was about to offer him a poisoned dagger which he would not dare to refuse; nor that this mon-

strous creature was soon to become, not only the hope and hero
of the Country Party, but of England itself. Shaftesbury's
affiliation with and loyalty to a perjured villain inaugurated a
phase in his career which has permanently blackened his fame.
Yet he could not, at this point, afford to look the ugly gift-horse
in the mouth.

In August 1678 Charles II was told that a certain Doctor
Titus Oates had news of a Jesuit conspiracy to murder him
(and the Duke of York, if he did not co-operate), organize a
Catholic invasion from Ireland, burn down the palace of Westminster, and re-establish Popery throughout his kingdom by
means of a mass *auto da fé*, as practised in Spain and the Low
Countries under Philip II. He added that the Queen and her
physician, Sir George Wakeman, had arranged to poison her
husband, and that the Fire of London had been caused by the
Jesuits. Having set out his information under eighty-one heads,
Oates presented it to Charles and the Privy Council in September.

No doubt the King, who remained permanently sceptical
about this informant's veracity, expected to see some kind of
an eccentric; he could not have imagined, save in a nightmare,
the spectacle of a half-deformed, squat, bandy-legged young
man (Oates was then twenty-nine) whose empurpled face was
split by an enormous mouth, and lengthened by a chin of vast
proportions. From this obscene mask issued a flat, drawling,
penetrating voice, raised in ceaseless discourse about the horrors
to come, interlaced with accounts of the speaker's own courage
and cunning, together with lists of those implicated, beginning
with the Pope—including a number of Jesuit fathers, Anglican
bishops and Catholic peers—and ending, convincingly as it
happened, with Edward Coleman, York's former secretary, now
in Mary of Modena's service. Oates provided the Council with
letters—all clumsily forged—from the plotters, and asked them
to prove his statements by inspecting Coleman's correspondence.
The secretary was then discovered to have been in close touch
with Louis XIV's confessor, Père la Chaise ('Father le Shee',
Oates called him) to whom he had confided his hopes of 'a mighty
work', i.e. the enforced conversion to Catholicism of Charles's
three kingdoms. Oates later described his own experiences as
a supposed Catholic convert, after which he had become a student
at the Jesuit college of St Omer. His coadjutor, a half-crazed

clergyman, Israel Tonge, confirmed his *bona fides* and his work as a spy in the cause of Protestantism.

In the uproar that followed the spread of this news from the Privy Council to Parliament, thence throughout London and eventually to the provinces, Charles kept his head and maintained his disbelief in Oates's information; he did not conceal his conviction that the Doctor was a scoundrel. (He did not know, nor did the Council, that Oates had been expelled from a curacy, two schools, two colleges and two chaplaincies for theft, drunkenness and sodomy.) If the King had not outwardly subscribed to the existence of the Popish Plot he would certainly have been dethroned, and possibly have followed his father to the scaffold. This became clear, both to him and to Shaftesbury, as the terror increased, engulfing the country in a miasma of hysterical hatred and alarm, enhanced by an obsessive, and sometimes enjoyable, belief in Oates's wildest revelations.

Shaftesbury's acceptance of these was based, not on unquestioning credulity, but on the knowledge that, eight years earlier, the King himself had, however falsely, agreed to the re-establishment of Catholicism with the aid of French troops; was still the pensioner of Louis XIV, and was still hinting at his own conversion. Although Charles was therefore in no danger of assassination, Shaftesbury seems to have thought that, in order to keep his throne, he might consent to divorce the Queen, exclude his brother, and submit himself to the jurisdiction of the Country Party. So Oates must be used, flattered and handsomely paid, while all those, simple and noble, whom he accused were to be tried for high treason.

Still, there were doubts, hesitations, shades of incredulity—until, on 17th October, the body of Sir Edmund Berry Godfrey, a magistrate of high repute and a firm Protestant, was found, strangled and pierced by his own sword, in a ditch near Primrose Hill. Medical evidence eliminated suicide. His murder—unsolved to this day—could not have been the work of a footpad: for his money and valuables were untouched. * It was at once announced that, before approaching the Privy Council, Oates and Tonge had laid their 'depositions' before Godfrey, and had asked him to witness them. The conclusion was inescapable. The Jesuits,

---

* It is possible that the Earl of Pembroke, a homicidal maniac, who had a grudge against Godfrey, may have killed him; but there is no definite proof of this.

hearing of the magistrate's co-operation, had killed him so that he should not inform on them.

Thus a rich feast was provided for all would-be persecutors of their Catholic neighbours throughout the kingdom. Shaftesbury hurried to set it before Parliament, while adding to it from his base, the Country Party's Green Ribbon Club, at Temple Bar, of which he was the President and the inspiration.

The question as to whether Shaftesbury, as a servant of the state, should have employed, not only Oates and his myrmidons, but a quantity of lesser and equally corrupt informers is now academic. He may (it is unlikely) have believed in the possibility of a Catholic invasion, and of a holocaust on the lines of the massacre of St Bartholomew and the burnings under Queen Mary. Yet he knew Oates to be a pathological liar and a sadist, drunk with his newly acquired power to torture and destroy all he chose to accuse. But just as, forty-two years ago, Shaftesbury, a boy of fourteen, praying for deliverance from ruin, had seen his wicked great-uncle struck down and carried out of the Court of Wards, so once more the Divine Will was expressed through the fantastic inventions of Oates and his gang. Belief in the Deity's support is sometimes essential—and always useful to men of devouring ambition. Shaftesbury therefore put on, as he himself would have said, the whole armour of God; and one of the most malignant figures in our history became his armourer.

When Danby dared to support the Popish Plot, Shaftesbury was enraged; for it was his peculiar property, and the basis of all his plans. 'Let the Lord Treasurer cry as loud as he pleases against Popery,' he exclaimed, 'and think to put himself at the head of the Plot. I will cry a note louder, and soon take his place.' He had not much difficulty in doing so; for Oates presently produced letters from James's confessor, Father Bedingfield, to Danby, which proved the minister's affiliation with France. That they were forged was not discovered; they sufficed to put Danby under suspicion of Papist activities.

For the next three years—from the autumn of 1678 to the spring of 1681—all Shaftesbury's brilliance, all his energies were devoted to what he and his allies called the Good Old Cause, that of forcing the government into a framework that partially materialized in 1688, while foreshadowing the

constitutionalism we now take for granted and describe as democratic and liberal. He had no private life at that time; nor did he
desire one. In this, his political apotheosis, he achieved supremacy
by unremitting attention to the slightest details, working day
and night in an icy resolve to bring down all those standing
in his path, and using any information, no matter how degraded
and suspect its source, to that end. The scum of criminal London
—the idle chatter of schoolchildren, of prostitutes, housewives,
apprentices, innkeepers and grooms—false witnesses of every
type, from prisons, taverns and, naturally, Ireland—all this
material was woven into the fabric of his organization. No individual was too obscure, too humble to be ignored; they were
brought before him to be bullied and terrorized, or flattered
and bribed, according to their value as Shaftesbury assessed it;
and his judgement of such persons seldom failed. His purpose
—that of defeating Stuart absolutism and eliminating French
domination—centred on three goals: Danby's dismissal, the
King's divorce and York's exclusion. Only so, in his view,
could English liberty be restored, because 'Popery and slavery,'
as he often told the House, 'go hand in hand,' together with
the activities of the King, the Duke and the Minister. His methods
were ruthless and unscrupulous; he did not so much touch
pitch as become immersed in it, rising from the gutters and the
slums of the City to triumph, if only for a time, over his enemies,
of whom one alone was more powerful, more coolly perspicacious, more cunning than himself—Charles II.

Because Shaftesbury's genius operated universally, his daily
life is best seen kaleidoscopically, in flashes, some dimly revealed,
others dazzlingly illuminated. To a Mrs Gibbons, who had
publicized her belief in Sir Edmund Berry Godfrey's suicide,
he said, 'You damned woman, what is this devilish piper you
have given in?', adding that if she did not disclose the names
of her associates, she would be thrown into prison for life.
Taking aside a more promising witness, he urged, 'Honest
Smug the smith, thou look'st like an honest fellow, thou shalt
shoe my horses, and I'll make a man of thee. Tell me, who
murdered this man, and who set thee to find him out? What
Papists dost thou work for?' And to Samuel Pepys's clerk,
refusing to supply evidence against his master (Pepys was
York's protégé), Shaftesbury used persuasion with 'Nay, nay,

leave us to make the use of it. Do you but confess it, you shall be safe.'

That many of those cajoled or threatened were either rewarded or only temporarily imprisoned does not detract from the cruel efficacy of Shaftesbury's brain-washing. After his death a number of similar scenes were recorded, most of them inventions; but there is no doubt that intimidation was part of his technique, and that Godfrey's murder (it is just possible that it had been planned by Oates) and Coleman's letters were a godsend, in that they enabled Parliament to force Charles to remove his brother from the Privy Council and, later, to send him into exile.

In December 1678 Danby was found to have collaborated with Charles and Louis XIV in arranging an annual subsidy of six million livres for three years, on condition that peace was maintained between the two countries, thus ensuring Charles's independence of Parliament. The King had to dismiss Danby; some months later he was sent to the Tower, where he remained for five years. Further efforts by the Country Party forbade Catholics to sit in either House, sent five Papist Lords to the Tower, and forced on Charles the dissolution of the eighteen-year-old 'Cavalier' Parliament in January 1679. Meanwhile, Shaftesbury became known as 'the great giant that speaks to all, with strange freedom and admirable eloquence'. He and Oates were now the idols of the London mob: and it was at this time that Shaftesbury recruited a new and very different ally—the Duke of Monmouth.

On 9th April 1649 Lucy Walter, mistress of the exiled Charles II, had given birth to their son, James; she died eleven years later. He was placed in the care of a courtier, Colonel Crofts, and returned to England in 1662 at the age of thirteen, to be created Duke of Monmouth and married to a Scots heiress, to whom he was consistently unfaithful. Adored and indulged by his father, he soon became a rake, fascinating almost everyone he met by his gaiety, beauty and liveliness. Light-minded rather than stupid, he was good natured—although, if drunk, somewhat less so, as he showed when, with some other courtiers, he was halted during a raid on a brothel by the beadle who, unarmed, begged for his life, and was run through the heart by this charming young scapegrace. Two months later, Monmouth 'pleaded

3

his clergy', and was pardoned. He then became a soldier, and a good one, though no tactician; he distinguished himself in several campaigns, and was greatly loved by the common people. In 1679, at the age of thirty, his popularity with them recommended him to Shaftesbury, who began to consider him as a substitute for York, on the grounds that his mother might be proved to have been married to the King. For by this time, Shaftesbury had begun to suspect that Charles would neither divorce Queen Catherine nor allow her to be sent away; and the 'Protestant Duke' was more than willing to look on himself as the heir to the throne. Shaftesbury's plans for him matured slowly; hitherto he had thought so little of Monmouth that, in making out his list of notabilities, he had put three V's (for 'vile') against his name. Now he might be reassessed and placed in opposition to his uncle; he was not, like Oates, a powerful weapon, but he could be presented as the potential saviour of the nation from 'Popery and wooden shoes'. Very soon, Monmouth was being toasted as Prince of Wales—and even when the King publicly denied having been married to his mother, hopes of his being legitimized were encouraged; for Shaftesbury seems to have thrown doubts on the veracity of Charles's declaration.

In May 1679 the Earl began to organize the reconstitution and enforcement of *habeas corpus*, the law that became known as 'Shaftesbury's Act', and which actually dated from the reign of Henry III. He succeeded in eliminating the abuses that had accumulated over the centuries, by making it possible for persons accused of any crime but high treason and felony (these were to be tried at the next sessions) to appeal to the Lord Chancellor, who must then order them to be brought up for trial within twenty days. No person could be recommitted for the same offence. Shaftesbury attempted, unsuccessfully, to provide against indefinite imprisonment by preventing those sentenced from being sent to Tangier, the Channel Islands or Scotland, and fining any judge who evaded these conditions. Naturally, his efforts to defend the liberties of the subject met with opposition in the Lords; they were only successful because one of the tellers, a new adherent to the Country Party, the wild young Lord Grey of Warke, chose to count a very fat Lord as ten, thus obtaining the necessary majority.

This partial reformation of the law added to Shaftesbury's

popularity with the Londoners, in particular with the apprentices, whom he called his 'brisk boys'. Driving in his coach from Aldersgate to Westminster, he would be surrounded by a yelling bodyguard of youths brandishing the 'Protestant flails' his propaganda had made famous, to a chorus of 'Thump-a-Thump-Thump!', while their hero, bowing and smiling—his smile was memorably sweet, yet somehow a little sinister—also took care to salute the watermen, and even the Covent Garden porters, throughout his progress towards another victory over the hated Duke of York.

All this time, Charles II remained high in his subjects' favour. In that respect Shaftesbury was helpless, the citizens' view being that their beloved King was threatened from within his own circle by crypto-Papists and murderous Jesuits, whom Lord Chief Justice Scroggs would shortly send to the gallows.

And so he did. In the spring of 1679 a number of innocent Catholics were hanged, drawn and quartered, to the rapture of the people, all Charles's efforts to save them having failed. His long training in danger and humiliation enabled him to sustain an outward serenity: but every now and then there was an explosion. Sitting among his gentlemen at a performance of *Macbeth*, he greeted the entrance of the First Murderer with 'Oddsfish! Why is it that whenever they bring on a villain in a play, they must needs clap on him a black periwig, when 'tis well known that the greatest rogue in England wears a fair one?'—speaking so loudly that the comment was heard and repeated. And to a friend who expressed his surprise at Shaftesbury's presidency over the new Privy Council, the King replied, 'They have put a set of men about me—but they shall know nothing,' thus subscribing to a priest's description of his great enemy as 'the plague of the royal authority, the scourge of the royal family, and bane of the whole nation'.

The panic inspired and organized by this frail, ageing man, who instructed his wife and her women friends to carry elegant little pistols in their muffs, spread throughout the country. 'We shall all rise in the morning with our throats cut,' cried a Member of the Commons, and another added that the King, Monmouth and Shaftesbury were 'the only true pillars of our safety'. The Court Party then accused the Lord President of offering pardons to the Jesuit fathers, in return for confessions of guilt. If he did, these proposals were ineffectual; the doomed men died declaring their innocence. And then came a lull, much deprecated by Shaftesbury. 'Now that the populace is satisfied,' he said, 'it will be hard to stir it up again, unless great efforts are made.' He need not have concerned himself, while Monmouth swayed the mob and Oates the House of Commons and the Old Bailey.

Those subscribing to all Oates's evil fantasies were censured for their credulity by later generations who had never seen or heard him. He had the gifts of a mob orator; his weird accent ('Aigh, Taitus O-ates'), his belief in himself, even his grotesque appearance, combined to impress an audience already willing to condemn anyone he chose to accuse—with the exception of the Queen; but even she, it was urged, should be 'removed', with her Catholic entourage, from her husband's Court. So Shaftesbury returned to the question of divorce, to be halted by Charles's prorogation of Parliament in May 1679. Then his rage broke forth. In the King's presence, he told the Lords that he would 'have the heads' of those who advised it, adding 'There is no need to hold a candle to His Majesty's face, for his intent is visible by his actions.'

Shaftesbury's schemes were further frustrated by the failure of the first Exclusion Bill, the acquittal of Sir George Wakeman, Monmouth's exile to Brussels in August, and his own dismissal from the Privy Council in October. When the Houses assembled to reconsider the King's proposals for a peaceful settlement, Charles's recollections of the Country Party's triumph in the February elections once more forced him to suggest limiting James's prerogative, if and when the Duke succeeded. These offers were sensible enough; but the King knew, and so did his hearers, that James would never consent, either to a regency or to Parliament's control of the forces. Such a plan, said one Member, resembled the binding of Samson with withes, and would have the same effect. 'It is a very hard thing to say,' Shaftesbury concluded, 'that we cannot trust the King, and that we have already been deceived so often.' This was indeed *lèse-majesté*; but the speaker went unpunished.

For the anniversary—17th November—of Queen Elizabeth's birth, Shaftesbury and Buckingham organized the usual Pope-burning procession on an unprecedented scale. This one cost several hundred pounds, was attended by some two hundred thousand persons, and had been ingeniously brought up to date, as is shown by the record of the programme.

Six whistlers to clear the way.
A bell-man ringing and shouting, 'Remember Justice Godfrey.'
A dead body, representing Sir Edmund Berry Godfrey, in the habit he usually wore, the cravat wherewith he was murdered about his neck, with spots of blood on his wrists, shirt and white gloves, riding on a white horse, one of his murderers behind him to keep him from falling, representing the manner he was carried to Somerset House from Primrose Hill.
A Jesuit priest giving pardons very freely to those who would murder Protestants.
A consort of wind music called The Waits.
Four Popish bishops in purple and lawn sleeves.
The Pope's chief physician with Jesuit's powder [quinine] in one hand and an urinal in another.
Lastly, the Pope, preceded by silk banners with bloody daggers painted on them for murdering heretical kings, and behind him, his counsellor, the Devil.

All the way along, the waxen figure of the Pope seemed to respond to the promptings of Satan, nodding and shaking on its throne. When the procession halted in front of Queen Elizabeth's statue at Temple Bar, where a huge bonfire had been lit, the Prince of Darkness sprang away, and the image of the Vicar of Christ was pushed into the flames. And then an appalling noise broke out—screech after screech, drowning the cheers of the crowd. The Pope's belly had been stuffed with cats—a fitting sacrifice, it was thought, to the Protestant cause and the Protestant Queen.

In December 1679 Monmouth was advised by Shaftesbury to return to London, in defiance of his father's orders; the Duke then struck the bend sinister from his arms. All the King, now desperate, could do was to prorogue Parliament till April 1680, beg Louis XIV for another subsidy, and thankfully accept the Country Party's retirement from the Privy Council. At this point the Country Party, with Shaftesbury, gave a dinner to Lord Chief Justice Scroggs, presumably in order to show their forgiveness for his dismissal of Oates's evidence at the trial

of Sir George Wakeman. When the toasts began, Lord Huntingdon, a new recruit and the great-nephew of Shaftesbury's godfather Mr Hastings, proposed Monmouth's health, to which
Scroggs, now very drunk, added that of the Duke of York.
Huntingdon, springing up, cried 'And confusion to Popery!',
upon which all the guests but Scroggs and Shaftesbury left
the room. The Earl then told Scroggs that he had been offered
£10,000 to get Wakeman off. 'You are an honester man than
I,' said Scroggs, adding that he could not have brought himself
to refuse such a bribe. This seemed a helpfully damaging admis-
sion; but Shaftesbury could not use it when, after the failure
of the second Exclusion Bill, he brought an action against
York as a Popish recusant, and described Louise de Kéroualle
as 'a common nuisance' and one of the most undesirable of
the 'chargeable ladies about the Court'—upon which Scroggs
dismissed the jury. Yet this attack was so widely publicized
as to add to Shaftesbury's power and popularity.

The fight between him and the King was no longer disguised.
One or the other must be brought down; and Shaftesbury,
sure that it would be Charles, had unwittingly began to lose
his grip on an extremely intricate situation by underrating
both his enemy's grasp of it, and the stubborn courage that
had carried him through the horrors of exile. Shaftesbury might
threaten the King—as he did when he told the French
Ambassador, 'We shall easily find the means, by the laws, of
making him walk out of the kingdom'—but he could not shake
him.

Parliament was dissolved in January 1681, and in the February
elections the Country Party triumphed again, with the result
that Charles summoned the Houses to meet at Oxford in March;
for this setting would be less prejudicial to his aims than the
turmoil of Westminster. In vain Shaftesbury protested; he
would not admit that his supremacy had been considerably
weakened by Halifax's successful opposition to the Exclusion
Bill, the withdrawal of the moderates from the Country Party,
and Charles's repeated denials of Monmouth's legitimacy. So
he fell back on the divorce. During a debate attended by the
King, he implored his audience to insist on it; and when one
of the Lords observed that His Majesty might not necessarily
have a child by a second wife, he pointed at Charles, and said,

'Can anyone doubt, if he looks at the King's face, as to his being capable of making children? He is only fifty. I know people upwards of sixty who would have no difficulty in making children.' There was a roar of laughter, in which Charles joined. He often told his friends that the Parliamentary debates were 'as good as a play', and attended them regularly. Characteristically he ignored Shaftesbury's attacks, receiving him in private, and pretending to consider a divorce. So the 'Dorsetshire eel', as the Court Party called him, was further deceived.

Both men had been ill, Charles so seriously that in August 1679 and May 1680 his life seemed in danger; he recovered completely; but Shaftesbury walked with a stick, and had lost much of his serenity. He flew into rages over details, would not rest or take advice, and even found fault with the devoted Lady Shaftesbury. The face under the great blond periwig was livid now, the eyes had sunk, yet his smile was as mysteriously sweet as ever.

By the time the debates at Oxford began, the members of the Country and Court Parties were known respectively as Whigs and Tories; originally, both names had been slang terms of abuse. Charles II's decision to meet his Parliament here rather than in London drew attention to his wish to prevent a second Civil War; this was a very clever move, in that the majority of his people would have preferred almost any hardship to such a catastrophe. Also, they had been seriously alarmed by York's threat of invading from exile in Scotland in order to establish his right with the aid of French troops. And in the Country Party, Algernon Sidney's proposal for a republic raised the dreaded ghosts of Cromwell and his major-generals. Shaftesbury's desire for Monmouth's inheritance (did not Henry VIII legitimize his younger daughter, whose reign had been England's glory?) prevailed over Sidney's schemes, as it did over those of Halifax for a regency under William and Mary. On 24th March he decided to approach the King with his 'expedient' for the succession.

As he had not then leave to speak to Charles, he asked the Marquess of Worcester to present His Majesty with a paper outlining his plans for Monmouth. Charles read it and, turning upon the Earl, said, 'Ay, marry, here is an expedient indeed, if one would trample over all laws of God and man.' Shaftesbury persisted with 'Sire—will Your Majesty give me leave to make it as lawful as we can?'

The chance to show himself as subject to the law was at once seized by Charles. With the majestic dignity that seldom failed of its effect, he replied, 'My Lord—let there be no self-delusion. I will never yield, and I will not let myself be intimidated. Men become ordinarily more timid as they grow old; as for me, I shall be, on the contrary, bolder and firmer—and I will not stain my life and reputation in the little time that perhaps remains for me to live.' Adding that he had law, reason and the Church (indicating the bishops) united behind him, he turned away.

Neither Whigs nor Tories knew that the King's boldness and firmness were partially based on an increased yield from the State's taxes and a further allowance from Louis XIV, who had agreed to give him £340,000 annually for the next three years. Also, Louis had promised his cousin financial support in the event of a civil war. Charles's threat of declaring war on France—a very successful piece of blackmail—had been made before he left London; so the announcement of the man who, four years later, himself became a Catholic, that 'the monarchy and the Church of England march together', silenced the Whig Party.

Yet Shaftesbury's popularity remained unaffected, and had been greatly enhanced by rumours of his being in danger of assassination during the brief and rather absurd drama of Dangerfield's 'Meal-Tub' or 'Sham' Plot, of which the instigator was a forger, a robber and a coiner. This incident was a source of profit to the merchants of silk armour; according to a contemporary, this invention ensured the weaver's safety, in that anyone attempting to stab or shoot him would succumb to helpless laughter at the sight of it.

Two days after his rebuff of Shaftesbury, Charles sent for him and asked if he had in mind any alternative to Exclusion. 'No,' said Shaftesbury, adding, 'the whole nation is of my opinion.' The King then suggested a private talk on the matter, to which each of them would bring a witness. Shaftesbury agreed, and proposed meeting at Lord Arlington's lodgings. 'Why there, of all places?' Charles asked. 'Because,' Shaftesbury replied, 'it is the most indifferent [neutral] place, my Lord Chamberlain being neither good Protestant nor good Catholic—and next, because there is there the best wine, which is the only good thing that can come of our meeting.' The King seems to have accepted this impertinence without comment.

He could afford to do so. On 28th March 1681 Charles II, taking both Houses by surprise, dissolved the Oxford Parliament, and left for Windsor. In vain, Shaftesbury urged the Lords to stay on and protest; one by one they slipped away. He then returned to London.

For the remaining four years of his reign Charles ruled without a Parliament. During the next few months he inaugurated his personal absolutism—and set in hand his revenge on the Country Party.

6

As Charles II was driving into Oxford, an elderly man called out, 'Remember your royal father, and keep the staff in your own hands!' 'Ay, by God I will,' the King shouted back, 'and the sword too!'

In the spring and summer of 1681 the sword—or rather, the axe—was being sharpened; and Charles intended that the first head to fall should be Shaftesbury's. Yet he had to proceed cautiously; for although the circumstances seemed propitious enough, some preliminary measures must be taken before his great enemy could be indicted.

Charles began by launching his Declaration, which was read in all the churches and widely circulated. In it he explained that he had dissolved his last two Parliaments because of their unreasonable insistence on Exclusion, their attacks on his judges and ministers—thereby implying Shaftesbury's leadership on these points—and their insolent addresses. Yet, he assured his people, he 'loved Parliaments', and intended to call them frequently. (His promise to Louis XIV that he would continue to reign without one was known only to the French Ambassador.)

This demand for obedience to all royal decrees exactly fitted in with the general lack of response to Shaftesbury's propaganda. Although only thirty-nine Catholics had been executed, and no damage done to national property, there was a feeling that enough blood had been shed; while disbelief in Oates's and other informers' accusations was increasing. In fact, Shaftesbury and the Country Party had overplayed their hand. They still commanded the City; but although these powerful allies denounced the dissolution of the Oxford Parliament, they submitted to the King's decision. There was no rioting; the apprentices offered him their services free; and several Whig noblemen, including that prudent peer, the Earl of Huntingdon, went over to the Court Party, begged Charles's pardon and were allowed to kiss his hand. Also, it was rumoured that Monmouth was about to ask his father's forgiveness and withdraw his claim.

In June an Irish informer, Fitzharris, was tried and condemned for false evidence about Godfrey's murder; and Shaftesbury's useless efforts to save him from the gallows amounted to another defeat. Halifax then advised the King that the moment had come to strike down the Whig leader. At six in the morning on 2nd July he was arrested, and his papers were seized.

Prepared for this, Shaftesbury had already destroyed all incriminating documents, and now gave the Serjeant-at-Arms his keys. Urged to eat something before his confrontation by the King and the Privy Council, he said, 'I have no stomach to eat, unless I can get a roast Irishman,' referring to Fitzharris's confession implicating the Whig Party. At eleven o'clock he stood before the Board over which he had so often presided, and faced the tall, dark man who had once taken him in his arms and 'sworn very deeply' that he would never quit his Lord Chancellor nor forsake his cause.

The witnesses supplying evidence of Shaftesbury's treason were those very Irishmen used by the Country Party against the Court during the Popish Plot. As he was not allowed to confront them, their charges were easily refuted. 'I have always been steadfast to His Majesty's interest,' he said, 'though in some things my judgement led me to take different measures to those advocated by some more near to His Majesty.' He added coolly that if their Lordships really believed him capable of employing Irishmen and Papists to subvert the Government, then 'I were fitter for Bedlam than prison'. This defence was ignored, and he was committed to the Tower; but several Councillors withdrew in order to avoid signing the warrant (for who knew whether Shaftesbury might not come back into power?) while others hesitated to do so. Enraged, the King exclaimed, 'Sign it, one and all!' and the remaining seventeen obeyed.

Shaftesbury was taken to an antichamber, where a meal had been prepared; at this point, Titus Oates came in, asked him how it was that he had been committed to 'Lob's Pound', and offered to visit and pray with him. Shaftesbury remained calm and cheerful. As he stepped into the barge that was to land him at Traitors' Gate, the people ran out to see him: and one cried, 'God bless your Lordship, and deliver you from your enemies!' Smiling, Shaftesbury replied, 'I thank you, sir—but I have nothing to fear. They have; therefore pray God to deliver them from me.'

In September he became seriously ill and, in order to escape a lingering death in the Tower, asked the King's leave to retire, either to St Giles or to his estates on the Ashley river in Carolina, of which the development had been his 'darling project' for many years. 'I must leave him to the law,' said Charles, and Shaftesbury then arranged to sell all his horses. Meanwhile, Charles told the French Ambassador that he now hoped to re-establish his own authority, adding, 'But this can only be done by cutting off some heads,' implying that others would follow Shaftesbury's.

The Government, refusing all Shaftesbury's requests for bail, postponed his trial till 24th November, when a bill of indictment for high treason was presented to the grand jury of Middlesex at the Old Bailey by Chief Justice Pemberton, who made it clear that they must bring in a verdict of guilty; as the hearing was a preliminary to Shaftesbury's trial by his peers (who were certain to condemn him) he was not present. He and his wife played piquet while waiting to hear his fate. The jury—Whigs to a man, empanelled by Whig sheriffs—brought in a verdict of *Ignoramus*; and on 28th November Shaftesbury was released. The people of London celebrated his freedom with bonfires and processions of green-ribboned men, shouting, 'No Popish successor—no York—a Monmouth—a Buckingham—God bless the Earl of Shaftesbury!'

He himself returned to Thanet House, and a few days later was the guest of honour at a great banquet in the Skinners' Hall. The Whigs then issued a medal, showing Shaftesbury's profile on one side, and on the other the sun emerging from the clouds, with the inscription *Laetamur* and the date of his release. So he triumphed; and the King and the Court Party had to contrive another attack. By this time, their most memorable support had been provided by Dryden, whose *Absalom and Achitophel* (followed by *The Medal* in February 1682) appeared in the last week of November. But Charles and his Council had in mind a deadlier weapon than the Poel Laureate's dazzling satires—the destruction of local government, and thus of the Whig party. This would ensure a new and irrefutable indictment of Shaftesbury for high treason.

The King's campaign began with the hunting down and imprisonment of Dissenters, and was followed by the seizure of city and borough charters throughout the country. As many of these were medieval, it was easy to pin-point certain minor illegalities and then to serve a writ of *Quo Warranto* on each corporation, thus forcing the surrender of the charters to the State. All were called in—some corporations gave them up voluntarily—and Whig sheriffs were replaced by Tories. No Tudor, not even Henry VIII, would have dared to exercise such tyranny over a people describing themselves as free. Charles II and his advisers enforced it unresisted. The conquest of the City of London took longer; eventually, a combination of chicanery and threats brought about the installation of a Tory Mayor and sheriffs, who would of course elect juries of the same persuasion: so that those elected could convict, rightly or wrongly, anyone the Court Party wished to destroy. Of these, Shaftesbury was, naturally, the first.

He may have been alarmed; he was certainly enraged and determined to fight back. He therefore formed what came to be known as his Council of Six—Monmouth, the Earl of Essex, Russell, Sidney, Hampden (grandson of the famous Ship-Money politician) and Lord Howard of Escrick, who had been imprisoned with Shaftesbury in 1681. Buckingham was no longer affiliated with this group, and had become a degraded and ludicrous figure, in spite of his newly acquired house in Dowgate ('Alderman George', Charles called him) and his popularity with its inhabitants. He stank worse than most seventeenth-century courtiers; and it was observed that his false teeth did not fit.

Two other noblemen, Sir Thomas Armstrong and Lord Grey of Warke, were also under Shaftesbury's command, and in some ways more belligerent than his Council. But Grey was a traitor, and Armstrong had no influence. Meanwhile, Monmouth could not make up his mind whether to be guided by Shaftesbury, or by those who disagreed with his tactics. So the Whig party was divided; and because they doubted his judgement their leader could not weld them together. Most of them were much younger than he, and could afford to wait till the King's grip on the country slackened, or was released by death. Shaftesbury could not. He had decided on immediate action, to open with a rising in the City, accompanied by similar movements in the West and the Midlands, where feeling against the Government had long been, and still was, very high.

It was at this moment that Shaftesbury's past rose to defeat him. He had overcome so many disasters, that he looked on them as mere setbacks—pauses in his progress. This caused him fatally to underrate his principal opponent. He never really sounded the depths of Charles's capacity for deceit, his extremely subtle use of his prerogative, or his ability to watch and wait, while appearing to yield. Also, although Shaftesbury was neither self-important nor conceited, he could not help knowing that, compared with his contemporaries, he was supereminent; and he utterly discounted the fact that age, overwork and ill-health had affected his genius, and were now urging him into the enforcement of his plans on a disintegrating Council. Heedless of correct timing and adequate support, he meant to set in hand a revolution. Despising the Stuart brothers, and disregarding the most suitable claimants, William and Mary of Orange, he had resolved to make Monmouth the heir, against all precedent, custom and tradition. He seems not to have had any great opinion of the Duke himself, preferring to manoeuvre him as a puppet in the political scene. Monmouth was his choice; and nothing must prevail against that decision.

Shaftesbury's self-knowledge was not on a level with his intellectual powers; nor was he malicious—Lady Russell once commented on his 'lack of gall'—and so he expressed surprise when his methods were denounced. 'If I have a fault,' he replied to one critic, 'it is that of tender-heartedness'—and he was perfectly sincere. His physical courage was that of one who, all his life, had defied the onslaughts of disease; and now he himself, he told his Council, would lead his ten thousand brisk boys into action. 'Your lordships may see,' he said, indicating his bent frame, 'that I *cannot* run away.' He then reassured the doubters as to the danger of a civil war. He knew the King better than they. 'He will sacrifice a hundred brothers rather than hazard his crown,' he went on, adding with a sneer, 'He will condescend to a compliance with the desires of his people in Parliament.' But the risings must be organized—and without delay. Charles summed up the situation more succinctly. The little Lord had been set free, he said, 'with a bottle to his tail', concluding, 'At the Day of Judgement we shall see whose arse is blackest.' He then obtained another £75,000 from Louis XIV, so as to avoid calling a Parliament. 'They are devils, who intend my ruin,' he told the French Ambassador. He knew that without those devils Shaftesbury had no solid political backing.

In August 1682 Shaftesbury made an unexpected and apparently pointless approach to York, who had returned from Scotland in the preceding April. In a letter that has not survived he warned James, according to the latter's biographers, that the Duchess of Portsmouth was planning to put forward the little Duke of Richmond, her son by Charles, as a substitute for Monmouth. He may have hoped to make mischief between Charles and York; but James merely told him to submit himself to the King, upon which Shaftesbury continued with his plans for revolution.

In September Monmouth made the last but one of his triumphant progresses, this time in the Midlands, where he was rapturously received. On the way back he was arrested for causing a riot. He then sent Shaftesbury a message to the effect that the country people had offered to 'draw their swords and rise instantly', but that he had decided to wait for the Earl's instructions. In a fury Shaftesbury abused him for his lack of initiative, and urged him to return to Cheshire as soon as he was released, so as to lead the rising. Advised by Grey and Russell, Monmouth remained in London. Shaftesbury then suggested seizing the Tower, only to be persuaded that this would be disastrous.

Already the Tory sheriffs had been sworn in; and Shaftesbury was told that the Privy Council had issued a warrant for his arrest. He therefore left Thanet House, and went into hiding in Cheapside; his meetings with the Council of Six took place at a wine-merchant's near by. Their arguments failed to convince him that they must wait till they knew how much support would be available. Implored by Russell to have patience, he exclaimed, 'Patience will be your destruction!' adding, 'I shall see ten thousand men at Whitehall gates ere I am many days older,' as he left the room. 'He will undo us all,' said Monmouth, and the others agreed. When news came in that neither the West nor the Midlands was ready to rise, Shaftesbury left Cheapside for Wapping. The Government spies reported that he had left England. In fact, he was waiting for the result of the City rising, now planned for 19th November. It was then postponed—it seemed indefinitely.

Still he would not admit defeat. He decided to cross to Amsterdam, where many of the Whig party had taken refuge, and continue his campaign from there. He was not aware—

he may have preferred not to be—that a sub-plot had been
formed by certain minor members of the Country Party to
assassinate the King and his brother as they returned from
Newmarket, in order to establish a republic. Shaftesbury would
have vetoed this plan if he had been consulted about it. His
whole career was dedicated to curbing and constitutionalizing
the monarchy, not (as he once told John Evelyn) to destroying
it; for, having worked under a republic, he knew its disadvantages; and he had always despised the impractical fanaticism
that produced such schemes. He did not live to see the failure
of this one, which resulted in the execution of the Rye House
plotters and the total defeat of the Whig party. So the Stuart
revenge was complete; and what one of Charles's courtiers
described as His Sacred Majesty's golden age began.

In the last week of November Shaftesbury made his final
arrangements. Having decided that Lady Shaftesbury was not
to accompany him, presumably because he expected to return
before long, he left Stringer in charge of her and of his affairs.
He said farewell to his 'dear, loving, faithful, virtuous wife'
calmly and cheerfully. Accompanied by two servants, Shepherd
and Wheelock, he then left Wapping for Harwich. Here he was
joined by a man whom, in his great days, he would never have
employed—a Scots dissenting preacher and pamphleteer, Robert
Ferguson, later known as Ferguson the Plotter. Landing at
the Brill on 28th November, the four men proceeded to Amsterdam and occupied rooms in The Bible inn, where they were
tracked down by a spy, whom Shaftesbury eluded by moving
to the house of a Dutch acquaintance. The regents of the city
ignored Charles II's request that the Earl should be extradited;
he was visited by several English refugees, and shadowed by
other agents; one of these reported that he and Ferguson were
drawing up an anti-papist memorandum to be presented to the
United Provinces. In the middle of December an Italian spy
told the English Government that Shaftesbury was suffering
from 'gout in the stomach'. In fact, he was being poisoned by
the stoppage of the draining from the wound in his side. But
not even Locke, himself too ill to travel, could have helped
him now.

Still he walked out on most days, supported by Ferguson
and a Whig friend, Sir William Waller. He could eat very little;

and in January 1683, unable to keep down more than a few spoonfuls of broth, he went to bed. On the 17th of that month, realizing that death was near, he made his will, and sent for his wife and son; but the letter was delayed, and Ferguson's reports had been so optimistic that they did not try to join him.

He was now so weak that it had become difficult to understand what he said; but one of the witnesses to his will heard him murmur something about 'enemies . . . serve my country . . . liberty'. He then relapsed into a sleepless calm. For two days and nights he lay with his eyes open, waiting for the end. On the 20th he spoke faintly but clearly to Ferguson, who at once began to examine him about his belief in eternity and the state of his soul. These unctuous adjurations had little or no effect on the dying man; he had often enjoyed theological discussion, and seemed ready to do so now; but the effort was too great, and again he sank into silence. All that night, Wheeler watched by him. At midday on Sunday 21st January he sat up, said 'I feel a little better,' and asked for some broth. Wheeler called Ferguson, who hurried forward with a cordial. Wheeler supported his master as he drank; he swallowed, gulped; then, sighing deeply, he died in the valet's arms.

He had left instructions that his body should be taken back to England and laid in the family vault at Wimborne St Giles. After he had been embalmed, his servants dressed him in the clothes he had recently discarded, and put on him 'a very fine new wig'. He was then placed in a simple wooden coffin with a glass top: so that those, and they were many, who came to pay their last respects, could see his face. As he lay there, with what one described as 'a very smiling countenance', it was hard to believe that he was dead.

Locke and Lady Shaftesbury arranged with the authorities in Amsterdam that he should be put on an English pink, the *Elizabeth*, and, attended by Shepherd and Wheelock, taken to Poole, thence to be carried to his home. On 21st February the little ship, flying a mourning flag embroidered with the Ashley Cooper arms, entered the harbour—and was immediately searched for incriminating papers. None were found.

The funeral costs came to £424. 19s. 3d. These included £2. 10s. for 'making and bricking up the grave, it being all arched over'.

There was much rejoicing at Shaftesbury's death, notably in the Whig party, who considered that his belligerence had harmed their cause; while for several years the Tory pamphleteers continued to issue rhymes about 'mighty Tapski's stinking guts', with such quotations as 'Of these the false Achitophel was first, A name to all succeeding ages curst'. Finally Dryden, in accordance with his duties as Historiographer-royal and Court poet, attached to his *Albion and Albanius* an ingenious drop-scene. 'Fame,' ran the instructions, 'rises out of the middle of the stage, standing on a Globe: on which is the arms of England: the Globe rests on a Pedestal: on the Front of the Pedestal is drawn a Man with a long, lean, pale Face, with Fiends' Wings and Snakes twisted round his Body; he is encompassed by several Phanatical Rebellious Heads who suck poison from him, which runs out of a Tap in his Side.'

Sir William Temple
(1628—1699)

And I turned myself to behold wisdom, and
madness and folly: for what can the man do that
cometh after the king? even that which hath
already been done ... Wherefore I perceive that
there is nothing better than that a man should
rejoice in his own works.

Ecclesiastes, ii, iii

Sir William Temple
attributed to Lely

In the second decade of the seventeenth century Blackfriars contained a number of medium-sized houses occupied by the families of those nobles who were not rich enough to refurbish the great Tudor palaces overlooking the Thames. One of these belonged to Sir John Temple, who had been born in Ireland and educated at Trinity College, Dublin. Returning from the grand tour in 1627, he married Mary, daughter of Dr John Hammond of Chertsey, formerly physician to James I; through him Sir John obtained a post at the Court of Charles I; he retained his Irish estates, and was later appointed Privy Councillor and Master of the Rolls in that colony. Shortly after one of his visits to Dublin his eldest son, William, was born at Blackfriars on 25th August 1628.

William's birth was followed by those of two children who died in infancy; then two more, John and James, were born and survived. In September 1638 Lady Temple, pregnant for the last time, left London to stay with her brother, the Reverend Dr Henry Hammond, formerly Dean of Christchurch, Oxford, at Penshurst in Kent. Eight days after the birth of the twins, Martha and Henry, she died. Her husband, writing of her to Dr Hammond's patron, the Earl of Leicester, as 'the desire of mine eyes, and the most dear companion of my life', never married again. He returned to Court, leaving his family in their uncle's care. So, at ten years old, William was virtually an orphan. He became devoted to Dr Hammond, a man of charm and kindness and a distinguished scholar, who delighted in the company of children, 'observing diligently', according to his biographer, 'the little deviations of their manners'. He desired rather to be loved than reverenced by the young Temples; and he was.

William, a handsome, intelligent and lively boy, came to prefer athletics, tennis especially, and outdoor sports, to his studies. His uncle's influence and methods provided freedom, gaiety and an easy discipline; and the peaceful remoteness of

Penshurst isolated him from the turmoil which led up to the Civil War. By the time he left the local day-school to become a boarder at that of Bishops Stortford, George Villiers, first Duke of Buckingham, had been murdered, the Fleet had mutinied and the Earl of Strafford was under sentence of death in the Tower.

William was still at Bishops Stortford when the Irish rebellion broke out. In 1642 Charles I, preparing for war with Parliament, ordered Sir John Temple to come to terms with the Irish; but that gentleman persisted in putting down the rebels—he later wrote a history of this movement— and was imprisoned in the Castle of Dublin. Parliament then deprived Dr Hammond of his living on account of his royalist sympathies. In 1644 Sir John was released, returned to England and arranged for William to be entered as a fellow-commoner at Emmanuel College, Cambridge. He was now seventeen; and he had fallen in love with Lord Leicester's daughter, Lady Dorothy Sidney, Waller's 'Sacharissa'—only to see her married to Lord Spencer, later Earl of Sunderland. His feeling for her lasted throughout his years at the University, and even beyond them; but it was rather a sentimental than a tragic passion. Meanwhile, his detachment from the disturbances of the war was maintained, although many of his fellow undergraduates, including the second Duke of Buckingham and his brother, Lord Francis Villiers, had run away from Cambridge to join the Cavaliers.

The inconclusive battle of Edgehill and the Royalist defeats at Naseby and Marston Moor had no effect on William's University career. With his 'chamber fellow', James Beverly, a wealthy young man, he continued his studies under Dr Cudworth, later famous as a philosopher, whose discourses were so dull that William escaped to the tennis court whenever he was released from the tutor's expositions on logic and metaphysics. While retaining and improving his Latin, he forgot such Greek as he had learnt at Bishops Stortford.

For several centuries—ever since the reign of Richard III, when the Temples had fought for him against Henry VII, and so lost their manor of Temple Hall—they had been comparatively poor; but Sir John's careful management enabled him to educate his children as became their breeding. When William left Cambridge without a degree, his father, who later resumed his Irish appointment under the Protectorate, arranged to send him on the grand tour for two years, and thus again removed him from the conflicts between King and Parliament. William, a sensitive, rather moody young man, therefore acquired an objective attitude towards religion and politics, which characterized his whole career. A staunch Church of England royalist, he was neither fanatical nor intolerant; looking on the struggles between Levellers, Independents, Presbyterians and monarchists from far off, his loyalty to the Stuart cause remained unimpaired, partly because at this time he did not become involved in it.

By the early summer of 1648 all the preparations for his travels had been made; valet and courier had hauled his baggage aboard the ship that was to take him to the continent, via the Isle of Wight, where his cousin, Colonel Hammond, was the Parliamentarian Governor of Carisbrooke Castle. Here Charles I, with his chaplain, another Hammond cousin, was imprisoned; and in an inn near by William found himself in a situation that suddenly became a drama. His share in it was that of an admiring spectator; yet it changed the whole course of his existence. The setting, the characters, were those of a romance in which Cavaliers and Roundheads, struggling for supremacy, achieved a peaceful conclusion. It was his first experience of the effects of national conflict on the individual.

Two years before William's arrival on the island, Sir Peter Osborne, the Royalist Governor of Cornet Castle in Guernsey, yielding to the Parliamentary forces, had taken refuge in St Malo, leaving his wife, his daughter Dorothy and his son Robin in England. The brother and sister—she was twenty-one and he a year older—now in the Isle of Wight on their way to join Sir Peter, were staying in the same inn as William: and all three at once became friends. His effect on Dorothy was immediate and lasting; his looks greatly pleased her. This tall, elegant young man wore his own hair which, falling in dark waves over his shoulders, set off the sculptured delicacy of his profile and his grey, deepset eyes. In her, he saw a more unusual beauty —black and white, Italianate, a little sombre. Her gaiety and wit so entranced him that, already half in love, he decided to accompany her and her brother to St Malo. These young people had much in common, in especial their hostility to Colonel

Hammond, whose treatment of the King they considered harsh and insolent—in fact, monstrous. So it was that, on their way down to the shore, Robin Osborne turned back, re-entered the inn and, taking out a diamond ring, engraved on a window-pane a quotation from the Book of Esther—'And Haman was hanged on the gallows he had prepared for Mordecai.'

This clumsy and provocative pun was discovered and reported before its perpetrator reached the quay, and he and his companions were brought before the Governor. Evidence against them had hardly been uttered, when Dorothy announced that she was the culprit—and there was a pause. William then seems to have used his relationship with Colonel Hammond to intercede for her. The Governor did not want to penalize a woman: and they were allowed to proceed.

From that moment, William Temple became utterly committed to this spirited and exquisite creature. He was now, in the contemporary phrase, her servant; and when they reached her father's house, he remained with her. His love, impetuously declared, was warmly received; she found him irresistible; and so, unable to relinquish this shared ecstasy—which was concealed from Sir Peter Osborne—William stayed on in St Malo. A week passed; then a month: and his journey was still postponed, it seemed indefinitely.

Meanwhile, Sir John Temple, who had been expecting to hear about his son's progress, made enquiries. Still in St Malo —and attached to an impoverished and therefore ineligible young woman! He was very angry. William was ordered to leave at once for Paris. His dependence on and duty to his father eliminated any thought of disobedience. Promising to write to one another, he and Dorothy parted. And so a correspondence that has become part of our literature began. Less than half of it survives.

Of the early letters William received from Dorothy, seventy-seven are extant; they date from December 1652 to October 1654. But as he remained abroad for the first eighteen months of what she preferred to call their friendship, their correspondence must have begun as soon as he reached Paris in 1648; and indeed, her first surviving letter shows that they had been writing to one another for some time. Only two of his to her have been preserved; yet her replies to those lost indicate the nature of his side of the interchange, and emphasize the contrasts—and sometimes the clashes—of their respective temperaments.

Dorothy had had a much harder life than William, whose fortunes were unaffected by the Protectorate's rather capricious treatment of the Royalists, many of whom retained their wealth and estates, while others were deprived of both. One of her brothers, Charles, had been killed fighting for the King; and her father, to whom she was devoted, was now a ruined man in failing health. His loyalty to the sovereign had received no support throughout his tenure of Cornet Castle; and when Dorothy and William first met, he faced the prospect of losing his manor-house of Chicksands in Bedfordshire, which had been sequestered by Parliament. In 1649 he managed, at crippling cost, to compound for it; and so, when the Osbornes returned to England, shortly after the execution of Charles I, Dorothy, her parents and her four remaining brothers, Robin, Thomas, Francis and Henry, had a home, but little else. Their lives were uneventful, secluded, and in her case confined. So the streak of melancholy in her character, unwittingly fostered by Lady Osborne, intensified, as the first year of William's absence passed, and any hope of being allowed to marry him receded, finally disappearing altogether. Yet, living for his letters and their rare meetings, she clung to their relationship that had become the background and the inspiration of her existence—one that had certain compensations, inimitably described by her in a series of sketches, jokes, gossip and reflections. She fought her periods of depression, sometimes mocking herself and those about her, not spitefully, but with as it were the shrug and the smile of a disillusioned yet unconquerable spirit. Meanwhile her daily routine, made up of little things, was so brilliantly reported to her lover as to ensure both his constancy and his certainty of their happy ending.

Dorothy did not share this belief. She never forgot—in fact, she was haunted by—a conversation with her mother (who died in the autumn of 1652) that shows the older woman's outlook as hopelessly resigned to the preponderance of evil. After telling William that 'the first thing I liked in you' was his good nature, and anathematising 'tricks, little ugly plots and designs', Dorothy recalls her mother asking her whether she did not think her 'too jealous [suspicious] and a little ill-natured'. As the girl said nothing, Lady Osborne went on, 'Come, I know you do, if you would confess it, and I cannot blame you . . . But I have lived to see that 'tis almost impossible to think people worse than they are—and so will you.'

Throughout a career that brought him many disappointments and frustrations, William Temple never subscribed to this view; and his sanguine temper and cheerful outlook were now enhanced by the gaieties of continental life. In Paris he made friends with a cousin of Dorothy's, Sir Thomas Osborne, later famous as Earl of Danby and Treasurer to Charles II. Together they played tennis, went sightseeing and were 'great companions', according to Temple, whose father recalled him to England in 1650.

William remained in London for several months; when Sir John Temple realized that he and Dorothy were meeting and that their relationship was unchanged, he sent the young man on a second journey, this time to Flanders, Germany and finally Brussels, then the capital of the Spanish Netherlands. Here William became as fluent in Spanish as in French; but he refused to acquire German. 'The Almain,' he later recalled, 'is a language I should never learn, unless 'twere to frighten children when they cry, yet methinks it should be good to clear a man's throat that were hoarse with a cold. I have heard some speak it so as it made me expect that their words should break down their teeth as they rushed out of their mouth.' Also he deprecated German drinking customs as gross, unseemly and harmful. In an age of gluttony and toping he remained abstemious, and in this he and Dorothy were alike; there is no mention of food or liquor in her letters.

'Sir,' she would begin, 'my very dreams are yours'—and later, 'Your last letter came like a pardon to one upon the block.' He was so eager to share all her interests that he set himself to read the novels she recommended and lent him—*Le Grand Cyrus* by Mademoiselle de Scudéri in ten volumes, and *La Cléopâtre* by de la Calprénède in twenty-three. This formidable task turned him towards what he called scribbled adaptations of the *Histoires Tragiques* of François de Rosset. Nine of these mercifully short romances were collected in a single volume and dedicated to his mistress, whose 'title to my heart', he informed her, had caused the 'unfortunate passion which has so long and so variously affected, busied, diverted, pleased and tormented me'. William's versions of such tales as *The Labyrinth of Fortune* and *The Generous Lovers* were modishly macabre, violent and unreal. Yet his ease of manner is already apparent, foreshadowing the grace and vitality of his maturer work; writing to please himself and Dorothy, he can still please those unable to face the productions of the novelists she admired and discussed in the intervals of lamenting their separation, imploring him not to quarrel with his father on her account and worrying about his tendency to catch cold. 'I shall hate myself as long as I live if I cause any disorder between your father and you,' she declares, concluding, 'I am very much your faithful friend and humble servant.' An account of her own difficulties was followed by 'I shall break through all inconveniences rather than deny you anything that lies in my power to grant.' Meanwhile, the barriers to her hope of marriage with him were reinforced by some ten or twelve 'servants' asking for her hand, and her eldest brother Henry's insistence on her choosing any husband but that highly undesirable Mr Temple, whom he continued to abuse.

Dorothy remained undefeated, describing her suitors in a series of vignettes. She was alternately amused, bored and repelled by this bevy; and her satirical accounts of them so entertained William that he forgot, at first, to be jealous. There was Sir Justinian Isham—'the Emperor'—a widower with four grown-up children ('the vainest, impertinent, self-conceited, learned coxcomb that ever yet I saw'); Henry Cromwell, the Protector's son, who sent her greyhounds from Ireland; her cousin, the Sir Thomas Osborne whom William played tennis with; also an unnamed deaf and dumb admirer, with whom she unwillingly conversed by signs; a 'melancholy, reserved man, whose head is so taken up with little philosophical studies that I admire how I found a room there'; another who said he would marry her as soon as his wife died; one who withdrew when he discovered that her dowry was inadequate; a gentleman threatening suicide when she refused him, and then thinking better of it; a poet; James Beverly, who had shared rooms with William at Cambridge; a Mr Freeman, a Sir John Tufton, a Mr Talbot, a Mr Bennet—and several more. Her dismissal of them infuriated Henry Osborne. 'It so wrought with him,' Dorothy told William, 'as to fetch up all that lay upon his stomach. All the people that I had ever in my life refused were brought again upon the stage like Richard III's ghosts, to reproach me withal; and all the kindness his discoveries could make I had for you, was laid to my charge.'

As she showed no sign of giving way, Henry became desperate, finally revealing an ambivalent attitude. While urging her to marry anyone but William, whom he accused first of atheism and then of indifference to her, he really wished her to remain attached to himself alone. On one occasion his fault-finding and lecturing 'came so near an absolute falling out', she told William, that he left the room, after 'making a leg' which she acknowledged with a curtsey. Later on, Dorothy had a good laugh over this ridiculous scene—'We are certainly now the most complimental couple in England,' she says; but her father's continued ill-health, her brother Robin's death, Henry's bullying and his attempts to confiscate William's letters made her very miserable, especially when Henry told her, 'People that marry with great passion for one another, *as they think*, come afterwards to lose it, they know not how.' He went on, 'I wish you a husband that loves you as well as I do'—but, Dorothy shrewdly observed, 'he never desires that I should love that husband with any passion.'

Henry then assumed an interest in his rival, remarking, 'I wonder he does not marry.' Dorothy replied, 'If I knew any woman that had a great fortune, and were a person worthy of him, I should wish her him with all my heart.' 'But sister,' Henry exclaimed, 'would you have him love her?' When Dorothy said, 'Do you doubt it? He were not happy else,' he laughed, and seemed pleased; but this did not prevent him setting on their neighbours to 'bait' and mock her for remaining single. During another argument, he burst out, 'I cannot see the ruin of a person I love so passionately'—but he could not, she perceived, 'forbear showing his malice.'

In 1653 William returned to London, to find that Sir John Temple had chosen a wife for him. He refused to consider the lady, or to accept his father's hints that Dorothy had ceased to love him; but he was disturbed by her telling him that she could not marry without Sir Peter Osborne's consent. ' 'Tis my duty,' she explained, 'from which nothing can ever tempt me, nor could you like it in me if I should do otherwise.' Yet she loved him so dearly that she now wrote of herself as his wife, adding, 'I would not live if I had not some hope left ... When that hope leaves us, then 'tis time to die.' 'Alas', another letter begins, 'I am too much concerned that you should love me.'

In March 1654 Sir Peter died, leaving Dorothy entirely dependent on Henry, who continued to 'torment' his sister, so that, while trying to forgive him, she confessed, 'I am afraid I shall never look upon him as a brother more.' As William's father still seemed adamant—in fact, he was beginning to give way —Dorothy decided that all hope of their marriage was at an end, and wrote to tell William so in a series of agonized letters. His reception of these coincided with the rumour that she was betrothed to someone else, and he concluded that she had given him up for good. In misery and despair he told his father—and Dorothy—that he was contemplating suicide; he could not live without her. Her letters implored him not to commit so great a sin, swearing that she loved him more than life, and promising to visit him, had no effect at first. Then suddenly he appeared at Chicksands, they spent the day together—and renewed their vows.

This Montagu-and-Capulet situation, which had now lasted nearly six years, was the result of the responsible and serious attitude towards marriage then accepted by parents and children in all classes. When runaway matches did occur, they disgraced the persons concerned. Lovers who were sincerely attached looked on their union as a contract for life, and such a contract must be based on the approval of those arranging the settlements. By eloping, William and Dorothy would have betrayed their love, quite apart from the fact that they would have had nothing to live on, and thus abandoned all chance of happiness for themselves and their children. They and their contemporaries took obedience to the Second Commandment literally; in their view, the sacrament of marriage was founded on what was then known as a treaty between their respective families, and therefore on the approbation and blessing of the Almighty.

At this point, William was on his way to join Sir John Temple in Ireland, believing that he would be able to obtain his consent to their marriage. Dorothy was not so hopeful, partly because she could not forget the time when her heart was 'like a country wasted by a civil war, where two opposing parties have disputed their right so long till they have made it neither of their conquests', and the chance of her marrying him depended on 'a thousand accidents and contingencies'. Then, begging him to preserve himself from 'the violence of your passion . . . which has been the ruin of us both', and 'made me, if it is possible, more wretched than I am', she had nevertheless promised to marry him—but 'this, to deal freely with you, I dare not hope for'. Now, within an hour of his departure, she was writing to him about her struggles with, and enforced deception of, Henry Osborne; for she allowed Henry to think that she and William had said their last farewells ('God be praised', Henry exclaimed) and so hoped to keep him from 'playing the madman'. 'I must have a ring from you,' she told William, 'a plain gold one . . . It shall be my wedding ring; or when I die, I'll give it you again.' Recalling their exchange of tokens, she desired him to take the greatest care of his beautiful hair, for—'I am combing and curling, and kissing this lock all day, and dreaming on't all night.'

Presently, William's report of his father's attitude encouraged her to dream of their life as like the story of Philemon and Baucis. 'I cried when I read it,' she confessed. 'Dear! Shall we ever be so happy, think you? Ah! I dare not hope it . . . I love you more than ever.' Meanwhile her daily routine, as described in one of her first letters, was maintained. Rising 'reasonably early', she would spend the day reading or working, and then —'About six or seven o'clock I walk out on to a common that lies hard by the house, where a great many young wenches keep sheep and cows, and sit in the shade, singing of ballads. I go to them, and compare their voices and beauties to some ancient shepherdesses that I have read of, and find a vast difference there . . . I talk to them, and find they want nothing to make them the happiest people in the world but the knowledge that they are so . . . When I see them driving home their cattle . . . I go into the garden, and so to the side of a small river . . . where I sit down and wish you with me . . . I sit there sometimes till I am lost with thinking.'

Surely it was the pictorial serenity of such passages as this that helped to ensure her lover's devotion, which was now leading them towards their union. Yet Henry had still to be convinced that he could not keep her to himself, and Sir John Temple persuaded of his son's determination. 'I hope this journey will be of advantage to us,' she wrote, 'when your father . . . told you you need not doubt either his power or his will . . . If neither, we may hope.'

In April 1654 Dorothy left Chicksands to visit relatives in Northamptonshire and London. In May William wrote to her in some agitation from Dublin; for her last letters had, he believed, miscarried. 'For God's sake,' he implored her, 'write constantly, or I am undone past all bearing.' He then declared that although his father had forbidden him to leave, yet 'I would venture all to be with you. I know you love me still; you promised it me, and that's all the security I can have for all the good I am ever like to have in this world. 'Tis that which makes all things else seem nothing to it, so high it sets me; and so high indeed, that should ever I fall, 't'would dash me all to pieces.' He concluded, 'For God's sake, let me know of all your motions, when and where I may hope to see you,' adding, with characteristic optimism, 'Let us but 'scape this cloud, this absence that has overcast all my contentments, and I am confident there's a clear sky attends us. My dearest dear, adieu.'

William was twenty-six and still in suspense when he wrote this letter. Meanwhile, his correspondence with Dorothy had brought about an extension of tastes and pursuits, first demonstrated by his translations from de Rosset and by the essays he wrote between 1652 and 1653. These epitomize some of the prejudices of a young man irritated by silliness and pretension, and not averse to declaring war on certain conventions. He greatly admired the *Essays* of Montaigne, and imitated his style, thus subscribing to Dorothy's detestation of formality. 'All letters,' she told him, 'should be free and easy as one's discourse.' And his early efforts, random and disjointed, rather resemble talk than work produced with an eye on the public. 'Going into a bookshop,' he writes—and it is as if he were describing the scene to Dorothy—'I asked for Montaigne's *Essays*. He told me he had it not. A young fellow that I took notice of for nothing but the lace upon his coat . . . said, "I have it at home." I asked him, "Sir, do you sell books?" He replied, "No, sir, but I buy books." ' But when the stranger compared Montaigne's *Essays* to the *Confessions* of St Augustine, William, disgusted by such ineptitude, turned away 'and made an end of the story'.

Yet, aware of his own intolerance, he sometimes paused to

wonder why it was that he so disliked the smell of tobacco, people of 'a stooping gait', religious bigotry, and the reverence accorded to the memory of Elizabeth I—'Bess Tidder', whom he thought overrated. (Boadicea, now—there was a queen indeed.) His scorn of a number of current projects included double-bottomed ships as much too slow, flying (leave that to those naturally winged), voyages to the moon (why concern oneself? There was nobody there), blood transfusions (death came at the appointed time) and the invention of a universal European language. (This would be a great waste of energy, as all those in a position to travel spoke at least three tongues.) William found these and several other notions not only 'wild', but 'enthusiastic', in the seventeenth-century, pejorative sense, and continued to mock them—kindly, of course; he knew that whatever career he followed—and until His Majesty was restored, no decision on that point could be made—he would always have to submit to the follies of others.

Turning to more trivial matters, he decided that Arabella and Marmaduke were his favourite Christian names; he was sure to take to anyone so called. His taste for gambling worried him; reckoning his losses over a single year, he decided to give it up, and stuck to this resolution. He was now becoming a connoisseur of wine; that and the love of fruit led him towards the study of gardens, which should contain, he believed, vineries, orchards and streams. Flowers interested him less; their culture should be left to ladies, who might use them for interior decoration. So, already, he seems to be visualizing a home of which Dorothy would be the adored and radiant mistress. And then, at last, his stay in Ireland from June to September 1654 was rewarded by his father's consent to his marriage.

Those months of anxiety had been considerably lightened by the company of his fifteen-year-old sister Martha, on whose affection and understanding he came to rely in his periods of depression. Dorothy's comments on this news were characteristic; she rejoiced to hear that his gay little sister sometimes teased William out of his melancholy; and she was sure, although he had not said so, that Martha was pretty. This may not then have been the case; but Lady Giffard, as she later became, grew into a very beautiful woman. She is now remembered as William's first biographer.

As Dorothy was an orphan and of age, she did not have to ask for Henry's consent to her marriage; he finally resolved to let her go, but not without a struggle. His ostensible objection was that he, as a Royalist, could not allow his sister to become the wife of a man whose father was employed by Parliament. Actually, he did not want to part with her dowry; for as long as she remained single he would have the use of it. Not unreasonably, Sir John Temple said that his consent depended on an equal settlement; and so the dispute, which lasted three months, began, while the lovers continued to correspond, eventually meeting in London.

Dorothy was staying with relations in Drury Lane, and enjoying many gaieties—private theatricals and parties in Spring Gardens—while she and William waited for the agreement about the marriage treaty to be concluded. In the first week of November 1654 she fell ill—so ill that her life was despaired of—and on the 9th of that month the disease was diagnosed as smallpox.

Regardless of the risk of disfigurement or death, William visited her regularly. He remained immune. Three weeks later, Dorothy recovered; but she was sadly changed, so much so that there was talk, among their friends, of the engagement being broken off. Martha, in whom William confided, later discreetly recorded that he was 'not wholly insensible' to the loss of Dorothy's beauty—in fact, that he had been greatly shocked by this, the first, though it was not to be the worst, of their tragedies. His love, perhaps enhanced by pity, remained unaffected.

The banns were read at the church of St Giles-in-the-Fields. And then, three days before the wedding, Henry Osborne announced that he was withdrawing his sister's dowry, presumably with the intention of preventing the marriage. Sir John Temple replied by cancelling his contribution; he would make no settlement on William until Henry completed his share of the bargain.

The situation was ironic; for some years earlier, Dorothy had told William that she thought it not only rash but wrong to marry without a settlement. Now, enraged, she refused to break her faith with him. On Christmas Day, early in the morning, she and William were married. They left to spend their honeymoon with her cousin, Lady Franklin, at Moor Park in Hertfordshire.

4

Sir John Temple then sued Henry Osborne in the Court of Chancery. In July 1655 he won his case, and renewed his promise of a settlement. So Dorothy and William were assured of an adequate, but by no means lavish, income.

2

William Temple had already stayed with the Franklins at Moor Park, which he later described as 'the sweetest place I have seen in my life'. From there he and Dorothy moved to London, and thence to Reading, where their son John was born on 18th December 1655. In May of the following year they made their long-promised visit to Sir John Temple's establishment in Dublin, where Dorothy, according to Martha, fitted into her husband's family life 'as if she had been born there'. It was then decided that she and William should make their home in Ireland, and he built himself a house on his father's estate in County Carlow. Their son was lively and robust; during the next seven years five other children were born, none of whom survived.

These losses brought the Temples very low; unlike most parents of that day, they rejoiced in the company of children, and liked to indulge and play with them. Their son—'little Creeper'—spent much time with his mother, and seems to have partially consoled her. But his father could not calmly accept the deaths of the others; he grieved for them all his life. Many years later, one of his essays concluded with an involuntary outburst of sorrow for those lost treasures. 'When all is done,' he wrote, 'human life is, at the greatest and best, but like a froward child, that must be played with, and humoured a little to keep it quiet, till it falls asleep—and then the care is over.'

Although William had determined to refuse all positions while 'the Usurper' ruled, he was fully occupied with the development of his property, and with the study of history and philosophy. At Dorothy's suggestion, he made some translations from the Georgics; and their lives were pleasantly serene. Cromwell's death in 1658 did not alter their prospects; but with the downfall of his son's government, William began to prepare himself for a career. This did not shape itself till a year after the Restoration, when he became Member of Parliament for Carlow. In August 1661 he crossed to England and met Charles II—formally—for the first time. Then the Duke of Ormonde, now Lord-Lieutenant of Ireland, and Arlington, recently appointed Secretary of State, agreed that he should be given a diplomatic post, and he returned to Carlow, 'with the resolution', he records, 'of quitting that kingdom and bringing my family to England'. During his absence, Martha had been married to Sir Thomas Giffard, who died a month after the wedding. Although her jointure was not large, she could easily have married again; she decided not to do so. She and Dorothy had become as devoted to one another as to William; and Martha became an indispensable member of their family.

William had to wait some time before getting employment. Meanwhile he, Dorothy, their son and Martha moved into a house at Sheen, where Dorothy's seventh child was born, dying a few months later: and once more 'little Jack' was a consolation. 'He is the quietest, best little boy that ever was born,' she wrote to her husband during one of his absences in London, adding, 'Can you tell me when you intend to come home? . . . Good dear, make haste. I am as weary as a dog without its master.'

It was not until March 1665, when England declared war on the Dutch, and triumphed at the battle of Lowestoft, that Arlington, whom William then admired and trusted, asked him if he would accept a secret mission—so secret that not even his wife must know where he was bound. The Secretary added that if this endeavour was successful, it would lead to something better. William agreed to go. He was then told to leave at once for Münster, whose ruler, Bernard von Ghalen, the Catholic Prince-Bishop of that territory, had consented—for a price— to invade the United Provinces with an army of 20,000 men. Temple was to approach him unofficially and incognito, in order to further this move.

By now, plague had broken out in London, and Dorothy was in the last months of her eighth pregnancy. Nevertheless she urged William to go, and he left in great anxiety, reaching Münster on 4th July, where he and von Ghalen signed the Anglo-German treaty. Then his difficulties began.

Temple's assumption that the Bishop would keep his word was not shaken when he realized that the second payment from England had been delayed; but a little later he became aware of the power of France over von Ghalen. For Louis XIV, temporarily allied to the United Provinces, had no intention of letting the Bishop invade, and prevented his doing so through bribes and threats. Temple then suggested to Arlington that he should be given the post of Ambassador to the Spanish Netherlands, on the grounds that he preferred Brussels to Münster, adding that as his business with von Ghalen was now concluded he might as well leave a Court where the heavy drinking he so much disliked was part of diplomatic interchange. Arlington agreed, and Temple moved to Brussels in October.

Presently von Ghalen's failure to invade began to worry him; and in April 1666 it became clear that he must return to Germany before that prelate made peace with the Dutch. The Marquis of Castel-Rodrigo, Viceroy of the Spanish Netherlands, supplied him with an escort, and he re-entered Münster to find that an agreement with the United Provinces had already been signed. Hoping to get von Ghalen to rescind this decision, he 'drank fair' with him at a great banquet, to the point of violent nausea. He then discovered that his host was still expecting the subsidy he had now forfeited to be dispatched through his agent in Brussels. Von Ghalen therefore persuaded Temple not to leave for that city until the money reached Münster. Temple 'seemed to accept all', but as soon as he returned to his quarters he set out alone, and rode all night through 'the wildest and most unfrequented country that ever I saw', collapsing (for he was suffering from a fearful hangover) in a peasant's hut near Düsseldorf. Here he was revived by his first taste of gin—'juniper water'—reached Brussels the next day, and stopped the English payment, thus saving King Charles a considerable sum. He was much praised by Arlington for this effort, given a baronetcy and told not to be mortified by the failure of his mission; but his salary was in arrears, and he had fallen into debt with the Brussels tradesmen.

Meanwhile Dorothy had given birth to a girl, Diana; with Lady Giffard, the ten-year-old John and the baby, she joined Temple in Brussels in the summer of 1666, where she miscarried of her last child. Her husband, disillusioned by von Ghalen's treachery, was thinking of retiring to Sheen. He longed for English country life, and the care of his vines and cherry trees. After the Anglo-Dutch peace was signed in July 1667, a new danger arose in the war between France and Spain, and he sent his wife and children home, while Lady Giffard remained to keep house for him in Brussels. Then, rather to his surprise, she suggested their making a trip into Holland, the largest and richest of the seven Provinces.

In Amsterdam William met and became the friend of the Grand Pensionary, John de Witt, principal spokesman in the States General. His consultations with the great Republican marked the first stage of his eminence in European diplomacy. His professional skill was enhanced by a combination of good nature and quick wit that made him excellent company. He had once told his wife that to seek popularity was a mistake, as if unaware that he himself possessed it without effort; in argument he retained a light touch, and could be very amusing. 'I am glad,' said one of his friends, 'that I am not a woman, for I am sure that you might persuade me to anything,'—and Lady Giffard adds that her brother did not mind 'whom he pleased nor angered'. Yet, while remaining detached from 'parties or factions', William Temple was always considerate of the feelings of others. So John de Witt, that severe and uncompromising potentate, found himself confiding in the representative of a country recently at war with his own. And while the two men discussed their problems, Lady Giffard explored the 'Indian houses', or curiosity shops, of The Hague and Amsterdam.

At this time, de Witt's difficulties might have been lessened by the gift of prescience, which he did not possess. He knew only that the Republic was surrounded by enemies, and that he must snatch at any support likely to diminish its dangers, as he had when making an alliance with Louis XIV. This peril was enhanced by the unique nature of the Dutch constitution—as it were a split running through the European hierarchy, seeming to defy all the accepted rules of government, and thus involuntarily challenging the imperial powers of France and Spain and the monarchical system of England.

The Grand Pensionary was the unofficial head of a small but very rich country divided, roughly, into two parties: that of Orange-Nassau, or the Princes, and that of the Regents, or political magnates, who ruled through their deputies in the States General. De Witt's authority was partially based on the wealth and power of Amsterdam, which dominated Holland, and therefore dominated the other six Provinces. So he had to deal with the latter's jealous competition, as well as with that of foreign states. While the prosperity of the Republic was enviably conspicuous, the country itself appeared more vulnerable than, in the event, was the case. And Sir William Temple was one of the few envoys aware of this, partly through his talks with de Witt, and also through his acquaintance—which grew into a friendship that endured for thirty years—with William Henry, Prince of Orange-Nassau, orphaned son of the Princess Royal of England, grandson of Charles I, and great-grandson of William the Silent.

That young man's position was anomalous, and as difficult, in some ways, as de Witt's; for the majority of the Dutch people looked on him as their future leader, and wanted him to inherit the power, with the titles, of Chief Stadtholder and Captain-General of all the United Provinces. The Grand Pensionary's political principles forbade this. His attitude towards the Prince was kindly, even fatherly; but he had determined to keep him in a subordinate position, that of a member of the nobility whose Stuart connections were a potential danger—possibly a threat—to the oligarchy de Witt had headed for some fourteen years.

When he and Temple met, de Witt's false ally, France, menaced his power from without, and the Orange-Nassau group, who wanted to replace him by the Prince, from within. So it happened that Temple, who was beginning to foresee the risk of Louis XIV's achieving a European dictatorship, put forward the scheme for his famous Triple Alliance, between England, Sweden and the Republic. While de Witt considered its ramifications Temple returned to London for instructions, and was accredited as emissary to The Hague in January 1668; here the Treaty was signed. In the intervals of conferring with Count Dohna, the Swedish Ambassador, and de Witt, he made his business to become the friend and, in due course, the adviser of the eighteen-year-old Prince of Orange.

'Dutch William', as his subjects called him when, twenty-one years later, he became King of England, was in fact of Italian, French, German, Danish and Scottish blood. Thinking of himself as a Dutchman and 'a plain man'—one of his favourite phrases —his tastes were cosmopolitan, inclining towards French culture, as did those of his intimates, of whom the chief was Count

Hans William Bentinck. (These two, growing up and working
together throughout their lives, always corresponded in French.)
The Prince's liking for, and increasing dependence on, Temple
were inaugurated by the Englishman's admiration for the
Republic. For William Henry's love of his country was a passion,
which Temple understood, and came, in a lesser degree, to share.
Within a few months he realized that Dutch administration,
Dutch standards, Dutch *savoir vivre* were far in advance of those
of any other kingdom, his own included. Indeed, there were
moments when this fastidious fine gentleman found Republican
hygiene, religious toleration, universal orderliness and care for
the arts and sciences unusual to the point of eccentricity. With
closer knowledge his approval overcame his prejudices.

This amazing country, which still retains its esoteric beauty
and charm, was then organized into three classes: the peasantry,
the merchants, and the aristocracy, each of which had its sub-
divisions. In his *Observations on the United Provinces* Temple noted
the convenience of this arrangement, and was particularly
impressed by the permissive attitude of the local authorities
towards religion. The national faith was that of Reformed Calvinism; but the Jews had their synagogues, and the Catholics,
worshipping privately, were employed in many capacities, while
remaining unmolested. So the Republic became a refuge for
such intellectuals as Descartes and Saint-Evremond, who had
been driven out of their own countries. National frugality was
tempered by practical expenditure on the poor and helpless,
in the form of homes for retired soldiers and sailors, and hospitals
run by doctors whose medical equipment was more extensive
than that of those practising anywhere else. Temple was especially
pleased when, visiting a seamen's home, the inmate who had
been showing him round refused a tip. 'What should I do with
money?' he said. 'All I want is provided.'

Patronage of painters, sculptors, musicians and writers was
another feature of the Republic; the houses of the merchants
and nobles contained libraries, pictures, Delft pottery, and
porcelain and silk carpets from the Far East. Finally, Temple
observed that Dutch colonizing and trading were more efficiently
organized than in England or Spain. The only aspect of daily
life in the Republic that puzzled him a little was the predilection
of its inhabitants for scrupulous cleanliness. It must be due, he

concluded, to 'the extreme moisture of the air'. One day, he goes on, dining with a Mynheer van Hoest, and suffering from 'a great cold', he proceeded, as was his custom, to spit. This caused 'a tight handsome wench (that stood in the room with a clean cloth in her hand) . . . to wipe it up and rub the board clean'. Such 'strange curious cleanliness' amused the guest, 'though the most trouble it gave me', he kindly adds, 'was to see the poor wench take so much pains about it'. On another occasion, he saw a man arriving at a house with dirty boots, and watched him being lifted over the spotless doorstep by the maid. And later on he came to appreciate 'the strange freedom that all men took in boats and inns . . . of talking openly . . . upon all public affairs'.

Temple's first acquaintance with these and other amenities convinced him that William of Orange was both fortunately placed, and worthy of the luxuries and pleasures he enjoyed; also, he had been carefully educated (he spoke six languages, and later became something of an art connoisseur), was adored by the common people, and not too much restricted in his choice of friends. 'I find him in earnest,' Temple reported, 'a most extreme hopeful Prince . . . something much better than I expected, and a young man of more parts than ordinary . . . that is . . . in good plain sense . . . with extreme good agreeable humour and dispositions . . . loving hunting as much as he hates swearing, and preferring cock ale to any sort of wine.' (This rather nasty drink was made by marinating a spiced chicken in sherry, adding ale and bottling the mixture.)

In fact, it seemed to Temple that the Prince was eminently fitted to lead a brave, civilized and industrious people. The high quality of his intellect was not then fully appreciated by the older man; not did Temple grasp until several years later either the problems of the Prince's status or the sufferings thereby engendered, which were enhanced by the frailty of his physique. Those caring for him since infancy had not expected him to grow up; and as he reached maturity he endured the onslaughts of asthma, toothache and haemorrhoids.

De Witt's arrangements prevented William of Orange from taking part in his conferences with Temple about Anglo-Dutch affairs; these became more frequent after Sir William had negotiated a treaty between France and Spain in May 1668 at

4*

Aix-la-Chapelle, and their discussions took place almost daily when Temple was appointed Ambassador to the United Provinces in the following August. He had hesitated to accept this post, because he now knew that certain ministers in England—among whom was Clifford of the Cabal—were hostile to the Triple Alliance. He could not have guessed that Charles II was preparing to undermine that alliance, nor that it would soon be a dead letter.

Temple was shrewd enough; but at this juncture his insight had been clouded by optimism, absence from England and loyalty to his sovereign, whose darker purposes were concealed from him. Nor was he aware that Arlington, his closest friend, supported, although unwillingly, the King's plan of betraying his allies in return for French subsidies. Temple's old-fashioned notions of honour and fair dealing were based on the avoidance of what he called 'tricks and juggling'—Charles's stock-in-trade. So he was completely deceived.

In January 1669 he began to realize the impossibility of obtaining a permanent settlement between England and the Republic about their respective East India Companies. 'God send me out of this briar!' he exclaimed. His prayer was unanswered. Still he struggled on, inclining towards what he considered the justice of the Dutch claim to Guiana, and deprecating Arlington's insistence on the immediate concession of that colony. By the spring of 1669 he had begun to distrust the Secretary (to whom Charles II had recently confided his intended conversion to Catholicism) and in January 1670 he wrote to him, 'My wings are cut, and that frankness of my heart which made me think everybody meant as well as I did, is much allayed.'

In May of that year the wings of the Triple Alliance were cut into fragments by the Dover Treaty, in which Charles II and Louis XIV agreed to destroy before dividing the United Provinces. Louis then seized Lorraine, upon which Temple, much distressed by a bout of neuralgia, was ordered home. 'As soon as you receive this, you must put your foot in the stirrup,' Arlington told him, and he arrived in London on 29th September, still unaware of the King's secret policy.

Arlington's reception of Temple had been carefully designed to show that the Triple Alliance was now to be abandoned, and that his protégé's failure to regain Guiana had lowered his prestige. Instead of being greeted, as on other occasions, with an embrace, the Ambassador found himself kicking his heels in an antechamber, while Arlington conferred privately with Ashley—the member of the Cabal of whom Temple most disapproved—for an hour and a half. When he was admitted, the Secretary's cold manner and offhand inquiries about his journey further disappointed him; and then, just as Temple was hoping to get down to business, Arlington sent for his five-year-old daughter, 'Tata', who was followed by a courtier 'on a common visit'—after which Temple went away.

Next day he was received in the Mall by the King, 'who stopped to give me his hand, asked me half a dozen questions about my journey and the Prince of Orange, and so walked on'. It was not until Temple interviewed Clifford that the Government's attitude was revealed. As the Minister continued to criticize his efforts, Temple lost his temper, exclaiming, 'In the name of God, what do you think a man can do more?' Clifford, equally enraged, replied, 'Yes, I will tell you what a man can do more, and what you ought to do more, which is to let the King and all the world know how basely and unworthily the States have used him, and that their ministers are a company of rogues and rascals!' Temple said, 'I am not a man fit to make declarations—I shall speak of all men as I find them,' and left the room.

Still his salary had not been paid; and when he decided to relinquish his embassy and send for his family to join him, permission for their return was not given till August 1671. During the crossing, Dorothy Temple was told by the captain that he had orders to shoot at any Dutch vessel, in order to create an 'incident' which would lead to a declaration of war. The ships met; shots were exchanged, the Dutch captain came aboard to protest and then left. 'What should I do?' the English captain asked Dorothy, who replied, 'You know your orders best; do as you think fit, without regard to myself or my children,' and the passage was effected without further misadventure.

Dorothy's intrepidity was much praised by Charles II. 'She showed more courage than the captain,' he told Temple, and went on to abuse 'Dutch insolence' with some warmth. With a smile, Temple replied, 'There is *some* merit in my family, since I made the Alliance—and my wife is like to have the honour of making war.' This was the only way, Temple perceived, 'to turn the discourse into good humour—and so it ended'. But he would have nothing more to do with what he saw to be gross double dealing, and the destruction of all his work. He therefore retired to Sheen, where he remained for the next three years.

3

William Temple could now devote himself to his favourite pursuits: gardening, writing, and the care of his family. This first, too short period of retirement was the happiest; for although he was distressed for all his Dutch friends, de Witt and the Prince of Orange especially, his days were busy and contented. Not without reason, he considered himself an expert on such subjects as European politics, the organization and history of the United Provinces, and international trade. He was prolific and authoritative; essays on the Empire, Ireland, Sweden, Denmark, Spain, France, and Flanders were succeeded by reflections on ancient and modern learning, recipes for health and long life, remedies for 'popular discontents', and plans for economic reform. Writing swiftly and easily, he did not shrink from the obvious, quoting King Solomon's platitudes with calm approval.

He then issued some rather peculiar judgements on poetry and the visual arts. He rated Sir Philip Sidney higher than Shakespeare, and noted that there had been no masters of painting or statuary for the last hundred years: so much for Bernini, Van Dyck, Reubens, *et al*. He had however a kindly word for Shakespeare's 'humour', which he describes as 'a picture of particular life', adding that people had actually been known to weep over his tragedies. He deprecated the elements of superstition, magic and 'enthusiasm', and ignored the Jacobean and Cavalier poets, presumably because of their recourse to these: but in Spenser's *Faery Queene* he found 'the execution excellent, his flights of fancy very noble and high; but the design', he went on, 'was poor, and his moral lay so bare that it lost its effect'. In fact, with Spenser's death there had been a decline in English literature, in spite of the quality of King James's Bible; for the Book of Job, and Deborah's song in that of Judges were truly admirable. Of course, Temple hastily conceded, the influence of 'true' poetry and music was good; yet in the end, Ovid, Virgil, Horace and their contemporaries had set an unapproachable standard.

Sir William's limitations and prejudices now add to the charm of his work. As in his youth, he wrote to please himself, and because he could not help it; taking up diplomacy as suited to his breeding, he much preferred authorship; and his pleasure in that profession can be shared by the reader.

Temple was also a student. He read all he could find about Mexico, China and Greece, and managed to get hold of translations of pre-Christian Runes and the Icelandic Sagas. Distrusting doctors—'I hope to die without them,' he remarks— he submitted various cures of his own, specifically for gout, finding the most effective that of Moxa, a moss from the East Indies. A poultice of this plant should be applied, and then set alight till it burnt down to the skin (the pain must be endured). In the event of failure, applications of nettles, holly and horse-dung (but the horse should be white) were recommended. For longevity, temperance was essential, added to a diet of herbs and cherries (but the cherries should be peeled before eating). Temple then threw in peace of mind; how to achieve it was left to the individual. Finally, in his notes for essays on *Life, Fortune and Conversation*, he wrote, 'Life is but a trifle that should be played with till we lose it,' concluding, 'Nobody should make love after forty, nor be in business after fifty,' advice he himself ignored.

Lady Giffard, recalling her brother's home life, described him as 'a passionate lover, a kind husband, a fond and indulgent father, and the best friend in the world'. This assessment is supplemented by the informality prevailing in the Temple household. In an age when children were so disciplined as to dread and sometimes dislike their parents, intimacy at Sheen produced various pet names. Sir William was 'Papa' to his wife and sister, John known as Child, and his six-year-old sister as Di or Nan. Both children were intelligent and responsive; but John had inherited his father's sensitivity, and he was too easily cast down. Sir William had ambitions for him, although his plans for the future were shadowed by the belligerence and corruption of the English Government. Its methods horrified him; and he did not hesitate publicly to condemn them whenever the opportunity arose.

In the fifth clause of the Dover Treaty Charles II and Louis XIV, having decided to 'reduce the power of a nation which has so often rendered itself odious', had agreed to launch a simultaneous attack on the United Provinces. On 20th March 1672 some English ships were instructed to fire on the Dutch fleet without declaring war. 'No clap of thunder on a fair frosty day,' Temple wrote, 'could more astonish the world.' In April France invaded, and within the next four weeks overran three Provinces.

In June King Charles intervened on his nephew's behalf; for he and Louis had arranged that after the conquest of the Republic William of Orange should become a puppet monarch —King of Holland was to be his title—under their jurisdiction. His consent was assumed; and Arlington and Buckingham were empowered to go to his camp at Bodegrave (he was now Chief Stadtholder and Captain-General) to put these terms before him. When he refused them, they were incredulous; he was too young and inexperienced to know what was best for him; and his cause, they assured him, was hopeless. As he remained unmoved, Buckingham persisted, 'Do you not see that it is lost?' to which the Prince replied that if that were so—and it well might be— he himself would rather 'die in the last dyke' than sell his country. Arlington expressed annoyance; Buckingham was sorry for the boy.

Louis XIV then issued his terms for peace. These included the cession of three cities and of an enormous tract of land, together with William's principality of Orange in Provence, 24,000,000 livres of indemnity, and—final touch of arrogance —a yearly embassy from the Dutch, whose envoys must present him with a gold medal in token of their gratitude for his clemency in allowing them to keep what remained of their dismembered kingdom.

William, who had just reached his majority, refused these terms. He ordered the sluices to be opened, and the terrain which had not been occupied by the French was flooded. He told his people that if this water-line were held—and those who tried to rescue their homes by stopping up the sluices were to be hanged—the French armies would be halted. In fact, as Temple pointed out, he saved his country by destroying it. Faced with a vast lake, the French generals argued, and paused. Louis XIV and his Court returned to Paris. In August the Dutch people, infuriated by de Witt's inability to maintain their defences, murdered him and his brother. (Neither statesman was to blame; they were the victims of the discrepancies in the administration.) Austria, Spain, Lorraine and several German principalities, all later known as the Confederates, then offered to ally themselves with the Dutch, and William, now acclaimed as a hero and a military genius, signed treaties with them. In December a frost, followed by a thaw, caused the French to withdraw to winter quarters, and the Dutch began to prepare their offensive, while William re-created and trained the army. In the spring of 1673 the French again failed to advance, but captured Maestricht. In September, after terrible fighting and many setbacks, William took the town and fortress of Naarden. It was his first decisive victory.

By this time, it had become clear to Temple that the English people were as bitterly hostile to the war as he was himself. His warnings against French aggression had taken effect; and he was supported in Parliament by the minister he still distrusted, Ashley, now Earl of Shaftesbury and Chancellor of the Exchequer, who had changed sides since making his *Delenda est Carthago* speech, and was urging peace. Charles II, while declaring that to desert his cousin and paymaster would be the act of 'a fool or a beast', began—unwillingly—to yield, and signed the Treaty of Westminster.

Then Temple's attention was drawn away from public affairs by the grief of Lady Essex, an old friend of his wife's. The death of her nine-year-old daughter had brought her to the point of suicide, upon which Dorothy implored her husband to intervene. He immediately sent Lady Essex a long letter of condolence, appeal and advice; this turned her thoughts towards her son, and she decided to live.

In February 1674 peace terms were worked out by Dorothy Temple's former suitor, Thomas Osborne, now Earl of Danby and Lord Treasurer. Temple was asked to discuss them with de Fresno, the Spanish envoy, before returning as Ambassador to The Hague. Meanwhile, the war between France and the United Provinces and their allies continued.

Temple's view of his embassy was not one of great enthusiasm. In his first talk with Arlington and the King, he said, 'I am grown a little rusty by lying still so long,' to which Charles replied with a smile, 'There is no man else to be thought of—I will answer for you.' Temple then suggested that he could more easily work for the general peace of which His Majesty would be the mediator if he went as an envoy rather than as an ambassador, thus avoiding the formalities that so often complicated negotiations. Consent given, he asked to speak privately with Charles; for he had now become aware of his master's tendency to intrigue against those he employed. Sinister rumours about the Dover Treaty had much disturbed him; and he decided that he must make his own principles and intentions clear.

He suspected that while both the French and the Confederates desired peace, Louis XIV did not visualize it on a long-term basis, or intend to give up his conquered territories, and that Charles might well support him in further aggression; also, he was beginning to believe (wrongly, as it happened) that the English King was still considering his promise to convert his subjects to the old faith. So he resolved to speak his mind, regardless of Charles's displeasure, and began by pointing out 'how ill Your Majesty has been advised to break measures and treaties so solemnly taken and agreed, how ill you have been served, and how ill succeeded'. Charles evaded this accusation by blaming his ministers. 'If I had been well served,' he said, 'I might have made a good business enough of it.' Temple, assuming that they had reached the religious question, said that to apply French methods of government, together with an enforced conversion to Catholicism, was totally unacceptable. Ignoring the King's impatience, he spoke at length, concluding, 'The English armies will never serve ends that the people hate and fear,' and added, 'It seems against all common sense to think by one part to govern ninety-nine that are of contrary minds.' Then, warming to this theme, he condemned the wickedness and folly of bringing over foreign troops to instil an alien creed. Finally, quoting Gourville, a Huguenot agent Charles knew and respected, he exclaimed, 'A King of England who will be the man of his people is the greatest King in the world—but if he will be something more, by God! he is nothing at all.' Charles did not answer for a moment or two; then taking Temple's hand, he said, 'And I will be the man of my people.'

No doubt Sir William was flattered and perhaps moved by this promise; yet he knew that such avowals were not always sustained. His loyalty did not blind him; he thought Charles likely to be influenced by one adviser after another, and therefore liable to break his word at any moment. This was not all the truth: nor yet half of it. Charles's political technique was subtle and ingenious; his awareness of how far he could go had long been based on a sleepless response to fluctuating circumstances. He could never be taken by surprise.

Temple, reaching The Hague in July 1674, tried in vain to see the Prince of Orange, who was rapidly liberating the Dutch towns and fortresses; he realized that this avoidance was the result of William's resolve not to discuss his uncle's terms until the Republic was no longer occupied by French troops; also, his Spanish allies wanted their territories freed; these included part of Flanders and Franche-Comté. So the Prince had decided to go on fighting until Louis's armies were entirely withdrawn. He knew that Charles II, although ostensibly on his side, would try to force a peace on him which would partially—and temporarily—satisfy Louis.

Prince William had not forgotten his visit to England in 1670, when, apropos of the religious issue, his uncle had said, 'I wish you would take more pains, and look to these things better, and not be led by your Dutch blockheads.' Eighteen years later, when he became King of that country, he was reported to have told Bishop Burnet that Charles had informed him of his own conversion. This seems unlikely; but such fragments of gossip sometimes have a basis of truth. In any case, the Prince's distrust of all but a few of the English ministers was well founded. He believed in Temple's integrity, as did the new Grand Pensionary, Caspar Fagel, with whom Temple discussed the peace while waiting for William's return from the front. In November the Prince, having completely liberated the Republic, entered The Hague in triumph. But he knew that with the spring the struggle must be resumed. His country was still partially encircled; and in no circumstances would he desert his allies.

Temple perceived a marked development in the youth he had described as having 'more parts than ordinary' and of 'good plain sense', such a short time ago. The slight, short, fine-drawn young man was still elegant and graceful; his masses of red-brown hair—he did not wear a wig till many years later—still flowed below his shoulders and on either side of his face. But now his large dark eyes were sunk, the curve of his nose was

more pronounced; and his expression and way of talking were
those of a person on whom maturity has been forced through
one ordeal after another. Much, indeed too much, and too suddenly, had been required of him, as Captain-General, civil
administrator and Head of State. At twenty-four, entering the
capital as the saviour of his country, he left behind him ruin,
desolation and slaughter. While the citizens of The Hague ran,
weeping and cheering, to kiss his hand, his stirrup, even his
horse's hoofs, he seems to have made no attempt to show the
gratification, far less the radiance, of the conqueror. The horrors
of the past, anxiety about the future, held and shadowed him;
and the present, although lavish in love and praise, carried yet
another burden, one of conflict and frustration. For his generals
were already in dispute about the spring offensive, and most of
his allies, the Spanish especially, had been impossibly difficult
to manoeuvre. Of his Stuart supporters, Charles II, having
once betrayed him (he had received £18,000 from Louis XIV
for breaking the Triple Alliance) was more than likely to do so
again; and James of York, while wishing him well, had hopes of
a new French agreement through the marriage of his twelve-
year-old daughter Mary with the Dauphin. Also, in the Prince's
own country, the anti-Orangist party, based in Amsterdam,
deeply resented his Stadtholdership, and even more the fact that
the States General had made it hereditary. The Regents of that
city (*ces coquins d'Amsterdam*, he called them) were ready to ally
themselves with France against him.

He had a few other English friends—Ossory, Ormonde's
heir, was one—besides the Temples. He was a frequent guest
at their house on the Voorhout, arriving unannounced to dine,
sitting over his cock ale, and pouring out his troubles to Sir
William, who sympathized, advised, and shared his tastes for
building, garden-planning and interior decoration. They talked
chiefly of politics; then they would discuss the Prince's purchases
of pictures and statues; even on campaign he had found time for
these. Temple was much impressed by his knowledge of, and
care for, the arts, and shared his love of music. The Prince had
been an enthusiastic dancer, composing and appearing in his
own ballets; he had no leisure for that now; his principal relaxation was hunting.

Meanwhile, Temple's position was anomalous. Secretly, he

agreed with the Prince's opinion of French aggression. Having been instructed to urge a separate peace on him, he met with an uncompromising refusal. His difficulties were increased by Arlington's jealousy of his friendship with Danby, whom Arlington regarded as a potentially successful rival. When Temple told him that his intimacy with the Lord Treasurer dated from their youth, Arlington was partially reassured. Then, resenting Temple's popularity with the Dutch and his influence over the Prince of Orange, he decided to undermine both by himself making an unofficial visit to The Hague. Temple, unaware of this plan, continued to assure the Prince of his uncle's 'personal kindness and esteem', his desire for friendship with the Dutch, and for a general peace.

William replied to these overtures with cold politeness, adding that if he himself could bring about an agreement 'consistent with the safety of my country, and my own honour towards my allies, I will do all I can to bring it about'. When Temple pointed out that his King was under an obligation to Louis XIV, William said, 'It were better to go on with the war, let it last as long and cost as much as it would. How it will fall out,' he went on, 'I cannot tell, and I must leave it to God. But I think we have as fair a game as the French.'

The discussion continued on these lines for some time. Temple then warned the Prince against Shaftesbury, who, he believed, had been intriguing with the Dutch in the hope of obtaining their help towards revolution in England. 'Who are these discontented Englishmen,' he asked, 'who corresponded with Your Highness during the war?' 'I cannot betray men who professed to be my friends,' William replied. Reverting to the war, he continued, 'The French might welcome peace. But Flanders must first be secured.'

Temple's reports of this and other interviews disappointed Charles and his ministers. Arlington then asked the King to let him try his hand at persuading the Prince of Orange to make a separate peace. He, his Dutch wife, and her sister, Charlotte of Nassau-Beverwaert, arrived at The Hague in December 1674, together with Ossory and his wife, another Beverwaert sister. This visit implied the failure of Temple's mission.

William was delighted to see Ossory, and tried in vain to arrange a marriage between Charlotte of Nassau-Beverwaert and Bentinck, who had fallen desperately in love with her. Her refusal added to the general dissatisfaction caused by Arlington's useless attempts to effect the separate peace which the Prince knew would further endanger his country. The Lord Chamberlain, as he now was, began by telling Temple, 'I must go to the bottom of the sore, and rake into things past, which you cannot do,' and then approached the proud young Stadtholder in a condescending and insolent manner, 'as if,' William told Temple, 'he had taken himself for the Prince of Orange, and me for Lord Arlington. I am a plain man,' he went on, 'and cannot bear his artificiality.' Arlington then complained to Temple that after three long interviews William remained 'dry and sullen', adding, 'I have absolutely given it over,' and left The Hague. Meanwhile Ossory, no diplomat, had told William that King Charles's hopes for the peace were partly based on a marriage between the Prince and the Lady Mary of York, now in her thirteenth year. 'My fortunes,' William replied, 'are not in a condition for me to think of a wife.' 'Thus ended,' Temple says, 'this mystical journey,' noting that on his return Arlington was coldly received by the King, and angrily by the Duke of York, who still believed that he would be able to marry his elder daughter to the Dauphin.

His failure so rankled with Arlington that in March 1675 he wrote to warn the Prince that he was in danger of losing his uncle's friendship by going on with the war, and that he should recall the fate of the de Witts. 'Upon this,' Temple says, 'he fell into the greatest rage I ever saw him in.' 'I am His Majesty's servant,' William declared, 'and if I can do him no service, I can at least do him no harm,' and denounced Arlington's mischief-making. His violence was partly caused by the fact that he was sickening for smallpox; for several weeks, nursed by Bentinck, who himself caught but recovered from the disease, William seemed unlikely to live. While his illness lasted, according to Temple, 'he had taken a fancy hardly to eat or drink anything but what came from my house', with the result that several Dutch friends warned the Temples that in the event of the Prince's death, their home would be destroyed and themselves murdered. Six weeks later, William was up and about; but he could not return to the front until May.

Temple was then sent for by Charles II to discuss what other measures could be taken to separate William from his allies. No solution was reached; but during his seven weeks' stay he discovered the English view of the Lady Mary's position and value. As it was now obvious that after thirteen years of marriage Catherine of Braganza would remain childless, the Duke of York must succeed—if he survived his brother; and in view of his habits and general health, this then seemed unlikely. His second wife, Mary Beatrice of Modena, had hitherto produced no living children; so the Lady Mary, now regarded as heiress-presumptive, had become a highly desirable match, in spite of the fact that her dowry would be a small one. And it was time, the Dutch considered, that the Prince should found a dynasty, though not all of them approved of an alliance with his English cousin.

Meanwhile Louis XIV, also bent on a profitable peace, offered William the hand of Mademoiselle de Blois, his daughter by Madame de Montespan. William refused, in formally courteous terms. Long afterwards, Saint-Simon—who was born in this year—was informed of, and recorded, a sharper answer. The Princes of Orange, William told the French Ambassador, were not in the habit of marrying bastards.

Soon after Temple returned to The Hague, William again refused Louis's peace terms, as did the Spaniards, and the war continued. Charles II and Danby then combined to lower Temple's prestige by sending over Sir Gabriel Sylvius as peace envoy in January 1676. 'God!' William exclaimed, 'I never said anything to Sylvius that I was not content my coachman should know.' Temple burst out laughing. 'Shall I tell my Lord Treasurer so too?' he asked. 'Yes, do,' William replied, adding wearily, 'We must try the fortune of another campaign.'

In April of this year, William, returning from the front to his palace of Honselaersdijck, asked Temple to meet him there for a private talk about his marriage. Several brides, he began, had been suggested to him. 'I know,' he went on, in his driest manner, 'it is a thing to be done, some time or other.' On the whole, the English match seemed to him the most suitable; but he would not make a decision without Temple's advice. 'Will you give it me,' he asked, 'not as an ambassador, but as a friend, or at least as an indifferent person?' This promise made, he explained that general mistrust of England militated against

his marrying the Lady Mary; in any case, he could not consider
the offer until he knew something more of her personally. This
breach of convention would of course be censured; but he was
determined to find out 'the humour and dispositions of the
young lady' before committing himself. 'I may not, perhaps,'
he added, 'be very easy for a wife to live with; I am sure I should
not, to such wives as are generally in the courts of this age.
If I should meet with one to give me trouble at home, it is what
I should not be able to bear.' After a brief outline of his own
difficulties and hopes, he concluded, 'If you know anything
particular of the Lady Mary on these points, I desire you to
tell me freely.'

Temple found himself in a quandary; for he had never met
the Princess, who lived at Richmond Palace, in charge of Lady
Frances Villiers, and seldom came to her uncle's Court; but
his wife and sister, he told William, had seen something of her,
and were on friendly terms with the Lady Governess. He could
only repeat their praises of the girl, adding that Lady Frances
had taken 'all the care that could be' of her upbringing. It was
agreed that on Lady Temple's next visit to England she should
find out all she could about the Princess, and report back to
her husband.

William then resumed what turned out to be a disastrous
campaign. Unable to prevent the French occupation of Flanders,
he had to agree to Charles II's proposal of a peace conference
to be held at Nimeguen, under Temple's supervision. After
several talks with Fagel, who said, 'There is not one man in
Holland who is against the peace,' Temple repeated this remark
to William in September. The young man burst out, 'Yes—I
know one, and that is myself! I will hinder it as long as I can.
But if anything should happen to me, they will do it in three
days' time.' Temple, more than ever inclined to support William
against Charles, was silent, and the Prince went on, 'I saw this
morning a poor old man, tugging alone in a little boat with
his oars against the eddy upon the canal—and when, with the
last endeavours, he was just got up to the place intended, the
force of the eddy turned him quite back again—but he turned
his boat as soon as he could, and fell to his oars again, and thus,
three or four times, while I saw him. And this old man's business
and mine are too like one another—and I ought to do just as

the old man did, without knowing what will succeed.' All his life, Temple remembered this speech, and the tone in which it was uttered; and so they parted.

On his return to Nimeguen, Temple was approached by a Monsieur Serinchamp from Lorraine, in some distress from gout —did he know of any remedies? Temple prescribed a Moxa poultice, which was then applied; but he was rather put out by his patient's lack of stoicism. When the burning moss reached his flesh, Serinchamp made a great to-do, 'roaring out' abuse of Sir William—who was, after all, only trying to help; discouraged, he decided not to advise holly, nettles or horse-dung.

While the peace conference floundered out of one abyss into another, Temple was further frustrated by Charles II's tightrope policy. The King wanted to justify his position, and placate his Parliament by mediating, while taking care not to work against the wishes, or rather the commands, of Louis XIV. In January 1677 he issued his own version of the French terms, which Temple was told to put before William, then in his hunting lodge at Dieren. The first item, that of an Anglo-Dutch alliance to be made after the peace, sounded promising enough; but as his uncle's conditions for it were read out, the Prince's face darkened. He got up and said, 'Dinner is ready —we will talk of it when we have dined.' At the door he turned. 'I would rather die than make such a peace!' he exclaimed, adding, 'I would rather charge a thousand men with a hundred, though I were sure to die in the action.' Later, he explained that what he now guessed to be a secret Anglo-French agreement was 'insupportable'. 'What hope is there,' Temple asked, 'in the present desperate situation?' William replied that he might have to appeal to the Emperor, 'If not,' he added, 'for my part, I must go on. When one is at High Mass—one is at it,' an analogy Temple found rather puzzling.

In February, Sir Joseph Williamson's proposals amplified those the Prince had already rejected. The Prince compared the Secretary's obsequious style to 'whipped cream for children', and went on, 'If His Majesty will not concern himself, I must leave it to God Almighty.' So Temple wrote warning Sir Joseph that His Highness could neither be fooled nor cajoled. 'He has a way of falling downright into the bottom of a business,' he explained, 'and is to be dealt with in no other way.'

Temple was then told that Charles II wanted him to succeed Sir Henry Coventry as Secretary of State; this post was priced at £10,000, of which half would be paid by the King. Temple refused; he could not produce the sum required. In July he was summoned to England, to find Charles in the best of humours, and still bent on persuading his nephew to desert his allies. 'Nothing can alter him,' said Temple, 'I spent all my shot last winter.' 'Go, get you gone to Sheen,' Charles replied, in his most beguiling manner. 'We shall have no good of you till you have been there. And when you have rested yourself, come up again.' On such occasions, Temple found his master irresistible. 'No Prince,' he recorded, 'has more qualities to make him loved.' After dwelling at length on the King's geniality and goodwill, Temple observes that his 'softness of temper' made him 'change hands . . . so that nothing looked steady in the conduct of his affairs, nor aimed at any certain end'. In fact, Charles's apparently capricious policy concealed an iron determination to stay where he was, withstanding economic and religious crises by temporarily giving way in order to assert himself as soon as he could be sure of success. Those who were much closer than Temple to this baffling and highly gifted man were similarly misled; they never plumbed the depths of his capacity to deceive.

The political situation in England did not admit of the steadiness which was Temple's ideal. Three ministers, Shaftesbury, Halifax and Danby, understood the various problems, but were unable to solve them. Some years later, Temple decided that his principles could only be adhered to by retiring from the indecency and corruption of conflicts in which he sympathized with no one. In the autumn of 1677 he withdrew from state affairs (Lawrence Hyde, Princess Mary's uncle, replaced him at Nimeguen, at his suggestion) taking no part in them till October, when the Prince of Orange arrived to inspect the Princess and come to an agreement with Charles II. Sir William then became indispensable and effective. Nevertheless, the differences between the King and his nephew remained basically insoluble.

Temple reported William as coming 'like a hasty lover' to join his uncles at Newmarket. He was indeed in a hurry to return home, with or without a bride, as soon as he had made arrangements for help against the French. When Charles began by

speaking of the marriage settlements, William said that he must
meet the Princess—who was waiting at St James's Palace—before
coming to an agreement on that or any other point. The King,
brought up short, was speechless; then he burst out laughing:
but with his usual good humour, he decided to give in to his
nephew's freakish eccentricity, and the Court returned to London.
There, William saw and spoke to the Lady Mary, who, as she
had not been told that their marriage was in question, received him
correctly but without interest. This plainly dressed young man,
a head shorter than herself, with a stoop, a hooked nose and an
asthmatic cough, had no appeal for a fifteen-year-old girl absorbed
in a passionate relationship with her 'dearest dear' Frances
Apsley, Court gossip, fashions and romantic literature. William
saw a slender, languorous, dark-eyed beauty, whose unselfcon-
scious grace and gentle manner greatly pleased him. He left her
to ask the King and the Duke of York for her hand. Charles
replied that political matters should be settled first; if William
wanted his niece, he must be prepared to bargain for her. The
Prince refused to consider this. 'It shall never be charged against
me,' he told Temple, 'that I sold my honour for a wife.'

The King remained unresponsive and, it seemed, perfectly
indifferent, for the next four days. Temple and Danby, who had
been counting on a speedy agreement, were in despair. William
then sent for Temple, and told him that he was about to leave.
'I regret ever coming into England,' he said. 'If His Majesty
and I are not to be the greatest of friends, then we must be the
greatest enemies.' Meanwhile, Charles was telling Danby that
the marriage would probably fall through; if it did, the Prince's
obstinacy would be the cause; he himself was not much concerned
either way. To Barrillon, the French Ambassador, he spoke
sadly of his being forced by Parliament to allow his niece 'to
sleep in Protestant arms'—but he was helpless.

Temple then implored the King to agree to William's demands.
With the amiable resignation of a man giving in against his will,
Charles replied, 'Go and tell the Prince that he may have his wife.
I was never deceived in judging a man's honesty by his looks,
and if I am not mistaken in the present instance, the Prince
is one of the honestest men in the world.' He added that he was
now ready to embark on the negotiations. When Temple told
William the good news, the Prince embraced and thanked him,

exclaiming, 'You have made me the happiest man in the world.' Arrangements between himself, his uncle and Temple for the liberation of Flanders were made in a very short time. (It did not occur to William till later on that Charles's decisions would be subject to Louis XIV's approval.) The Duke of York then gave his unwilling consent to the marriage, and told Lady Frances Villiers to bring the Princess to his closet, where he informed her that she was to be married to her cousin in a few days' time. Mary, aghast, burst into tears, and wept all the next day. Louis XIV, equally appalled—as if, said his courtiers, at the loss of an army—remarked, 'There are two beggars well matched,' and held back Charles's current subsidy. That monarch, having pleased his Parliament and silenced the protests of the French Ambassador, could congratulate himself on another triumph.

Temple, in high spirits, attended a series of celebrations, and then returned to Sheen, where he remained for most of the next eight months.

4

In June 1678 Louis XIV, having taken five strongholds in the Spanish Netherlands, ordered his Court painters to show the Dutch cringing before him, while he graciously consented to their request for a six weeks' truce; this composition was to be added to those lining the Galérie des Glaces as Versailles. So the agreement about the barrier towns in the Anglo-Dutch treaty became invalid. Charles II then accepted a new subsidy from Louis. 'Since the Dutch will have a peace on the French terms,' he said to Temple, 'and France offers money for my consent to what I cannot help, I do not know why I should not get the money.' The Spanish also submitted to the French, and the Prince of Orange, deprived of his authority in the States General, was helpless—until, on 25th July, Temple arrived at The Hague with instructions to organize a peace which would include the return of the barrier fortresses.

This volte-face had been caused by Louis XIV's demand that the English forces should be reduced to 8,000 men. 'Odds-fish!' Charles said to Temple, 'Does my brother of France think to serve me thus? Are all his promises to make me master of my kingdoms come to this? Or does he think that a thing to be done with 8,000 men?' His anger was genuine; and Temple, persuaded that His Majesty had been 'perfectly cured' of dependence on France, told William that at last Charles and Louis were divided, and that what the Prince had described as 'a mischievous peace' would be reconstituted through a new Anglo-Dutch alliance. Perceiving that William remained 'something troubled', Temple then conferred with the States General, who, concerned for their trade, complained, not unnaturally, of English 'tricks and insinuations'. Temple turned against the deputies. 'They would make a man lose all patience,' he wrote. 'They deal with men just like so many children, and make them believe any stories of cocks and bulls.' He managed to persuade them to resist, and it was agreed that if the towns were not evacuated within fourteen days, Anglo-Dutch forces would together make war on France.

The French, taken by surprise, signed a treaty of peace at midnight on 10th August. William, uninformed of this, defeated them at St Denis on the 15th; but the Spanish had already signed away their possessions, with the result that Franche-Comté and twelve of their towns remained in Louis's hands. So the war ended; William considered it a miserable and dangerous peace.

Then, on 24th August, Lawrence Hyde arrived at The Hague, with instructions for Temple from Charles II not to let the Dutch ratify the Franco-Spanish treaty, promising to declare war on France within three days, and complaining that William was not sticking to the agreement made between them in the autumn of 1677. (Charles had of course no intention of attacking France; his gesture was intended to appease Parliament.) Temple protested 'I grow too old and infirm, and am not fit for these sudden commands,' he said. William waited till Hyde left the room to visit the Princess Then, throwing up his hands, he exclaimed, 'Was there ever anything so hot and so cold as this Court of yours? Will the King, that is so often at sea, never learn a word that I shall never forget since my last passage, when in a great storm, the captain was all night crying out to the man at the helm, "Steady, steady, steady"? If this despatch had come twenty days ago,' he went on, 'it had changed the face of affairs in Christendom, and the war might have been carried on till France had yielded to the Treaty of the Pyrenees [of 1659], and left the world in order for the rest of our lives. As it comes now, it will have no effect at all. At least, that is my opinion—though I would not say so to Mr Hyde.'

Temple had no answer. In fact, far from being old and infirm, he was at the height of his powers; but as he could not defend his master's chicanery, he asked leave to retire. Danby begged him not to give way to 'humour', and he left for Nimeguen, where the peace was signed in February 1679. Returning to The Hague, he was again offered the post of Secretary of State, which he refused. He would not work for a corrupt ministry, nor for a King who made a habit of breaking his word. When Danby urged him to change his mind, he lost his temper. 'I stand always upon the ground of having never done either an unjust or an ungentlemanly action in my life,' he told the Lord Treasurer, 'or an unfaithful one to my master and my country.'

He was speaking the truth. Yet some of his biographers have been jarred by a declaration they describe as complacent and vain; and in an age when self-deprecation is rated higher than self-knowledge, Temple's reply, made in angry haste, seems tasteless enough. In fact, he went so far as to record it in his memoirs, so that his own judgement of his reputation should come down to posterity. The result has of course been the opposite of what he intended; for he is now remembered as a conceited prig, whose diplomatic achievements were at the best unimportant, and in the long run ineffectual.

In his own day, Temple was respected, admired and loved by those who knew him best. His patriotism remained uncorrupted; his care for his country's prestige, although unappreciated and perhaps mocked at by many of his contemporaries, had a certain effect when he chose to exercise it abroad, as he did over matters that now seem rather trivial. When he called the Procurator of the Court of Holland 'an insolent fellow' for summoning one of his valets without leave, and added that King Charles's representative must not be treated like 'one of your burghers'; when he refused to light a bonfire for some Dutch celebration without instructions from his government; when he saved the lives of five English soldiers unjustly condemned for desertion; when he reminded Arlington that the Republic was a country 'where the fruit ripens slowly, and cannot be preserved if it be gathered green'; when he cut down the ceremonial of arriving at Nimeguen in a coach and six, so as not to delay the other envoys—on all such occasions he showed a scrupulous regard for his professional duty, and some scorn for convention.

These strictures did not affect the genial informality prevailing in his household. 'Ill humour ought never to come to the table,' he used to say; or his simplicity—'I hate the servitude of Courts, I was made for a farmer,' he told his sister—or his sympathetic understanding of other people's difficulties. Lawrence Hyde, who was jealous of his success, has described him as dull and garrulous; but this charge is based on a single conversation, when Temple 'held me in discourse a great long hour, of things most relating to himself, which are never without vanity . . .

and some stories of his amours, and extraordinary abilities that
way, which had once upon a time nearly killed him'. In speaking
of his youthful exploits—or possibly of his courtship of Dorothy
—Temple was no doubt, as is sometimes the case with elderly
people, both tedious and prolix. Hyde never saw, or perhaps
preferred not to see, Temple's dryly amusing side, and resented
his chaff; he did not like being teased. Nor did he appreciate the
other's anecdotal vein, which was shown when Danby described
England as being in the throes of 'a cruel disease' (i.e. the turmoil
of the Popish Plot) which only Temple could cure. Sir William's
reply took the form of a dialogue, with which he must often have
entertained his friends. 'A certain lady came to Dr Prujean
(the greatest of that profession in our time) in great trouble
about her daughter. "Why, what ails she?" "Alas, doctor, I
cannot tell; but she has lost her humour, her looks, her stomach;
her strength consumes every day, so as we fear she cannot
live." "Why do you not marry her?" "Alas, doctor, that we
would fain do, and have offered her as good a match as she
could ever expect; but she will not hear of marrying." "Is there
no other, do you think, that she would be content to marry?"
"Ah, doctor, that is that troubles us; for there is a young gentleman we doubt she loves, that her father and I can never consent
to." "Why, look you, Madam," replies the doctor gravely (being
all among his books in his closet) "then the case is this, your
daughter would marry one man, and you would have her marry
another; in all my books I find no remedy for such a disease
as this." '

As a family man, Temple was probably at his best. He had
become very proud of John, whom he was training in diplomacy;
his adored treasure was the fourteen-year-old Diana, an exqui-
sitely pretty child, whose only extant letter to him conveys a
delightful freshness and gaiety. Writing from Sheen in 1678,
she begins, 'Sir', and thanks him 'for all my fine things', going
on to describe how happy they have made her. 'And now,'
she continues, 'If Papa was here I should think myself a perfect
Pope, though I hope not to be burnt, as there was one at Nell
Gwyn's door the Fifth of November, who was sat in a great
chair, with a red nose half a yard long, with some hundreds
of boys throwing squills at it. Monsieur Gore [a dancing-
master, who had taught the Princesses Mary and Anne] and

I agree mighty well, and he makes me believe I shall come to something at last ... All the fair ladies petition for him ... Come when you please, and you will meet with nobody more glad to see you than, Sir, your most obedient and faithful daughter.'

Temple endorsed this letter 'my Di', and put it away. Four months later the writer died of smallpox. Replying to an enquiry about business, her father wrote, 'My heart is so broken with a blow in the most sensible part of it, that I have done nothing since as I should do, and I fear never shall again.'

This loss may have made him change his mind about retiring from the political scene when he returned to England in 1679. Before leaving The Hague—for the last time, as it happened— he had had to make formal farewells to a number of people; one of these was William's uncle, Prince Maurice of Nassau-Dietz, the owner of a celebrated parrot, reputed to converse in Brazilian. The stories about this creature were endless; Temple recorded them rather sceptically. He then parted from the Prince and Princess of Orange without, it seems, much regret; and this may be accounted for by the fact that since his marriage William was no longer so much in need of his old friend's companionship. Also, Temple had been unable to interest himself in the Princess, who within a fortnight of her departure from England had fallen passionately in love with her husband, and taken to life in the Republic as if she had been born there. Two miscarriages in as many years, fluctuating health, and anxiety during William's absences at the front had not prevented her feeling secure and useful. She was much loved: but not by Temple, who may have found her combination of piety and childishness unappealing; he preferred sophisticated women. Mary realized this; when he asked for the honour of attending service in her chapel, she consented, remarking, 'I know he will not come,' and she was right. (Temple had always been an orthodox churchman: but not an assiduous church-goer.) His wife and sister were devoted to the Princess, corresponding with her when they returned to England. She seems to have felt more at ease with them than with him; shy, over-sensitive and inclined to morbidity, she found herself at a loss with intellectual men; and Temple was not susceptible to her charm or her beauty.

He would now have been in desperate straits for money, if

his father's death in 1677 had not left him better off; as it was, the Treasury owed him some £7,000, of which he eventually received less than half after he left The Hague. 'Upon my arrival in England,' he wrote, 'I met with the most surprising scene that ever was.' The hysteria caused by the Popish Plot had increased the furious enmity between Whigs and Tories; the former party, led by Shaftesbury and Monmouth, was now in the ascendant, the Cavalier Parliament dissolved, Danby impeached and in the Tower, and the Duke of York about to go into exile. Temple refused to believe in the possibility of a Catholic invasion (or that the Jesuits had murdered Sir Edmund Berry Godfrey) and was appalled by the persecution of that sect. Later on, he became convinced that York's conversion and his fanatical adherence to the old faith made him unfit to succeed. Now, his first object was to bring about moderation, and effect general agreement on policy through both Houses of Parliament. Stunned and distracted by his daughter's death, he could not take in the whole situation, or even guess at the aims of the four ministers, Essex, Sunderland, Finch (later Earl of Nottingham) and Halifax, with whom he became affiliated soon after his return. He believed that revolution and chaos were being planned by the evil genius of Shaftesbury, whose candidate for the succession was the Duke of Monmouth. Detesting the one and despising the other, Temple proposed to Charles the installation of a new Privy Council, consisting of thirty members; half of these should be officers of the Crown, and half a selection from landowning lords and commoners. As to the Plot, Temple did not think that the King believed in it, any more than he himself did; but when he consulted his friends on this point, they replied that 'it must of necessity be pursued as if it were true, whether it is so or no', and that therefore Charles should subscribe, outwardly at least, to its veracity. Temple had to accept this view; but in his first talk with the King he made it clear that he preferred to advise His Majesty unofficially, and so refused the Secretaryship for the third time.

Charles accepted Temple's plan of a new Privy Council, and together they worked on the details in secret—or so Temple believed. He did not know that the King had evolved a policy of his own, which would seem to spring from Sir William's

5

scheme, nor that the Duke of Monmouth was privy to it. Monmouth urged his father to let Shaftesbury have a place on the Council, and Charles agreed to this. When he told Temple to inform Finch, Essex and Sunderland of their now completed plan, they were all delighted. 'It looks like a thing from Heaven!' Finch exclaimed. Next day, at a meeting consisting of these three, Temple and Halifax, Charles suddenly announced, 'There is another who, if he is left out, may do as much mischief as any—Lord Shaftesbury. He will never,' Charles went on, 'be content with a Councillor's place among thirty, and therefore I propose to add one to the number by making him President.'

Those ministers who did not want to fall out with Shaftesbury agreed. Temple launched into agitated protest. 'He will destroy all the good that we expect,' he began, and went on to speak passionately and at length against this proposal—but on concluding found himself unsupported. Heedless of etiquette, he got up and went to the door. There he turned, and said, 'I desire Your Majesty to believe that I have had no part in Lord Shaftesbury's coming into your Council or your affairs. Your Majesty and the Lords have resolved it without me. I am still absolutely against it.' Charles laughed, and, Temple records, 'turned my answer into a jest'. During the next few days Temple discovered that Monmouth had not only known about the Council, but had talked of it to a number of people, including, naturally, Shaftesbury.

In electing the great Achitophel as President, Charles II, far from being influenced by his favourite son, planned thereby to hamstring Monmouth's patron and his own most implacable enemy. He believed that, as President, Shaftesbury would be enticed away from his efforts to destroy Stuart despotism, and so lose his power and popularity. This was one of the King's few mistakes; for Shaftesbury continued to work against him with renewed vigour and authority, with the result that the Whigs described the Council as 'a new Court juggle', while their leader again urged Monmouth's succession on the public, most of whom were more than willing to accept it. Eventually, Charles dismissed Shaftesbury from the Council. Temple then warned the King that this would not affect Little Sincerity's progress. 'I would hold any wager,' he said, 'that I shall yet see that Lord in Your Majesty's business.' 'What makes you think so,' asked Charles. 'I knew,' Temple replied, referring to the Chancellorship of which Shaftesbury had been deprived in 1673, 'that he was restless while he was out, and that he would try every door to get in; he hath wit and industry to find out the ways. He is rich enough to make bribes, and has skill enough to know where to place them.' Temple concluded with a bitter condemnation of Shaftesbury's tactics and character. Every move that Lord had ever made, he told Charles, sprang from ruthless ambition. He was a renegade and a traitor.

No one, either then or later, could doubt Shaftesbury's ambition; but his determination to win the fight between himself and the King was based on a policy English people have long taken for granted—that the monarchy should be ruled by Parliament, and in certain respects be merely symbolic. When Shaftesbury's efforts to bring this about were defeated, Temple saw in his downfall a victory for good government and right principles. Ironically, he and Shaftesbury were in accord about the danger of French domination. Temple wished, above all things, to free England from the power of Louis XIV. Shaftesbury, believing that power to be bound up with the enforcement of Roman Catholicism, subscribed to the popular view that those of that faith fell into two sections, then described respectively as the Old (and therefore inoffensive) Catholics, and the 'Jesuited Papists'.

Temple's instinctive tolerance, and his long absences abroad, both before and after the Restoration, made it impossible for him to understand or to take seriously the fear of Catholic tyranny exploited by Titus Oates and used by the Whig party to defeat the Tories. He trusted in the good intentions and common sense of a number of men in both groups. Shaftesbury knew that these did not now prevail, and was taking advantage of the general corruption, whether Whig or Tory, to transform the Government into an oligarchy, ostensibly headed by Monmouth, who would be guided and advised—in fact, ruled—by himself. Temple's hopes rested on the supposition that if James did not succeed Charles, his elder daughter and her husband would become joint sovereigns, and that if she and William —who was fourth in line to the throne—had no children, then the Princess Anne, an equally staunch Protestant, would be

Queen. Shaftesbury, mistrusting all the Stuarts, was resolved
to avoid either solution. He believed William to be potentially
despotic, and knew that Mary was subordinated by him. So
Monmouth, the people's idol, now known as the Revolting
Darling, must be legitimized and accepted as Prince of
Wales.

Temple then warned the Council that Louis XIV might
again invade the Dutch Republic. He had set up a Chambre des
Réunions, whose members were advising him about the territories in the Spanish Netherlands; they said that he could take
over certain towns and fortresses on what they described as
lawful grounds, and his armies acquired them without much
difficulty. It seemed to Temple that 'a strong and resolute pro-
tection' provided by England was needed; but both Houses of
Parliament, he noted, 'had no eyes but for the dangers of popery
upon the Duke [of York]'s succession to the Crown; which
humour was blown up by the arts and intrigues of the Duke
of Monmouth and Lord Shaftesbury'. At this point, Charles
told Temple, 'The haughtiness and insincereness of the French
are not to be borne—and I will at one time or another bring
their old House about their heads,' although he knew very well
that he could not afford to do so. Sunderland, Halifax and Essex
then informed Temple that he and they should ally themselves
with Shaftesbury and Monmouth by permanently banishing
York. 'I will not,' Temple said, adding that he would never
have anything to do with either Shaftesbury or his protégé,
nor 'enter into matters of difference between the King and his
brother'. He advised Charles to prorogue the predominantly
Whig Parliament, upon which Shaftesbury swore that he would
have Temple's head as the price of his interference.

Sir William then told the Council that no Catholic priest
should be arrested unless it could be proved that he was plotting
against the Government. This enraged Halifax, who said,
'If you will not concur in points necessary for the people's
satisfaction, I shall tell everybody that you are a papist.' Temple
replied—'with some heat'—that he would not meddle with
the Plot, and was about to retire, which he did by degrees,
attending the Council at longer intervals. On one occasion,
he was forced to exchange a few words with Shaftesbury about
a new treaty with the Dutch; then he avoided him, even in

the Council Chamber. Presently he heard that he himself might be impeached as a crypto-papist and a supporter of absolute monarchy. He ignored the rumour and made up his quarrel with Halifax. Hoping to effect some agreement on policy, he decided, on the dissolution of Parliament in 1680, to stand as Member for the University of Cambridge; he was elected, spoke several times in the Commons—and was disregarded. When Charles fell ill and York returned, Temple perceived that the majority of the Councillors had ceased to consult him; 'spited to the heart', he returned to Sheen, permanently this time: or so he hoped. But as soon as the King recovered he was recalled; and Halifax, exercising all his charms, told him that they would burn down his house rather than let him desert them.

After a year of unsuccessful effort, Temple began to wonder whether the Exclusion Bill might not solve the problem of the succession. When Charles II ordered one of his secretaries to convey his refusal to grant it to the Commons, the Council vetoed that functionary's appearance as 'too unacceptable', and two others were chosen instead. Next day Charles sent for Temple, and told him to carry the message. Temple said, 'I do not well understand why a thing agreed upon last night at a Council table should be altered in Your Majesty's chamber,' adding, 'I am very sensible how much of Your Majesty's confidence I formerly had, and how much I have lost. I will confess I have not so good a stomach in business as to be content only with swallowing what other people have chewed.'

This was his final protest. When Cambridge University summoned him to stand for the Oxford Parliament of 1681, he asked the King 'to let him know his pleasure'. 'Do what you will,' Charles replied. 'I will do what Your Majesty would like best,' Temple persisted. After a pause, the King said in his kindest manner, 'Considering how things now stand at this time, I doubt your coming into the House will not be able to do much good. Therefore, let it alone.' 'I will do so,' said Temple, and departed to Sheen, whence, he goes on, 'I sent the King word by my son that I would pass the rest of my life like as good a subject as any he had, but that I would never meddle any more with any public affairs—and I desire His Majesty will not be displeased with this resolution.' 'Tell your father,' said Charles, 'that I am not angry with him—no, not at all.'

So Temple, at fifty-three, feeling himself 'an old, beaten horse', settled down to country pursuits. Eight years of happiness lay before him. Then he was struck by the heaviest blow of all.

The Prince and Princess of Orange were much concerned when they heard that Temple's efforts to retire had been followed by his dismissal from the Council. William then asked him whether he should visit England. He had been advised to do so by Henry Sidney, an old friend of Temple's, now Ambassador to The Hague, on the grounds that a certain coolness had arisen between him and his uncles which could only be dissipated by personal contact; and William himself wanted to raise the question of his wife's dowry, which had never been paid.

Temple, who knew that the Prince's refusal to support the King over the Exclusion Bill had greatly displeased both Charles and James, hesitated to give an opinion. Finally, he advised against the visit. He did not think that William and Charles were likely to agree on policy; for the King's dissolution of the Oxford Parliament, while defeating the Whigs, has also caused a split in that party. Although the extremists, led by Shaftesbury, still wanted Monmouth to succeed, the moderates preferred Mary, represented by her husband. William's uncles would therefore look on his arrival as an attempt to establish their joint claim: a highly distasteful gesture.

Neverthless William, persuaded by Sidney, and anxious to explore the situation for himself, asked and obtained leave to wait on the King, who told the French Ambassador that to deny his nephew would arouse suspicions about his promise to Louis XIV not to call another Parliament. In the event, Temple proved to be right. The visit was disastrous, partly because the Whig party enraged Charles by their welcome of his nephew; also, William urged the King to reassemble Parliament, which his uncle was not in a position to do. Temple did not wait on the Prince, who left England in deep depression, without even the promise of his wife's dowry. And he had to accept the fact that Temple's withdrawal from politics was permanent. The difference between himself and the Government, Temple had written, 'is too great ... one thing is fit for a pilot, and another for one of the crew . . . Such a perpetual fluctuation as I have met in our councils is what I am not able to deal with.' Temple then referred to the current prophecy that William would one day rule over three kingdoms, adding that he himself did not expect this to happen.

The man who for sixteen years had arranged the affairs of nations and maintained a European reputation was now absorbed in, and corresponding about, such subjects as droughts and frosts, new remedies for gout (in his case the Moxa poultice had been disappointing), the progress of his cherry trees, and a cure for Henry Sidney's weak eyes. 'Put a leaf of tobacco into each nostril as soon as you wake,' he wrote. '. . . It will make you a little sick, perhaps at first . . . but it is presently past.' Still distrusting the faculty, Temple had become something of a homeopathist; and he was much concerned by the reports of the Prince of Orange's poor health and his wife's third miscarriage. Later on, Sidney reassured him. 'I have but to get a boy,' the Prince had told him, 'and I will give you a recipe for it.' But this couple on whom so much depended remained childless.

Temple could now devote the greater part of his leisure to writing; and seeing him thus happily employed, his son begged him to set down his memoirs while the events of the last ten years were freshly remembered. Temple, preferring dilettantism (his efforts at verse-making, except for a charming piece on Lady Giffard's lory, show little talent), demurred. The young man persisted; and his father eventually produced a detailed record of his diplomatic experiences in the Dutch Republic, Germany and England, dedicating it to John, as to one expressing 'a reasonable desire'. For Temple believed that his son would become famous and successful in the profession he himself had abandoned. 'I do not remember to have refused anything you have desired of me,' he wrote, 'which I take to be a greater compliment to you than to myself.' John Temple was then accredited to the English embassy in Paris, where he acquitted himself adequately enough; but he was inclined to be over-anxious, and to exaggerate the consequences of any mishap. He took himself and his work much more seriously than his father had, and seems to have wished to emulate him, however unpropitious the circumstances. Also, he was influenced by Sir

William's rather sweeping verdict on failure. 'None that has failed once,' he used to say, 'ought ever to be trusted again.'

Meanwhile, the Temple family were able to contemplate the national upheavals objectively and from far off. In 1683 Charles II's revenge on the Whigs was completed by Shaftesbury's flight and death, the destruction of local government, and the execution of Sir Thomas Armstrong, Algernon Sidney and Lord Russell on the grounds of their supposed share in the Rye House Plot; while Essex—whose mother had been one of Temple's closest friends—cut his throat in the Tower rather than come to trial on the same charge. So Louis XIV's promise to make Charles master of his kingdoms was fulfilled; for the Stuart monarch reigned in undisturbed absolutism till his death, while York's succession was assured through Monmouth's disgrace and exile.

During these years, Temple quarrelled inconclusively, and perhaps not unenjoyably, with a neighbour, Lord Brouncker, about a right of way; then he began to consider arranging his son's marriage with a Huguenot heiress, Mademoiselle de Rambouillet, with whom John had fallen in love. Her family, supported by Louis XIV, were unwilling to conclude the match; so Temple appealed to Charles II, who in January 1685 asked his brother of France to approve it, which he did. A month later, Charles was dead. James II succeeded him unopposed, and with every intention—or so it seemed—of allowing his Protestant and Dissenting subjects to worship in peace. For five years, Temple recorded, he himself left his London house untenanted; then, still working on his memoirs, he set down an account of the late King's temperament and behaviour.

He considered that Charles II's most outstanding characteristic was his dislike of flattery; he always, Temple noted, changed the subject when this attempt at pleasing him was applied. In fact, the King, unlike his brother, that monument of stupidity, was far too clever to be taken in by such methods; he also knew that the sycophant and the toady, finding themselves at a disadvantage through his rejection of their advances, could be further set back by his taking on their role; for his easy, familiar ways amounted to flattery of a far subtler kind, one that endeared him to thousands, and was lovingly remembered long after his death. Astute though Temple was, he did not

5*

perceive that the King's agreeable informality had been a screen for his manipulation of those in whose power he sometimes found himself; his wit, his rallying, pleasant approach took them by surprise, creating a friendly atmosphere which concealed his real intentions. Another contemporary has described Charles as 'not cruel nor bloody'. Indeed, the King disliked cruelty, and only used it when his prerogative was threatened. One of his most faithful servants observed that 'he knew men to a hair'; and this tribute sums up the true nature of Charles's brilliance. There was no mercy for those of his adversaries who did not yield to his persuasiveness; and of these, Shaftesbury was the most conspicuous example. Temple concluded his obituary by deprecating the King's indifference to his 'glory'. That Charles was no patriot, and had thereby kept the crown on his head and his head on his shoulders, did not occur to him. Finally Temple joined, with a few reservations, in the chorus of praise for this strange, melancholy, devious, totally disillusioned being.

Four months after James's accession, Monmouth's belief that the Whig party's support, combined with his apparently unfailing appeal to the people, would ensure a successful invasion resulted in the holocaust of Sedgemoor, and Judge Jeffrey's celebrated 'Campaign in the West'. This, the last demonstration of Stuart mercilessness, did not affect the King's position till three years later, when it became a useful weapon in the hands of those determined to get rid of him. Nor did it strike such onlookers as Sir William Temple as particularly horrible, any more than had the lynching of the de Witts, or the torture and murder of Dutch women and children by French soldiers. It was not his habit to comment on the inevitable and the usual; he accepted both, as did most of his contemporaries, and kept his oath to a King he saw to be increasingly reckless and misguided.

In the autumn of 1685 he and Lady Temple, having celebrated the marriage of their son and his French bride, decided to let the young couple occupy Sheen, while they and Lady Giffard (who recalls that her sister-in-law had never 'been kind' to that place) moved to an Elizabethan manor-house in Farnham. Here they re-created what Sir William described as 'the private path of stealing life' he preferred. He called their new home Moor Park, in memory of the house where he spent his honeymoon, and began improvements by adding terraces, a bowling green and a summerhouse overlooking the stream that ran through the garden. The Temples saw a few neighbours, paid a courtesy visit to the King at Windsor, and rejoiced in what seemed to be the happy marriage of their son.

It was not until 1687 that the effects of James II's basic policy became plain to the French Ambassador, who reported the general discontent and alarm caused by his defiance of the laws. 'Though we now have a Prince . . . whose assiduity in business makes him his own chief Minister,' wrote the second Earl of Chesterfield, 'yet Heaven . . . hath found a way to make all this more terrible than lovely.' In the summer of 1688 Louis XIV promised James that, if need be, he would send over enough troops for him to 'subdue his enemies', and thus enforce Roman Catholicism on his subjects. Meanwhile, through the ageing King's wild fanaticism the nightmare re-created by historical memories of the Gunpowder Plot and the massacre of St Bartholomew seemed to be coming true; the ghosts of Anne Askew, Ridley, Little Bilney and the Guernsey victims rose to warn the English Protestants, reinforced by news of the *dragonnades*; and the Catholics, foreseeing hideous reprisals, were equally appalled. Temple remained uninfected; as he saw James busily sawing off the branch on which his brother had balanced so gracefully, he retained his privacy. Neither his former Whig associates nor the Prince of Orange told him of their plans; and it was not until November 1688, when he heard that William and his forces had sailed from Helvoetsluys, that he decided what his attitude should be.

As Moor Park lay between the Stuart army and that of the Prince, the Temples and Lady Giffard returned to Sheen, to find John preparing to meet and welcome William. Temple forbade him to do so; it was the first time in all their lives that they had disagreed. After James II fled the kingdom (one of his followers noted that he did so with an idiot grin on his haggard face) Temple relaxed his embargo, taking his son to wait on William at Windsor. 'In kindness to you,' the Prince told him, 'you were not acquainted with my design.' The Temples then accepted the joint sovereignty of William and Mary.

Before his coronation, William visited Sheen in order to persuade his old friend—one of the very few Englishmen he could trust—to become his Secretary of State. Temple refused; he would not break his oath by working for James's daughter and son-in-law; while his principles and religion made it impossible for him to become a Jacobite. William was followed by Henry Sidney and Halifax, who pointed out to him 'how much the Prince ... your country and your religion must suffer by your obstinate refusal to engage in their defence'. Temple replied that, apart from his oath, he had promised James never again to accept public office, and that this promise would be kept. He resumed his friendship with William, visiting and entertaining him privately; his wife and sister were received by Queen Mary, who corresponded regularly with Lady Temple; none of their letters has survived.

Sir William did not allow his self-restrictive principles to stand in the way of his son's career. He counted on the young man's achieving the distinction and fame for which he seemed perfectly qualified; for John Temple was conscientious, highly trained, and eager—perhaps a little too eager—to excel. Louis XIV's persecution of the Huguenots had resulted in his wife's brother and sisters taking refuge in England; he became almost as fond of them as of his own family; and he was now the father of two little girls. With his appointment as Secretary for War, his professional success seemed assured; but neither his parents nor his wife appear to have guessed that he was, and perhaps always had been, basically vulnerable, and therefore quite unsuited to the burdens of political responsibility. He now spoke of resigning to Sir William, who, 'with the tenderness of a father,' according to a friend, urged him to continue, 'If you are not yet capable of officiating yourself, you might be so in two or three months,' he said, 'and in the meantime, your clerks will do the business.' This rather casual optimism had no appeal for John Temple, and may indeed have increased his self-distrust; and perhaps pride forbade his handing over his work to subordinates.

So it was that when William III prepared to cross to Ireland to repel the Franco-Jacobite armies, John Temple found himself, as he believed, utterly disgraced. For General Richard Hamilton, employed by him on behalf of the Government, was a Jacobite spy who, on arrival in Dublin, gave valuable information to James's Viceroy, Tyrconnel.

Did young Temple recall his father's dictum, that a failed man should never be trusted again? When he realized what had happened, he filled his pockets with stones, took boat towards Westminster, and jumped into the river, leaving a letter with the waterman. This was later endorsed by Dorothy Temple, 'Child's paper he writ before he killed himself', and began, 'My folly in undertaking what I was not able to perform has done the King and the kingdom a great deal of prejudice. I wish him all happiness and abler servants than John Temple.' He went on to explain that 'this violence' was caused by his having been 'long tired of the burden of this life; 'tis now become insupportable'. He sent loving messages to his Rambouillet brother and sisters-in-law, and to his parents, from whom he had had, 'especially of late, all the marks of tenderness in the world'. He concluded by saying that he 'despaired not of ease in a futurity'.

They had been so proud of him—so sure of his happy future. And they were spared nothing when they received the account of his last moments. After making enquiries about the tide, he engaged 'the first oars who plied him' between six and seven in the evening; as they were about to shoot the rapids under Tower Bridge, he gave the waterman a shilling and his farewell letter—and sprang overboard. Then, suddenly desperate for life, the Temples were told, 'he ris up again; but the eddies sucked him in before the waterman could bring his boat about—and so he drowned.'

Lady Giffard tried to comfort the two people she loved best in the world, and to support John Temple's young widow. 'With this load of affliction, and my own,' she wrote, 'and all of us with our hearts broken, we returned at the end of that year with Him [her first thought was for "Papa"] and his desolate family, to Moor Park.'

A contemporary report describes Sir William's stoicism. But just as, long ago, he had warned Lady Essex that 'your life is not your own, but His that lent it to you ... therefore, by all laws, human as well as divine, self-murder has been agreed upon as the greatest crime', so he now sank beneath the thought of his son's guilt, together with his loss. Lady Temple, completely broken, told one of her Osborne nephews that she had 'deserved' this irreparable sorrow. 'Having no tie to the world,' she added, 'I may the better prepare myself to leave it.' She had borne, in all, nine children. One by one, they had been taken from her.

Her husband took refuge in his writing, and began to revise the memoirs his son had urged him to complete. It was not much of a consolation; gradually, as he became further involved in the work, he realized that he needed an amanuensis; and while he was looking out for a well educated and biddable secretary, Lady Temple received a letter from a distant cousin, long widowed, asking for a place for her only son, who after seven years at Trinity College, Dublin, was in need of employment. Negotiations ensued; and the youth, who had obtained his degree in spite of trouble with the authorities (he had been punished on twenty occasions for insubordination), was engaged, and joined the Temple household. His appearance was not prepossessing, nor were his manners; but he seemed sufficiently qualified for the post. His name was Jonathan Swift.

The Temples now decided to hand over their London house to their daughter-in-law and her children, while they made their permanent home at Moor Park. For some years, they had been served by Edward Johnson and his wife, Bridget; he was steward of the household at Sheen; when he died, his widow accompanied her employers to Moor Park as Lady Giffard's waiting-woman.

Mrs Johnson's daughter, Hester, was between eight and nine years old when Swift became Sir William's secretary. As she spoke with a lisp—thus greatly endearing herself to the Temples, who seem to have been thereby reminded of their lost Diana—she was known as Esther, or Hetty. 'Her imperfect language and natural way of talking', according to Lady Giffard, so delighted Sir William that he made a pet of her, with the result that she was thought to be his natural daughter, and referred to as such after he died, partly because he left her £1000 in his will. He had indeed virtually adopted her soon after Diana's death, that is, before the births of his granddaughters. No evidence to support the rumour of her illegitimacy exists; it was not subscribed to by Swift, who became her tutor, and was to immortalize her as Stella, re-creating her lisp in the 'little language' of his Journal. Another dependant, a distant cousin of Lady Temple's, was Rebecca Dingley. She and Swift were the same age—twenty-two—when he joined the household.

He observed the conventions of the day by the immediate production of a pindaric ode to his employer. This effort was unremarkable. It was followed by the writer's reminder that his agreement with Sir William was temporary, a stepping-stone to a post in Ireland, as soon as the reconquest of that colony had been completed. In May 1690 he left England with a letter of recommendation from Temple to Sir Robert Southwell, then Secretary of State to King William. Nothing came of this scheme, and he rejoined the Temples in December 1691.

Sir William's need of Swift's services resulted in his remaining
at Moor Park for the next two and a half years, and he soon
became indispensable. His resolve to make a figure in the world,
and to use Temple's influence to that end, was combined with
an intense admiration for the older man. Involuntarily, Sir
William fascinated Swift, who became morbidly dependent on
his favour. Temple seems to have been unaware that his rather
uncouth, extremely able young secretary was subject to corro-
sive ambition, and a furious resentment of any slight, real or
imaginary. The poverty and neglect, the lack of care and affection
in his early life had so embittered Swift as to make him violently
opposed, not only to patronage, however kindly, but to the mere
fact of being an employee; and his devotion to Temple was
poisoned by his longing to be equally famous and powerful.
When Sir William, sometimes in pain from gout, and sometimes sunk in gloom for his son's death, fell into silence, or responded coldly to Swift's advances, the young man suffered
all the agonies of the egotist; he never forgot the effect on himself
of Temple's moods of depression, or attempted to understand
them. Years later, recalling that time, he told Stella that his
first employer had 'spoiled a fine gentleman' by his indifference.
That the nature of Swift's genius eliminated any question of
gentlemanliness, fine or otherwise, did not occur to him. Every
now and then Temple had, he believed, humiliated him, treating
him, he remembered, as a schoolboy; so Sir William's many
kindnesses, his familiar talk, his giving Swift a start in life,
added to the secretary's rage at having to accept benefits he
came to look on as insults. Yet in these early years at Moor Park
he seemed to settle down gratefully and amicably enough,
idealizing the Temples while secretly rebelling against them.

The fact that his status later became that of a friend—almost
an equal—was ignored; he continued to think of himself as
unjustly deprived of the rights to which his talents entitled him,
while exercising the latter in verses addressed to 'Mild Dorothea,
peaceful, wise and great', and to Lady Giffard as 'Dorinda' ('Thus
when Dorinda wept, joy every face forsook'), whom he afterwards referred to as 'that old Beast' in his Journal. His ruthless
honesty compelled him to acknowledge Temple's distinction,
first as a statesman, but primarily as a writer. 'I prefer him,'
he told a friend, 'to all others at present in England.' He could

not help venerating the man who had four times refused a great office, and had maintained his integrity by leaving the gambling-hells of Court and Council to find peace in an exile Swift himself desired to leave.

Once more, Temple agreed to further his career, and helped him to obtain an Oxford degree, so that he might eventually take holy orders; also, he promised to ask the King to grant Swift a prebendary stall at that University.

As Temple became increasingly dependent on Swift's services, he delayed the fulfilment of this promise. 'He is less forward than I could wish,' Swift complained in a letter to his cousin Thomas. Meanwhile, he continued to copy out his employer's *Memoirs* and some of his *Miscellanea*, which Temple then revised for publication.

In 1693 William III came to Moor Park to consult Temple unofficially, and Swift was desired to attend them. This privilege might have helped to provide the opening for which he longed; but because he was still employed as a copyist, he continued to chafe against Temple's use of his services. Yet he impressed the King, who, as they walked about the garden, paused to observe a bed of asparagus. English people, he told Swift, knew how best to grow this vegetable: but they spoilt the result by cutting it wrongly; and he advocated the Dutch method. He then reverted to the bill for triennial Parliaments, about which he could not make up his mind. A day or two later, he sent Bentinck to Moor Park for further consultation. In theory, King William was against the bill, as being an encroachment on his prerogative; he desired a written statement on the matter.

Temple complied, strongly advising His Majesty's consent to the bill. His letter was carried to Court by Swift; yet still the secretary remained dissatisfied and resentful. This may have caused him to ask Dryden, on the grounds that they were distantly related, to read some of his poems. The Laureate's judgement struck him to the soul. 'Cousin Swift,' he said, 'you will never be a poet.'

This merciless verdict—no crueller than many Swift himself was to pronounce in his own days of greatness—sent him back to Moor Park with the news that he was leaving, to obtain ordination and independence in Ireland. Somewhat disconcerted, Temple offered him the non-resident post of Master of the Rolls in Dublin: a sinecure which would provide both a salary and his continued employment as amanuensis. Swift refused, suggesting that his cousin Thomas should take his place—and departed in May 1694. Thomas Swift was engaged, and proved inadequate. With his usual good humour, Temple accepted the inconvenience.

Shortly after his arrival in Ireland, Swift discovered that the living of Kilroot in Belfast was available; but no bishop would ordain him without a testimonial of character. So the fiercely proud young man was forced to apply to Temple for yet another favour; he did so on 6th October 1694 in pitiable terms. Having explained his dilemma, he went on, 'I shall stand in need of all your goodness to excuse my many weaknesses and follies and oversights . . . This is all I dare beg from your Honour under circumstances of life not worth your regard.' Temple sent the recommendation by return, Swift was ordained on 25th October, and settled in at Kilroot, where he remained for the next two years.

By this time, Temple's *Essays* and his *Observations on the United Provinces* had been translated into French, and were being widely read on the Continent. A young Swiss writer, Monsieur Muralt, so admired them that he asked and obtained leave to call on 'this famous diplomatist and philosopher' in the summer of 1694. 'I went to his house,' he continues, 'and received every sort of courtesy.' When Muralt mentioned his works, Sir William said of his translators, 'They have mutilated me cruelly.' He then conducted Muralt round his property, which his guest described as 'the ideal of a pleasant retreat . . . cultivated by the master himself'. Noting that Temple was as free from official business as from ambition, Muralt goes on, 'I saw . . . le Chevalier Temple both healthy and gay; and though he is getting on in years, he tired me in walking, and except for the rain . . . would, I believe, have forced me to ask for quarter. This good old man thought I should not be sufficiently rewarded for my trouble if I saw only his little house.' 'I assure you,' Muralt told his host, 'that I am more interested in men than in buildings.' 'Before leaving London,' Sir William replied, 'you should go to Petworth, the country house of the Duke of Somerset.' He supplied his guest with horses and servants for the journey, and then, suddenly fearing that the Duke might be at Court, asked Lady Temple to write a note of introduction to the Duchess.

Having inspected Petworth, Muralt records, 'In that magnificent palace, the quiet house and little garden of Monsieur Temple constantly recurred to my memory.'

Lady Giffard's memoir of her brother, part of which she wrote several years before his death (it was not published till 1736), adds some more intimate touches to Muralt's account. Temple's humour, she says, 'was naturally gay, but a great deal unequal, sometimes by cruel fits of spleen and melancholy ... He grew lazier and easier in his humour as he grew older ... Riding and walking were the exercises he was most pleased with, after he had given over tennis ... He ... wore always the plainest stuffs, and for many years the same colour.' The combined effect—informal, glowing, serene—of a sister's loving study and a visitor's eager response, resembles a painting of the Dutch school.

In the Christmas week of 1694 the Temples heard that Queen Mary had succumbed to smallpox. For a short time, the reports gave the impression that the attack was not serious; then, in the early hours of 28th December, she died.

The national mourning was deep and sincere, and one of those most affected was Dorothy Temple. Her relationship with the Queen seems to have supported her through her own last, agonizing loss; now, deprived of hope and courage, she sank, giving way to an incurable melancholy. Long ago, in reply to her husband's remark that 'to be miserable is not the way to be good', she had written, 'Most people make haste to be miserable, they put on their fetters as inconsiderately as a woodcock runs into a noose.' That was the judgement of youth. At sixty-eight, the fetters of grief constrained her resistance to illness. In February 1695 she died, and was buried beside her daughter in Westminster Abbey.

Sir William did not expect, or wish, to survive her. Turning to his sister for comfort, he found that he was wrong; more closely united than ever before, they achieved happiness, even, sometimes, a mild gaiety, in the company of a few old friends. As usual, Lady Giffard's spirit rose to meet this crisis; and her brother, having made a new will, published his *Introduction to the History of England*, which Swift had prepared for the press before his departure. As Temple's plan for following up this essay with others of the same kind required a more skilled helper than Thomas Swift, he wrote to Jonathan suggesting that he should return to Moor Park. At this time, Swift himself was seeking a change of occupation; for he had received a major setback in his private life.

For some months, bored and irritated by the limitations of his parish, he had been corresponding with and courting a Miss Jane Waring, whom he called Varina. Her uncertain response to his increasingly passionate approach was driving him to desperation, when Temple's letter arrived. He then told her that he would give up what seemed to be his last chance of a career if she would consent to marry him and settle in Kilroot. She refused, and he returned to Moor Park in 1696.

No other woman was to have the same appeal for him; and he never forgot the humiliation and misery caused by her dismissal. He therefore renewed his relationship with Temple in furious rebellion against a fate he felt to be undeserved. For neither then nor later could he take in his effect on other people; and the only person able to put up with his tormented ardour was Sir William.

On arrival at Moor Park Swift found himself more considerately treated. There are indications that he no longer ate at the housekeeper's, or second, table, but took his meals with Temple, Lady Giffard and their guests; so he became acquainted with, and thereby impressed, members of the Court circle. At the same time, he had more leisure than formerly, and was able to continue working on the first of his great books, *The Tale of a Tub*. Stella Johnson, now in her sixteenth year, still charmed and amused him; she had, he says, 'every feature in perfection', although he could not help adding that she was a little too fat.

The influence of his employer's works on those of Swift prevailed long after Sir William's death. Temple could not know that he himself was leaning on a stick which, once lit, was to soar and explode in a pattern of multi-coloured stars. He remained kind and patient with the secretary who had replaced his cousin; but he had need of all his tolerance when Jonathan Swift retreated into the sullenness and resentment caused by his patron's concern for others. It was Sir William's custom, when he and his guests sat down to a game of One-and-Thirty—a very mild form of gambling—to supply the players with a shilling each, so that the standard of expenditure should be tactfully set, and also because this was, in his view, an act of courtesy. Swift took his gesture as an insensitive demonstration of patronage and meanness, recalling it long afterwards with sneering mockery. Fortunately the vicissitudes of Temple's career had taught him, on this as on other occasions, to ignore such absurdities; so he accepted his secretary's withdrawal into yet another grievance with a serenity that may have further embittered that impossibly difficult young man.

Meanwhile, Lady Giffard's use of Swift's services furthered his ambitions. 'I have sent him,' she wrote to a niece (Martha Jane Temple, who later became Bentinck's second wife), 'with another compliment from Papa to the King, where I fancy he is not displeased with occasion of going.' At this time, she was chiefly concerned to spare her brother's energies; for his gout had become increasingly troublesome. 'Thank God,' she informed the same correspondent, 'Papa is not very bad, I hear him just going downstairs, though with a lame knee.' Temple's refusal to diet was an anxiety; his consumption of roast beef, 'with a very good stomach ... he is now a great deal better, whatever comes after it', is recorded by her in mingled relief and foreboding; she adds, 'Papa is so well as to have dined below every day since you left.'

Visiting and playing cards with the Somersets at Petworth was another pleasure. 'We are got hither at last,' Lady Giffard reports, 'and Papa I thank God very well, and insufferably pert with winning twelve guineas at Crimp last night.' That she still teased him about his enjoyment of little things was a great happiness to them both, as was his interest in literary and political discussion. In 1698 he told Lord Dartmouth that he had just finished reading Algernon Sidney's *Discourses on Government*. 'Have you seen it?' he went on. 'I have read it all over,' Dartmouth replied. 'I cannot help admiring your patience,' said Temple. 'What do you think of it?' 'It seems to me writ with a desire to destroy all government—' Dartmouth began, and Sir William put in, 'That is for want of knowing the author.' He had never had much use for that uncompromising republican, whom the Whigs reverenced as a martyr to the Old Cause; nor had he been impressed by his last words on the scaffold, when the headsman, waiting for Sidney to finish his prayers, had respectfully enquired, 'Will you rise again, sir?' 'Not till the Resurrection—strike on!' was the highly Cromwellian reply.

'There is a passage in [the *Discourses*],' Temple told Dartmouth, 'which explains the whole.' He then stressed Sidney's belief that Divine Right belonged, not to the monarch, but to the man most fitted to govern. 'Now I that knew him very well,' he continued, 'can assure you that he looked upon himself to be that very man, so qualified as to govern the whole of mankind.' This was his last recorded judgement, as admiringly remembered as any in his books, which are now almost forgotten. He had made Swift his literary executor, while Lady Giffard had charge of his manuscripts. She was very angry when the secretary arranged to publish them without consulting her: and he complained bitterly of her daring to protest about his discourtesy.

In the last weeks of 1698 Sir William remained active; but with the New Year he became an invalid. Lady Giffard, giving no details, reports that 'the gout wore out his life'. At one o'clock on the morning of 27th January 1699 he died—'and with him,' Swift wrote, 'all that was good and amiable among men.' He was buried beside his wife and daughter in Westminster Abbey; in his will he had directed that his heart should be interred under the sundial at Moor Park. No information survives as to the disposal of his son's body; possibly it was never recovered.

Among the mass of Temple's obituaries Swift's in the best known and the least intimate. While crediting the man who had done so much for him with 'wisdom, justice, liberality, politeness, eloquence', love of country and universal esteem as the most accomplished writer of his time, he failed to record any personal obligation. A simpler and more moving tribute came to Lady Giffard from Henry Sidney, who wrote, 'I never loved anybody better than I did him.' She did not live to see a rather surprising account of her brother from the greatest memoirist of her own or any other age, who never set eyes on Temple, and whom Sir William himself would have regarded as a national enemy.

At twenty-four, Saint-Simon, then beginning his career at the Court of Versailles, wrote as follows. 'England . . . lost, in a special sense, one of her principal ornaments, I mean the

Chevalier Temple, who had a high reputation in science as in literature, and in politics and administration, and who became famous as an Ambassador and mediator in the general peace. He was witty, subtle and brilliant, yet simple too, having no desire to parade himself, and who liked to live happy and free, in the English fashion, not caring to acquire properties, riches or fame. He had many friends, some greatly distinguished, who were proud to know him.' This, the ultimate salutation, needs no comment—and remains unsurpassed.

Sir John Reresby
(1634—1689)

My heart is inditing of a good matter; I speak
of the things which I have made touching the
King; my tongue is the pen of a ready writer.

Psalm xlv, 1

Sir John Reresby
attributed to Faithorne

Sir John Reresby was born at Thrybergh in the West Riding of Yorkshire on 14th April 1634. He eventually inherited an estate that had belonged to his ancestors for some six hundred years. His father, another Sir John, claimed descent from Sir Adamus de Reresby, first heard of in the reign of Edward the Confessor; the establishment of his family in Yorkshire is proved by deeds dating from the thirteenth century.

The younger John Reresby was what we now call accident-prone. In his third year a fall from a window, disjointing his left knee, was the first of a series of breakages, which seems to indicate a brittleness of bone; his performances as a duellist were unaffected by this disability, and may be ascribed to the rather belligerent resolution he inherited from his father, who, hurrying to York to join the war against the Scots in the autumn of 1639, found that peace had been concluded, and that his services were no longer required. He then met with what his son later described as an unfortunate and costly mishap; its results perfectly illustrate the prevailing attitude towards the privileged class of which he was an outstanding example.

Sir John's heir (whose birth was to be succeeded by those of six brothers and two sisters) was only five when his father's accident happened; but its effects on him, combined with his lameness and short stature, presently produced a compensatory determination never to give in, accept an insult or refuse a challenge. He must have heard that 'adventure' recounted many times; it set a pattern he followed all his life.

As Thrybergh was a day's journey from the rendezvous at York, the elder Sir John, with two officers in the same regiment, decided to stay the night in the principal tavern of that city. They were celebrating their freedom in an upper room set apart for them when an unknown, drunken gentleman forced his way in upon their feasting. Desired to leave, he refused, upon which Sir John took him by the shoulders and threw him downstairs, splitting his skull. A few days later he died, and Sir John was arrested for murder.

It was all very awkward. Here was a gentleman of property, breeding and eminence, charged with a crime he had committed through mere impetuosity, and in defence of his rights against a sottish interloper. Then, at the trial, the surgeon, giving evidence as to the cause of the victim's death, announced that he had been suffering from smallpox; signs of the disease remained in his head. Therefore he had died from that, not from the split in his skull—and Sir John Reresby was acquitted, to the general satisfaction.

His little namesake, duly impressed, was thereby convinced that to take the offensive—in self-defence—was the duty of every brave and honourable man, whatever the consequence. Five years later his father fell into what might have been more serious trouble as the result of joining the Royalist army. Arrested by the Parliamentary forces and brought before their General, Lord Fairfax, who committed him to prison, he was again reprieved, this time through the intercession of his friends, remaining under restraint in his own house. When the Royalist army had been defeated he went up to London, to compound for his recently sequestered estate. Refusing to take the oaths to Parliament, he returned to Thrybergh, where he died of food-poisoning in April 1646. So, at twelve years old, his eldest son became the head of the family.

There is no doubt that he missed his father very much. Throughout his life he remembered him as handsome, amusing, accomplished and popular, although too easily roused to anger. The youthful Sir John modelled himself on his favourite parent; his love for Lady Reresby was less whole-hearted because, from the moment of her husband's death, she put an end to any hopes he might have had of ruling the household; her decisions were paramount, and extremely sensible. She came of a wealthy and distinguished family, the Yarburghs of West Riding, and now used her portion to settle her husband's debts and arrange for the better education of her sons. She engaged for John and his next brother, Edmund, a tutor who remained with them for three years.

In those days, the West Riding was part of a separate kingdom. Yorkshire gentry had their own standards, their own culture; the background of John Reresby's early years there provided an odd mixture of rough living, care of the arts, exuberant

hospitality, proud independence and a certain scorn for out-
siders. One saying quoted with approval as late as the nineteenth
century, typifies contemporary feeling. 'Keep a stone in thy
pocket seven years; turn it, and keep it seven years longer,
that it may be ever ready to thine hand when thine enemy draws
near.'

When John Reresby began to compose his *Memoirs* he did
so 'for posterity'; but he did not mean the general public. He
was concerned only that his descendants should know what
he had done, and what he represented. As to himself, he could
not promise 'an exact and particular' account. 'I shall only draw,'
he says, 'the gross lines of my own little story.' In fact, it is not
so little; for he had many adventures, some ludicrous, others
dramatic. He recounts them with complete unselfconsciousness
and a rather engaging complacency.

He was fifteen when Lady Reresby came to the conclusion
that his education had not been adequately dealt with, and that
he and Edmund must be put to school in London. With her
elder daughter, Elizabeth, she and these two sons left Thrybergh
in 1649; she then entered John and Edmund as day boys at
Whitefriars. Here John was able to develop his passion for
music, beginning with the violin; but his mother decided against
Whitefriars, and moved him and Edmund to a boarding-school,
the Blue House at Enfield Chase, where they remained for the
next two years, while she returned to Yorkshire. She then arranged
that Edmund should be apprenticed to a wool merchant; John
was entered at Gray's Inn as a law student. Here he would have
been happy enough, if he had not heard that Lady Reresby
had married a Mr James Moyser of the West Riding. He abhorred
the thought of a stepfather; but soon after he came home for
the summer vacation he found that gentleman 'both kind and
just'; and during the next six years the birth of four sons and
a daughter did not diminish his mother's care for him. In 1653
she sent him back to Gray's Inn, with a bodyservant and an increased allowance. He was now nineteen; and although he made
many friends, his aggressive tendencies ruled his behaviour.
Looking out for slights, he was ready, indeed eager, to respond
as became a man of honour; his definition of such a person was
based on an immediate challenge. 'I will show you my sword,' he
would say, at the faintest sign of what he took to be disrespect

from his more sophisticated companions; and so a fight, which sometimes developed into a mêlée, would begin.

On one of these occasions he was set upon by three students, and thus forced to retreat; next day, in a manner that would have delighted Dumas, he challenged the principal attacker, Sir Thomas Spencer, who, unwilling to break the laws against duelling, asked a friend to mediate between them. Very well, said Sir John; then young Spencer must make 'public submission' to him before those who had shared in the quarrel. This was done, good humour prevailed, and Sir Thomas stood drinks all round. Altogether, it had been a most satisfactory affair. But it left Sir John with the feeling that life in Gray's Inn did not really suit him; and as a staunch Royalist, he disliked being under the Cromwellian regime. His mother consented to his going abroad; and in April 1654, accompanied by a tutor and two servants, he set off for Paris.

He became very fond of his tutor, a Mr Leech, who had taken holy orders after leaving Cambridge, and whom he describes as a great scholar. His wish for a higher standard of instruction, in languages and music especially, could not be granted at Gray's Inn; and his combative instinct was combined with a fastidiousness that rejected both the lechery and the puritanism he found there. With Mr Leech's help, he hoped to achieve a more civilized, less constricted way of life in continental society: but not necessarily in Paris, where he stayed just long enough to fit himself out with fashionable clothes before going to the Palais Royal to watch the exiled Charles II playing billiards with Prince Rupert and the Duke of York. Here, his native caution prevailed: he made no move towards a presentation; if he had done so, the Parliamentary agents would have reported it, and he would have been recalled to England and heavily fined.

He and Mr Leech then moved to Blois, where they stayed some months, so that Sir John could study the language, improve his dancing and learn the guitar; but this peaceful existence was disrupted by his threatening to challenge a fellow lodger, upon which the tutor arranged a visit to Saumur, where they stayed with a member of the Leech family for nearly a year. Besides working at philosophy and mathematics, Sir John learnt to play the lute and took lessons in fencing. Then he broke out again, this time over a lady.

His looks were not outstanding; but his approach to women, one of respectful gallantry, generally met with encouragement —so much so, that several young ladies came to prefer his company to that of the local youths: as in the case of a Mademoiselle de Boragan, who asked him to escort her to a ball, with the result that he received a challenge from the gentleman expecting to accompany her. When the jealous rival did not keep the appointment his inamorata, disgusted, would have nothing more to do with him.

Sir John then became involved with two more ladies, one married, the other single; he was walking in the meadows with the latter, when he overheard a tipsy gentleman criticize her; he sent him a challenge, which remained unanswered. Next day, with his servant and fellow countryman, he gave the offender some smart blows with a cudgel as he came out from Mass—upon which, having convened a party of friends, his enemy attacked in force. Sir John and his companion took refuge in a nearby house, only to hear that their adversary was about to sue them for assault. Finally, the dispute was settled in their favour by the local authorities.

Sir John now came to the conclusion that he should leave France for Italy; and as he could not afford to take Mr Leech with him they parted, the pupil regretfully. 'I shall ever own,' he says, 'the blessing of being so long under the conduct of so learned and so pious a man.' He had been looking forward to seeing Italy ever since leaving England. It did not disappoint him.

As he had no intention of making the journey alone, he stopped in Lyons in order to join a group of Englishmen who were preparing to cross the frontier. They delayed their departure for nearly three months; and so Sir John found himself at a loose end. His life would have been rather dull if he had not made 'a particular acquaintance' (the contemporary euphemism for an affair) with a Carmelite nun in that city. He was twenty-two; and his cursory reference to this incident gives the impression that it was by no means the first of such relationships, the only difference being his choice of a conventual mistress. His dislike of what he calls debauchery implies precaution against venereal disease; and so his frequentation of a Carmelite suggests that the lady was both well bred and healthy. As 'a woman of wit and beauty', she was just what he needed 'to pass the time away' in the intervals of improving his performance on the lute.

He and his friends were on the point of departure when they heard that plague had spread over Italy, and was chiefly prevailing in Rome. The greater number decided to cancel the journey; Sir John, with a Mr Berry, resolved to make it, aiming for Padua, as being free from infection. The two young men had been close friends ever since their first meeting in Saumur, which had begun with disagreement, boxes on the ear and the inevitable challenge, cancelled by the tutor's intervention. Once more on the best of terms, they reached Padua on 13th November 1656, found lodgings, and entered the University in company with other foreign students; for their plan of going on to Rome was now abandoned.

Here Sir John was in his element; he responded as eagerly to the extravagant display of the social scene as to the wild violence (accompanied by elaborate ceremonial, with special rules for bowing, kissing hands and general politeness) of student life. Pageantry, splendour, the baroque intricacy of architecture, paintings and dress made a brilliant setting for theft, murder and lust. While studying mathematics and fortification, he unconsciously modelled his behaviour on that of the young gentleman satirized by Mercutio when he tells Benvolio that he is like a man who 'when he enters the confines of a tavern, claps me his sword upon the table and says, "God send me no need of thee!" '—and accuses his friend of being 'as hot a Jack in thy mood as any in Italy'.

Reresby's share in the general exuberance was shadowed by concern about Mr Berry; for that young man had taken up with a prostitute, the daughter of their landlady. She came regularly to Padua, and was the mistress of a Dutch merchant in Venice. She now transferred her favours to Berry, and was bent on getting all his money out of him. He then promised her more wealth than that provided by the Dutchman, with the result that she came to live with her mother, in order, it was obvious to Sir John, to ruin his friend, whom she persuaded to escort her back to Venice for the Carnival. He agreed to take a house for her there, and Reresby, rather perturbed, went with him.

For a short time, he was so overwhelmed by the fantastic glories of the Carnival as to forget the dangers threatening his companion. In this glittering, fairy-tale world, given up to feasting, fornication, practical jokes, music, and masquerades in every variety of fancy dress, the rather conventional young Englishman became one of a frenzied, vociferous throng, whose chief resort was the Piazza San Marco, crowded from early morning till the small hours with jigging, shouting, riotous figures. Here, although there was hardly room to move, dancers and singers, threading their way through the maze, sustained their rhythms, swirling in a conglomeration of colour and light, to the sound of trumpets, drums and violins. Engulfed in the medley, Reresby and Berry were swept towards the water, and from their gondola watched the slowly moving Bucentaur, gilded and hung with crimson satin, carrying the Doge to wed the sea, while the bells clashed against one another, the cannon thundered, and a thousand rockets exploded over the city. This extravaganza ended with a concert on the lagoon, and the sudden, soaring eruption of Fame, who, from an illuminated cloud, declaimed, in verse, the triumphs of the Republic. Meanwhile, in the smaller squares and streets, the Venetian courtesans, celebrated throughout Europe for their gifts and graces, paraded in gowns of red and yellow. Their breasts were bare, their heavily scented headdresses made of tinsel flowers. Some carried kittens dressed as babies, others pretended to swoon in the arms of their pursuers. Years later, struggling with local government under grey Yorkshire skies, Reresby—ageing, invalidish, careworn—was to recall those bejewelled, beckoning creatures with cool detachment. He had never been drawn to ladies of pleasure.

He now decided to contribute to the grotesque aspect of the Carnival by arranging for his page to play the bagpipes—an instrument never yet heard in Venice—which he so concealed that no one could tell where the noise was coming from, with the result that he and the boy were mobbed and nearly 'pulled to pieces' by the crowd. After this triumph, he persuaded Mr Berry to return to Padua, with a view to resigning from the University and leaving for Florence; but the young man refused to part from his mistress. Sir John therefore resolved to prove her worthlessness by making love to her himself, and then reporting her betrayal to his friend, 'The whore, being subtle', he says, first took a bracelet from him as the price of her consent, and then told Mr Berry of his advances, having 'aggravated the

6

story with all the ill circumstances imaginable'. Sir John at once described his plan to Mr Berry, adding that he had used it 'as a persuasion not to lose his time any longer in staying with so perfidious a slut', and once more urged him to leave her. The young man, convinced, flung his arms round Sir John, and agreed to go. His mistress then tried to poison Reresby, or so he believed (it was after all an Italian practice), and he and Berry left for Florence as soon as he recovered from what may have been an attack of continental dysentery.

Shortly after their arrival, the two friends were received by the Grand Duke Ferdinand II, one of the last Medici rulers of Tuscany. As Reresby's Italian was now fluent enough for him to talk at length with the Duke, he became a favourite guest; and Ferdinand, who was anxious to remain on good terms with the English Government, invited Sir John to his palace in the hills, and sent him presents of food and wine. His stay in Florence was the happiest time in all his travels; here and in France, his frequentation of three persons—the Grand Duke, a little Stuart princess and a beautiful young Englishwoman—had a permanent effect, and was recorded with characteristic simplicity.

Ferdinand II was an extremely able and popular ruler. He had been the supporter and patron of Galileo; after his death in 1642 the Duke continued to finance his inventions by ordering new kinds of telescopes, weather glasses, retorts and thermometers, some of which Sir John inspected in the Pitti. Ferdinand's palace in Pisa contained an anatomical theatre and a foundry for chemical experiments, while his brother Leopoldo was responsible for the famous scientific Academy of Cimento. Ferdinand's tolerance of what is now known as permissive behaviour was shown by his refusal to punish or even frustrate his homosexual subjects. When his horrified mother brought him a list of these persons, he scanned it, remarked, 'One name is missing,' added his own in capitals, and threw the document in the fire.

The Tuscans took his side when his wife quarrelled with him over a handsome page, and he continued to lead them in their pursuit of entertainment—football, racing, ballets (in these, horses played the principal part) and torchlit concerts on the Arno. Reresby was especially impressed by the gardens of Ferdinand's younger brother Cardinal Gian Carlo—which contained, besides elaborate water-works and rare plants, an elegant 'house of pleasure' for his mistresses—and much admired his collections of paintings and statues; a ceiling picture showed a group of nymphs busily castrating the Grand Duke's favourite dwarf. No sightseer in the conventional sense, Sir John preferred outdoor amusements, such as the battle between Africa and Asia on the one side and Europe and America on the other, which was held in the amphitheatre of the Boboli gardens; and he much enjoyed a chariot race which he watched from the Piazza Santa Maria Novella, 'where', he noted, 'if a driver escape a mischief by the fall, he seldom doth being run over' —and thus losing his life in an attempt to win a prize of thirty crowns. Also, Reresby greatly admired the Grand Duke's economies. 'He does not think it below him to play the merchant,' he says, and added that Ferdinand sold what he could spare of his wine, advertising it by hanging a bottle outside the Pitti Palace, just like an innkeeper.

Open-air banquets, visits to the Zoo, rhyming contests on the Ponte Santa Trinità, fireworks, tournaments, hunting, pageants, and public recitations of impromptu verse—all entranced Sir John; but poor Mr Berry was not so happy. He pined for his 'miss', and the rapturous licence of Venice. Presently he began to look on his companion as a tyrant who had cheated him into deserting her. As he could not quite make up his mind to tax his friend with this manoeuvre, he approached him during his music practice and reverted to their quarrel in Saumur, which must now, he said, be revenged. Sir John replied with a sharp answer, Berry continued to abuse him—and finally, as it became clear that swords must be drawn, they descended to the courtyard. Their landlord, hearing the dispute, came too, and persuaded them to forgive one another, which at last they agreed to do. But Mr Berry left for Venice, while Reresby made short stays at Pisa and Leghorn before returning, briefly, to Florence. Then, determined to see as much of the continent as possible before his money ran out, he set off for Germany, the Dutch Republic and the Low Countries.

He reached The Hague in October 1657, where he was received by two members of the Stuart family, Elizabeth, the exiled Queen of Bohemia, and her niece, the widowed Mary of Orange. Reresby seems not to have been aware of the existence of the

Princess's son, the seven-year-old William Henry, who, three decades later, was to upset all his plans by becoming King of England. He then made his way, slowly, towards Paris (ready, as ever, to challenge anyone who jostled him or trod on his foot), where he was presented to Queen Henrietta Maria, who had retired, with her youngest daughter, Princess Henrietta Anne, to a convent in Chaillot. Having engaged two footmen, and living 'as handsomely as I could till I went for England', he reached London to find that his mother had arranged to marry him to a Miss Sarah Hotham, whose dowry, £3,000, made her a suitable match, and who at once took a fancy to him. Sir John did not reciprocate, and ignored the gossip caused by her advances.

Annoyed by the London workmen, who, objecting to his fashionable dress, shouted 'French dog', and stoned him and his valet, Reresby joined his mother and stepfather in York. There he met the man whose influence and power eventually helped to found his career. In his thirty-first year George Villiers, second Duke of Buckingham, was engaged on a delicate and apparently hazardous negotiation—that of regaining his income and his estates through marriage with Mary Fairfax, only child of the Parliamentary General. Her father, endowed by Cromwell with all that Buckingham had once possessed, soon fell under the nobleman's spell. So did Reresby, who described him as 'the finest gentleman of person and wit I think I ever see'—but, unlike the General, who gave his consent to his daughter's marriage with the Duke, presently perceived that Buckingham 'could not be long serious or mind business'.

Villiers might have been a great man; he preferred to be an adventurer. His subjugation of the Fairfaxes (all three became attached to him within a few weeks) was one of his many triumphs, and may be partly accounted for by poor plain Mary's falling hopelessly in love with him. His brilliance and beauty, his amusing account of his adventures and escapades during the exile made him irresistible, and to her, fatal. She learned to endure without complaint all the misery he caused her, hoping to please him by her choice of flamboyant dresses and jewels (she had no taste in such matters) that were to make her a figure of fun at the Court of Charles II. Bedizened, childless and neglected, she behaved with dignity, remaining devoted to her outrageously unfaithful husband.

In November 1659 Sir John, disliking the confusion caused by the downfall of Richard Cromwell's government, returned to France. In Paris he was received at the Court of Queen Henrietta Maria, who had now moved to the Palais Royal, and encouraged him to wait on the fifteen-year-old Princess Henrietta Anne. He was much taken with this frail, slightly deformed child, with whom he danced and played duets on the harpsichord; what she liked best was to walk with him in the palace gardens, where 'the innocent diversion' of a swing had been put up for her. There he would swing her, high, high, while her ladies stood watching them. He and the Queen often talked of English affairs; and she presented him to a niece of the Duke of Ormonde, Elizabeth Hamilton, with whom he immediately fell in love. He wanted to marry her: but the obstacles were insurmountable, for she was a Catholic, and very poor. Yet he hankered after her, thought of himself as her 'servant', found it difficult to enjoy the balls and masques at the Palais Royal if she were not there, became more belligerent than ever when walking about Paris, and finally succumbed to an illness (undiagnosed) which kept him indoors for some weeks.

When news came from England that Charles II was to be restored, the exiled Queen gave a great ball at the Louvre, attended by Sir John, who was desired to dance with the most beautiful of Cardinal Mazarin's nieces, Hortense Mancini. On 2nd August 1660 he took leave of the Queen, who gave him a letter of introduction to Charles—'vous êtes un des nôtres', she told him—after which he called for the last time on the lovely Miss Hamilton. She received him, as was then the custom, in bed. He still thought her 'the finest woman in the world', but left without declaring himself. Several years later, she married the Comte de Gramont, immortalized by her brother Anthony in his celebrated *Memoirs* of that nobleman.

After a fearful crossing, Reresby came to Whitehall and presented Henrietta Maria's letter to the King, with whom he talked for a few minutes. He was on the point of returning to Yorkshire, when he met Frances Brown, eldest daughter of a barrister, Sir Wolston Brown. Her charms made him forget all about Elizabeth Hamilton. Determined to ask for her hand, he reached Thrybergh to find his mother urging him to marry —but not with Mistress Brown; she had a choice of ladies in mind for him, whose dowries were much larger. Sir John refused to consider any of them. Lady Reresby persisted. He remained firm. He would marry for love—or not at all. It was the first serious quarrel he and his mother had ever had; and the battle was to be painful and prolonged.

2

Disregarding his mother's embargo, and encouraged by Frances Brown's reception of his advances, Sir John now began his courtship of that young lady; quite soon he became aware that, given their respective parents' consent, she would be willing to marry him.

He proceeded as custom required by giving her a semi-classical name—Coelia—and sending her letters and verses. He expressed himself adequately in prose; his attempts at poetry are of the same standard as those of Noel Bastable in E. Nesbit's famous series, although they lack the schoolboy's vigour and clarity. Whether they impressed Reresby's mistress or not, he continued to produce them at regular intervals. 'Although my knotty Muse has got the ricketts,' he begins, 'I'll tell you of a subtle plot in verse . . .' Knotty, indeed. But he knew that he was doing the right thing in so addressing her. Everyone in his world wrote verses; and he would too, although it must have been hard work at times. Some relaxation was essential; he found it during an expedition to a horse fair at Malton.

After being involved in a fight with some townspeople in York—he was struck on the head by a cudgel, and defended himself with his sword—he had a dispute with another visitor to the fair, who took exception to Sir John's throwing a glass of wine in his face during dinner. 'We should have fought the next day,' he says, 'but we were reconciled.' He then set off for London, and on the way took a fancy to a pretty woman in the party, whom he persuaded to ride pillion behind him. Thus isolated, they seem to have dismounted—presumably the weather was fine—rejoining the company after an agreeable interval at the roadside, 'managed', he adds, 'with discretion . . . an adventure which I cannot but relate', as if rather proud of this brief diversion.

Established in London with several servants—one, a present from a friend in the Barbadoes, was a negro—and a coach and four, he called on Queen Henrietta Maria, and began his career as a courtier. He was genially received by the King, who, Reresby noted, 'followed his pleasures. Besides that his complexion led to it,' he goes on, 'the women seemed to be the aggressors . . . and did sometimes offer themselves to his embraces.' Sir John's love for Frances Brown did not prevent his joining in all the activities of the Restoration Court, now in its heyday. While continuing to write to her ('One smile from you can do more than all the caresses in the world from others') he joined a circle in which gallantry and wit were set off by elegance, beauty —and concupiscence, this last unrestrained by the King's marriage to Catherine of Braganza, a plain, convent-bred girl, who was so unfortunate as to fall in love with her husband. ('I thought they had brought me a bat instead of a woman,' Charles said to a friend.) 'She had nothing visible about her to make the King forget his inclination to the Countess of Castlemaine,' Sir John observed, 'who was the finest woman of her age.' This fine woman's coarseness and brutality did not distress Reresby; he took them for granted, as he did her partial domination of the King, who forced her into his wife's household, regardless of poor Catherine's sobs and protestations. In this galaxy, Buckingham, who treated his Duchess with equal cruelty, was, literally, Charles's Lord of Misrule. Sir John's position was then strengthened by the Duke, now Lord Lieutenant of the West Riding, who made him his Deputy. Yet still Lady Reresby refused her consent to his marriage.

At this time, and for the next twenty years, Reresby alternated between London and Yorkshire, undeterred by the hardships of the journey. In the 1660s his interests at Court predominated; his account of his share in the kaleidoscopic variations supplements, more intimately, those of such writers as Bishop Burnet, Madame d'Aulnoy, Anthony Hamilton, Evelyn and Pepys. He saw its diversions as part of the good life brought about by the Restoration; and today, in plays and novels, that aspect is still described in terms ranging from mild disapproval to nostalgic longing for its gay excesses.

That vision has been enhanced by the production of certain artists, who cared rather for grace and splendour than for accuracy, so that the result tends to mislead. The rhythms of Grabu and Purcell; the canvasses and miniatures of Lely, Cooper and Greenhill (Lely painted Lady Castlemaine as the Madonna, with

one of Charles II's bastards as the Holy Child); the protean
brilliance of Dryden, Rochester and Wycherley; the gloating
comments of diarists who remained outside the Court circle,
glimpsing it in flashes—all these contributions have created
a dream-world inhabited by charming, lively, sophisticated
beings, swaying in draperies of satin and velvet to the sound of
lutes and violins: carefree, exquisite, alluring. Acceptance of
this picture precludes any awareness of its basic quality, one
of appalling tedium, hideous corruption and gross insensitivity.

This discrepancy was observed by an anonymous contemporary
in an etiquette manual, *The Refin'd Courtier*. Here the writer,
seeing through the surface glitter, describes, while deprecating
them, the dirty habits and insolent behaviour of those privileged
to wait on royalty at Whitehall, Hampton Court and Tunbridge
Wells. And Reresby's *Memoirs* substantiate the underlying
squalor and crudity of seventeenth-century high life.

The author of *The Refin'd Courtier* begins by describing his
readers' table manners. He begs them not to be like those who
'put their noses into a mess of broth, and never once lift up
their faces or eyes, much less remove their hands from the dish:
and ... with their cheeks distempered and swollen—grease
themselves up to the elbow and make their napkins look like
dishcloths, and yet are not ashamed to blow their noses on them
and sometimes to wipe off the sweat which ... trickles down ...
to their necks.' He goes on, 'There are those who when they
cough or sneeze ... do not turn away ... but bespatter the
faces of those they talk with.' He adds, 'Beware of jeering
instead of jesting,' thus recalling Reresby's attempt to 'divert'
the company by hoaxing, at enormous length, the half-witted
Earl of Carnarvon. The courtier, urged not to 'protract the time
with empty preambles', should already have been warned by the
Comte de Gramont's ineffably boring anecdotes, sometimes
lasting for half an hour, which, according to his Hamilton
brother-in-law, made the King 'hold his sides' as he listened.
(On such occasions, that monarch's politeness must have been
sorely tried.) And contact with the storyteller could be as disagreeable as his prolixity. 'When you are discoursing with anyone,
you must not draw so near that your breath may reach him'—and
'be careful that no unsavoury rank smell shall come from you
... and refrain from spitting as much as you can.' The author

then notes that 'it is inadvisable ... to prepare for the easing of nature in public view, or to truss up our clothes before others when we return from performing that office.' Also, 'He who would be a well bred man ought to refrain from loud and frequent yawning (a crime the Romans severely punished).'

In fact, what with recalling all these precepts, there can have been little energy left for deciding what dreams to recount and what not, and trying not to launch such conversational gambits as 'Do you know my friend Mr Such-an-One? O! then you can know no one!' Finally, one of the most unattractive habits was that of assumed propriety, sharply satirized in *The Country Wife*. When Mrs Dainty observes that it is more enjoyable to sleep with a lover than with a husband, Lady Fidget exclaims, 'Fie, fie, fie, for shame, sister! Whither shall we ramble? Be continent in your discourse, or I shall hate you!'

Indeed, continence of any kind was seldom practised in the palaces of Charles II. Like his spaniels, his courtiers and their ladies were not house-trained; they danced and gambled and flirted over a noisome morass. There were those—oddly enough, Nell Gwyn was one—who objected to the effluvia of excrement and urine; but this player's criticisms merely drew attention to the fact that she had been brought up in a brothel.

In these circumstances, Reresby kept his health by taking the waters at Scarborough, where Frances Brown and her family were now established, returning south to hunt in Enfield Chase with the King and Buckingham. A few days later, dining with Sir Henry Bellassis, he quarrelled with, and was challenged by, an Irishman. Seconded by their host, he fought him in Hyde Park. The aggressor nearly died of his wounds, 'which made us,' Reresby says, 'abscond ... but at last it pleased God he recovered'. This incident was preceded by a free fight in Holborn, from which he only just escaped with his life.

These records are typical of the age. Reresby, neither a fire-eater nor a drunkard, was merely conforming to standards evolved over the centuries. He is exceptional only in his ability to describe, simply and without pretension, his 'own little story'. He fitly represents the aggressive, excitable nature of the national temperament, often commented on by visiting foreigners, who, not unreasonably, found the English aristocracy violent, unreliable and inclined to extravagance. Yet they could rise to a crisis, as Sir John did during the anti-monarchist rebellion in Yorkshire in 1664, which he helped to put down under Buckingham's command. With the outbreak of the second Dutch war in the following year, he attached himself to the Duke of York, thus rising in his mother's estimation, with the result that their dispute about his marriage ended, and he and Frances Brown became husband and wife on 9th March 1665. They then moved into Thrybergh, which they found 'in a ruinous condition', but 'with this stock', says the bridegroom, 'we began the world'.

During the plague year the Reresbys entertained the Duke of York and his first wife, Anne Hyde—'a very handsome woman, with a great deal of wit'. They were especially impressed with the Duchess's cool handling of her host's pet snake, and with her discreet reception of her Groom of the Bedchamber's advances. This gentleman, 'Beau Sidney', was 'so much in love with her', Sir John observed, 'as appeared to us all', and she 'not unkind to him, but very innocently'.

Not so innocent was the Duke of Buckingham's connection with Anna Maria Brudenell, Countess of Shrewsbury, who became his mistress in October 1666; with her husband, and her brother, Lord Brudenell, she, Buckingham and his Duchess visited York, and were attended by the Reresbys. Lady Shrewsbury, already notorious, sat to Lely several times. Her personality was such that his technique—that of presenting his female sitters as drowsy and brainless goddesses—was defeated.

Buckingham was the fifth of this sinister creature's lovers, all of whom had been accepted by her pathetic cuckold of a husband. These adulteries were an excuse for her insistence on bloodshed. The man aspiring to her favour was expected to challenge the one she intended to discard, not only with the aid, as was then the custom, of a second, but also of a third. In these duels, several had been seriously wounded, and one killed. 'She might have a man killed for her every day,' de Gramont told Hamilton, 'and only hold up her head the higher for it.' The tendency later described as sadistic steals out from beneath Lely's brilliantined flatteries, particularly in a full-length portrait, now in the possession of the Marquess of Bath. Here Lady Shrewsbury is shown as almost plain, not noticeably elegant, and more like some exotic animal than a human being. To possess her would, it seems, have been easy: to tame her impossible;

although Buckingham, according to Reresby, believed that he could do so, when he invited her, her husband and brother to his house in York. 'I sent ... for my wife to wait on the Duchess of Buckingham,' says Sir John, 'who, good woman, perceived nothing of the intrigue between her husband and the Countess of Shrewsbury.' But very soon the tone of Buckingham's houseparty caused him to send Lady Reresby back to Thrybergh; their company was 'no good school for a young wife'.

Lord Brudenell then came to Sir John in some perplexity as to whose side he should take in the affair. He had already seen Villiers and Lady Shrewsbury in one another's arms, and on the following night was 'sent for from a tavern very late to his sister's chamber to make her and Lord Shrewsbury friends, they having had a great quarrel of jealousy concerning the Duke; and yet,' Sir John adds, 'the Countess had so great power with her lord that he stayed [in York] some time after that.' Nevertheless, the wretched worm was beginning, at last, to turn. Naturally, this enhanced his wife's pleasure in Buckingham's love-making. She seems to have foreseen the prospect of another duel, and further notoriety for herself.

Soon after the Shrewsburys left for London Buckingham gave a dinner-party; among the guests were Reresby, Sir George Savile (afterwards Lord Halifax) and Lord Falconbridge, an elderly man, married to one of Oliver Cromwell's daughters. Buckingham, generally at his best on these occasions, was in a state of simmering irritation. As the entries in his Commonplace Book show, he could not trust Lady Shrewsbury out of his sight ('My believing in you and you believing in your glass will undo us both', he wrote) and was ready to pick a quarrel with anyone. Arguing with Falconbridge, he broke up the party, and next day received a challenge from that nobleman through Sir George Savile, who was followed by Sir John, offering the Duke his services. But Villiers's mood had changed. 'I do not know whether it will come to fighting or not,' he said, adding that Savile had already been engaged as his second.

Reresby then went to morning service at York Minster, where he was pursued by Sir George in some agitation; his sword was not of the kind used in duels, and he wanted Sir John to lend him a longer one. This was done, and Savile hurried off to the field where the principals were waiting. Reresby, following him at a distance, hid himself behind a hedge—and was horrified to see Falconbridge, his second and Savile draw their swords, while that of the Duke remained in the scabbard. A 'parley' he could not hear took place, agreement was reached and the combatants separated.

Sir John, distressed 'to see my captain come off so calmly', complained of Buckingham to a friend, who repeated his criticisms. The Duke sent for him, and after some discussion accepted his apology and an invitation to dinner. Buckingham then returned to London, followed by Reresby, who reminded the King and the Duke of York of their promise to make him High Sheriff of Yorkshire. Charles had done nothing; his brother, 'more punctual' in these matters, confirmed the appointment, and thus ensured his protégé's loyalty for the next twenty years.

Returning to York in state, Sir John took a house near the Minster for the Assizes, ordered a new coach and a consort of violins, and gave a ball, followed by 'entertainment to all the ladies', at a cost of £300. Now his position was such that he could afford to dispense with Buckingham's patronage; and this was just as well, for the Duke, who has been acting as chief minister of state, fell into disgrace through neglect of his duties, was sent to the Tower for brawling, and emerged to accept a challenge from Lord Shrewsbury. Villiers, who generally refused the kind of dinner-table provocation of which no one could remember the cause the next morning, had decided that this particular issue must be resolved in blood. The King, determined to prevent the duel, gave orders that Buckingham should be confined to his house. His commands miscarried, and on 21st January 1668 Buckingham and Shrewsbury met in a close at Barn Elms. Buckingham's second was killed, and Shrewsbury so severely wounded that he died two months later.

His widow joined the Duke at his house in the Mall on her return from France. The Duchess then brought herself to protest. 'It is not for me and that other,' she told her husband, 'to live together.' 'Why, Madam, I did think so,' Buckingham replied, 'and have therefore ordered your coach to be made ready to carry you to your father's.'

Sir John, an affectionate and faithful husband, while disapproving, was careful not to criticize the Duke, and they remained on good terms. (Buckingham had, after all, killed his man, as became a gentleman of breeding.) With the death of his mother in this year, Reresby inherited enough to improve and add to his mansion of Thrybergh, and 'kept open Christmas' there. His eldest son, William, the second of nine children, was born in January 1669.

In 1670 Sir John's attendance at Court was marked by the visit of William of Orange, whose cold propriety and unconcealed contempt for Restoration manners and the dirt and shabbiness of his uncle's palaces annoyed his hosts. It did not matter to them that all the carpets were faded and stained; but William and his suite were openly disgusted by the habits of Charles's spaniels, who 'pupped and gave suck' in corners, thus making the rooms 'very nasty and stinking'. Several ladies complained to the King of the Prince's lack of response to their attempts to flirt with him. So it was that, towards the end of his nephew's visit, Charles told Reresby and Buckingham to arrange a banquet which would ensure William's drinking more than he could hold. His favourite cock-ale was replaced by floods of champagne and rivers of sack, with the result, says Reresby, 'that, once entered, he became more frolic and merry than the rest of the company . . . broke the windows of the maids of honour . . . and had got into their apartments had they not been timely rescued.' The picture of a boy of twenty being brought to this point by a group of middle-aged tosspots is not a pretty one; and William never forgot that his uncle's courtiers had made a fool of him. His opinion of them had not changed when, two decades later, he became their King; it was then their turn to be humiliated and scorned. Sir John's comment on William's outbreak shows that his marriage to his cousin Mary of York was already in question. 'I suppose,' he says, 'that his mistress did not less approve of him for that vigour.' At this time the Princess was eight years old.

Such observations emphasize Reresby's detachment from the Court circle, and his simplification of political matters. Although he was constantly in London—he spent the whole winter there in 1672—he became increasingly occupied with local affairs as he grew more powerful in Yorkshire. He combined litigation (generally successful) with the purchase of land and the improvement of his estate, in order to leave his descendants a prosperous inheritance. In this respect, he was far-sighted, rather grasping and extremely practical, with the result that his view of the ruling clique in the capital tended to be superficial.

Sir John preferred the Duke of York to Charles II, because he felt the former to be more reliable, and therefore more useful to himself. While thinking of the King as 'my great master', he deprecated his easy-going, pleasure-loving side. Charles seemed to him lazy to the point, sometimes, of inefficiency—which was far from being the case. Reresby liked to see his superiors working hard and getting results; the King's apparent dilatoriness puzzled and disheartened him, as did his habit of telling the same story twice, and occasionally three times running. That, and Charles's punctilious attendance on his mistresses appeared to Sir John a sad waste of time; while James, whose lusts ranged far further than, if not so successfully as, those of his brother, was always busy, generally to his own detriment. In 1673 York's acknowledgement of his Catholicism was a great disappointment to his protégé; thereafter, Reresby attached himself to a neighbour, Sir Thomas Osborne, who became Earl of Danby and Lord Treasurer in that year. Two Yorkshiremen long known to one another must surely rise together; and the fact that Buckingham was temporarily affiliated with Danby further strengthened, or so he believed, Reresby's position when he became Member of Parliament for Aldbrough and Governor of Bridlington.

These and other duties distracted his attention from the undercurrents of national issues. The interrelations of Arlington, Shaftesbury and Halifax: the machinations of foreign ambassadors, the rivalry between York and Monmouth over the succession – all these complications interested him less than the actions of such personal acquaintances as Danby and Buckingham, who were estranged and soon to be enemies. It is characteristic of Sir John's attitude that a cursory reference to his former patron was followed by 'This year I began to build two little houses at the east and west ends of the house for closets.' In the following year he made a full but private report of the debates in Parliament on finance, naval estimates, 'the height and boldness of the papists', and the prorogation of the Houses. Meanwhile, his personal affairs proceeded smoothly. It was not until the autumn of 1676 that he faced disaster in the form of an accusation which came near to causing his arrest for murder.

Reresby's care for his dependants, of whatever degree, ensured the support of the majority; but he had enemies and rivals both locally and in London, who resented his rise at Court and his acquisition of places. One of these was the Duke of Norfolk, with whom he had already had 'some suits and differences', and who was planning to undermine his position. The sudden death of Sir John's sixteen-year-old negro servant seemed to the Duke a suitable means of revenge; he told the Privy Council that the boy, having been castrated, had died as a result of the operation.

Such a charge had some plausibility, in that those owning male slaves were apt to prevent the propagation of their species by gelding them. Reresby, who knew that his black boy had died of a tumour on the brain some weeks before Norfolk's story went the rounds, sent for the coroner and a jury, exhumed the body, and so proved his case. 'When they came to uncover the breast,' he records, 'it was so putrified that they could go no further, but . . . several having the curiosity to see him, gave in their verdict *ex visitatione Dei.*' Yet this did not suffice. A surgeon in Norfolk's employ 'under pretence to view the cod better . . . would have lifted it up', only to find it 'as sound and firm as when he was born'.

This hideous process, calmly gone through by both Reresby himself and Norfolk's witnesses, caused a great deal of talk lasting several months. Sir John ignored it, as did Danby, who in February 1677 sent for him and described his own difficulties in his struggle against the Country party. He warned his friend that they were bent on creating 'discontents between the King and his people. Confusion,' Danby continued, 'might be the issue, and therefore I desire you not to embark with that sort of people.' Reassured, the Lord Treasurer then personally escorted Sir John to wait on Charles in the lobby of the House of Lords, presenting him as a staunch Tory. 'I have known him long,' said the King, and turning to Reresby, continued, 'It is said I intend the subversion of the religion and government by an army and arbitrary power—but every man, nay, those that say it most, know that it is false.' This reference to Shaftesbury was not perceived by Sir John, who replied, 'I shall never, to the best of my knowledge, do anything but what becomes a true and faithful subject.' 'You shall have access to me,' said his master, 'when and wherever you desire it.'

In the following May Reresby, very much set up by the King's confiding in him, but still plagued with the castration story, complained of its circulation to Danby, who assured him that His Majesty had discounted the rumours. Sir John raised the matter with Charles himself, and was again reassured. A month later, he was told that Lord Yarburgh was 'one of those who had begged my estate upon the story of the Moor'. Taxed by Reresby, Yarburgh denied the charge, adding that he would find out and denounce the authors of the calumny; Sir John then discovered that he was one of them. However—'I considered', he says, 'that stirring further in it would but make more noise', and ceased to trouble himself about an attack so characteristic of his circle.

He then proceeded north, pausing on the way to meet the Duke of Newcastle, with whom he rode into Derbyshire. On the Peak his horse slipped and fell on him, breaking his kneecap. Carried to the nearest inn, he was attended by the local bone-setter, who set his knee wrongly, as did another man after he reached Thrybergh. Finally, a third practitioner reduced the swelling 'indifferently well', so that 'by God's mercy I had good use of [both] knees after all this'.

Sir John's recourse to duelling was in no way affected by these mishaps, as he later showed in a dispute at the playhouse about the seating arrangements with a Mr Symons, who told him, 'You are uncivil.' 'You are a rascal,' Reresby replied, and desired him to come outside. Here they drew their swords, but were arrested by a captain in the Duke of Monmouth's regiment, who next day brought them before his commander. Monmouth 'made us friends', Reresby says; and a few days later, when he and Symons met in the street, that gentleman offered to share a bottle of wine with him, and apologized for his discourtesy.

After a long session in London, where he had to deal with a number of complications and intrigues about his governorship of Bridlington, Sir John returned for the Assizes in the summer of 1678 to York, where he discovered that a Mr Bright had been and still was 'the great agent contriving and managing that invention of the Moor'. Reresby at once brought an action against Bright, from which he won 'a hundred marks, and, more than that, my credit, all the world being convinced of the malice and falsehood of the inventor'.

In October of this year Reresby fell ill, 'of an unaccountable disorder in my head', recovering to receive news of the Popish Plot. As it became clear that he must return to London, and that for a considerable time, he took the road with his wife and family. He then became the spectator of a drama which threatened to destroy the monarchy, and with it all he himself had obtained. His account of the Parliamentary decisions and debates gives the impression that he did not succumb to the general panic. But it was an anxious time, and there were moments, especially after the murder of Sir Edmund Berry Godfrey, when he did not quite know what to believe.

3

Reresby prefaces his version of the Country Party's attempt to overthrow the Government with 'To give a particular account of this Plot is not the business of this work'. He then provides a brief outline of Titus Oates's 'discoveries', as revealed to the general public in October 1678.

On the 23rd of that month Sir John's attendance at Court followed a new routine. He no longer waited on the King in the royal apartments, but obtained leave to see him privately in those of Louise de Kéroualle, Duchess of Portsmouth, Charles's *maîtresse en titre*, who was supposed to be the power behind the throne. Both the French Ambassador and the English ministry, seeing her as the envoy of Louis XIV, believed that her influence was paramount, as did Louis himself. In fact, Louise, a plump, rather prim little woman, to whom Charles remained devoted until his death, was not even his confidant, except where his religion was concerned. His other policies, fluid, subtle and secret, had always been concealed from those with whom he appeared most intimate: and never more so than during these years of crisis, when he masked his real intentions by a frankness —a loquacity, even—which deceived and flattered all his circle. He gave Reresby the impression of being completely unguarded and rashly indiscreet, first by receiving him in his mistress's bedchamber—sometimes while her hair was being dressed— and then by his contemptuous references to Oates's revelations. 'I think it some artifice,' he said. 'I do not believe one word of the Plot,' and on another occasion he told Sir John that one of Oates's allies was a rogue who had given false evidence about Godfrey's murder.

These tactics, sustained over three tumultuous years, were very effective in that they strengthened the loyalty of such persons as Reresby, while pleasing and encouraging the Court Party, of whom Halifax and Danby were now the most powerful. The vast majority, in the Commons and elsewhere, choosing to believe Oates's wildest inventions, were distressed and alarmed by the King's carefree attitude, and thus all the more determined to protect him from his enemies. So it was that Shaftesbury's and Buckingham's efforts to discredit him ended, after a desperate struggle, in failure and disgrace.

Reresby's *Memoirs* show that he discounted Charles's most dangerous adversary. He does not even trouble to abuse Shaftesbury: but this can be accounted for by his devotion to his local duties. In Yorkshire, he was a great man, almost a potentate; in London, Newmarket, Windsor or Tunbridge Wells he was merely a steadfast member of the Court Party—and also the friend and confidant of the hated heir-presumptive, whose apostasy he deplored but tolerated. Sir John still admired James, and he was very sorry for him.

Having placed all his hopes on Danby, he was appalled by Ralph Montagu's dramatic betrayal of that nobleman's dealings with Louis XIV. This news, says Reresby, 'put the House in a flame, and it was presently moved that he ought to be impeached of high treason'. In the debates of January 1679 Sir John spoke in the Lord Treasurer's defence, and then returned to Yorkshire, only to hear that Danby was thought to be 'bringing in popery'. Rejoining the Court in April, he found Danby committed to the Tower, 'where I went to visit him. He appeared not much concerned.' 'The King,' remarked another courtier, 'is no more concerned for him than for a puppy dog, nor for what becomes of the Duke of York neither.'

In fact Charles, by imprisoning Danby, had saved him from execution. Meanwhile, Reresby had now no patron; and he felt that the King was to blame. 'It is very unhappy,' he wrote, 'for a servant to serve an unconstant or unsteady Prince,' adding, 'This great change . . . made me seriously reflect upon the uncertainty of greatness.' He himself had nearly attained that condition; but now—'This confirmed me that a middle estate was ever the best,' and so it was inadvisable, in view of his children's inheritance, 'to climb over the heads of others to a greatness of uncertain continuance'.

In June Reresby found a patron in Halifax, to whom he wrote, 'My Lord, I must confess myself a true servant of the Government (so long as I find it doth not intrude upon the liberty of the people) and . . . I know not how better to convince your Lordship of that real respect I have for your Lordship, and of the deference I have ever had for your judgement.' This approach was well received. Sir John maintained his position and, attending the King's *coucher*, 'wondered to see him so cheerful amongst so many troubles'. He did not expect any special notice; but Charles came up to him and said, 'I assure you of your command—and I will stick to my old friends.'

A week later Reresby left for Thrybergh. The Duke of Monmouth, returning from his victory over the Scots Covenanters (having burnt several Acts of Parliament and declared for 'Jesus Christ and the Kirk' they then, as usual, ran away), paused at Doncaster, where Sir John hurried to meet him 'with half a buck and some extraordinary sorts of wine'. He waited for the Duke till midnight, and then 'got into the bed designed for his Grace', who appeared before he could rise and dress. Monmouth's behaviour was characteristically winning. After a hasty meal, he 'sat up but a short time, and would not have the sheets changed, but went into the same bed'. Reresby thought the Duke 'very handsome and accomplished as to his outside, [but] his parts were not suitable . . . to his claim to the Crown'. Still convinced that James should succeed, he entertained him and his second wife on their return from Scotland, but noted that they were 'very coldly received' by the people. The Lord Mayor of York, forced to vacate his house for Their Highnesses, took away all his furniture when he left it. Sir John tried to make up to James for this discourtesy by presents of venison and wine— 'but it was not worthy of his notice'. He then kept Christmas at Thrybergh 'with the usual solemnity'.

In May 1680 he joined the Court at Windsor, where he found the King apparently unmoved by the rising strength of the Country Party, whose meetings now revolved round Monmouth's and Shaftesbury's schemes for proving the Duke's legitimacy. Sir John hurried to tell the Duke of York how to 'obviate' these plans, was thanked, and then shown round the Castle by Charles, whose improvements included murals by Verrio and a great copper statue of himself in the courtyard. The King was in excellent spirits; he went fishing, even when it rained, and walked in the park unattended. James then told Reresby that he might be given an embassy abroad; when he took leave of the King, Charles, clapping him on the shoulder, said, 'Your services shall be recompensed.' Assured of this promotion, Sir John

returned home to renew his friendship with the Duke of Newcastle, now his most powerful ally in the north.

On the whole, life was very pleasant—he attended the Sheffield
cutlers' feast, and entertained the Newcastles—when he was
thrown from his horse, breaking his elbow. 'No man,' he says,
'had more misfortunes of this kind than I, yet it pleased God
to restore me after them all.'

On his next visit to London, Reresby took a house in Leicester
Fields. He had no sooner settled in than he was attacked in the
Commons for refusing to censure the policy of the Court Party.
He spoke of this to Charles, who said, 'Do not trouble yourself.
I will stick by you and my old friends, for if I do not, I shall
have nobody to stick by me.'

Then came what Reresby describes as one of 'the greatest
days that was ever known' in the House of Lords—the debate
on Exclusion between Halifax and Shaftesbury, ending, after
a ten hours' duel, in Shaftesbury's defeat by the man who had
formerly supported the Country Party. A little later, Reresby
was threatened with the loss of his governorship of Bridlington,
and once more appealed to the King. 'Let them do what they
will,' said Charles. 'I will never part with any officer at the
request of either House, for my father lost his head by that
compliance—but as for me, I will die another way.' And Halifax
added, 'I will venture my life with my friends.'

When the question of the King divorcing Queen Catherine
arose, Reresby attempted, vainly, to stop the talk of Charles
'seldom or never [making] use of her as his wife, she having
a flux of blood in her private parts'. A few nights later, at Charles's
coucher, he was much impressed by His Majesty's discourse about
those who pretended piety. 'They are generally the greatest
knaves,' he said. Meanwhile, Halifax, whom he saw almost
every day, was gloomy but determined. 'If it comes to a war,'
he told Reresby, 'you and I must go together.' 'I am ready to
follow you,' Sir John replied, 'but if the King expects his friends
to be hearty and steady to him, he ought to encourage them a
little more,' and went on to speak of the promised embassy. 'We
must have you nearer home,' said Halifax, adding that he himself
was thinking of retirement. 'I shall go my own pace,' he continued, 'and not be kicked out when they please.'

Then, dining with the Bishop of Ely, Reresby met Titus

Oates for the first time. The idol of the Country Party held
the floor—he was very drunk—beginning with abuse of the
late Queen Henrietta Maria, and going on to denounce Catherine
of Braganza, while the guests sat silent and embarrassed. Finally,
Sir John told him he was a liar. Purple with rage, and very
much surprised, Oates left the room. 'This is his usual discourse,'
said the host apologetically, and the party broke up. A few
months later, Reresby returned to Yorkshire with the Duke
of Newcastle, whose progress resembled that of royalty. 'He
travelled indeed,' Sir John noted, 'like a great prince, with three
coaches and about forty attendants on horseback.' Confiding
in Reresby at some length, the Duke concluded, 'I like not
the measures now on foot, I think the times but slippery.'
Sir John then visited Halifax at Rufford, to hear further complaints of the King. 'It will ruin us all,' said that nobleman,
'if His Majesty continues to advise with those of one interest
this day, and hearken to those of another tomorrow—nor can
his ministers be safe under such uncertainties. If he would be
advised—' Halifax meant by himself—'it would be in his power
to make all his opponents tremble.'

Brilliant and perspicacious though he was, Halifax did not
grasp the real nature of Charles's policy. His opponents were
not given time to tremble. They were struck down in the moment
of what seemed their greatest triumph. And that moment was
now approaching.

Reresby recorded the dissolution of the Oxford Parliament
in March 1681 as if he were not fully aware that it embodied
Charles's first great triumph over the Country Party. 'It was
plain,' he says, '. . . that the King would not relinquish his
brother, and did not think of calling another Parliament for
a long time.' He did not know that Charles, now more or less
solvent through the beneficence of Louis XIV, would soon
be in a position to rule as a dictator; he believed that if Parliament
had not been dissolved, the monarchy would have been replaced
by a republic. Later on, he realized that the Whigs had planned
a constitutional régime, which would transfer the control of
the forces from the King to Parliament; this would have resulted
in the loss of all Sir John's offices in the north. He therefore
trusted in Charles's 'declaration full of fair promises . . . and
of his intentions of governing according to law', and continued

to build up his own position; although he was rather disturbed by the fact that his embassy abroad (Denmark had been suggested) did not materialize. While waiting for this advancement, his chief concern was still that of local government; his powers in Yorkshire remained under Halifax's control.

So he proceeded to add to his administrative duties, combining them with attendance on Halifax and the King; as the strain increased, his health broke down. He recovered to hear that he might be given the Governorship of Yorkshire, a place for which he had been angling for some time. Then came a personal misfortune. 'I set forward to York, leaving my wife and family at London,' he says. 'She had behaved herself with care during my sickness; but we had a falling out at our parting, which gave me some trouble.' No doubt he was always a difficult patient; and he and Lady Reresby had been much distressed by their eldest daughter, Frances, succumbing to smallpox. 'It pleased God,' noted her father, 'to restore her without prejudice to her features and complexion.' Frances was a beautiful girl, and they were very proud of her.

Hawking with the King at Newmarket, and in daily touch with Halifax, Sir John now embarked on a new project, that of becoming Justice of the Peace for Middlesex and Westminster. Charles, speaking of what he called the 'unjust verdicts' of the London —and presumably Whig—juries, said to Reresby, 'It is a hard case that I am the last man to have law and justice in the whole nation.' Sir John's increasing intimacy with the King—he dined with Charles on the royal yacht, and attended him at the Lord Mayor's banquet—seems to have curbed his belligerence. He intervened in several disputes ('I sent one Mr St Johns to the gaol for wounding another gentleman') and noted disaprovingly that no less than ten duels were fought in London in the last week of 1681. After presiding over the Westminster sessions in the following month, he was summoned to wait on the Moroccan embassy, who presented the King with two lions and thirty ostriches. Charles received the ambassadors with his usual courtesy; but when the huge gilded cages containing their gifts were brought in, he burst out laughing. He said to Sir John, 'I know nothing fitter to return to them than a flock of geese.'

Reresby now began to criticize the Duchess of Portsmouth who, he says, 'to show her power over the King' would influence him against certain courtiers—'and yet', he adds, 'His Majesty was not at this time charmed with her bed, for it was generally believed he had not lain with her [for the last four months]'. Then on 12th February 1682, Sir John was suddenly involved in a murder case of such gravity as to be recorded by a plaque still to be seen in Westminster Abbey.

The heroine of this episode was a recently widowed heiress, Lady Ogle, now married to Mr Thomas Thynne ('Tom of Ten Thousand'), the powerful Whig ally of Monmouth and Shaftesbury. According to Sir John, she, 'repenting of the match, had fled from him into Holland before they were bedded'. Another suitor, Count Johann Königsmarck, a Swedish nobleman, who had been living in England for some time, may have planned to join her there; enraged at being forestalled by Thynne, he instructed three accomplices, Stern, Borosky and Vratz, to kill his rival. Between seven and eight o'clock in the evening Thynne and Monmouth were in the former's coach on their way to St James's, when the Duke asked to be set down, and Thynne, preceded by a servant carrying a flambeau, went on to visit his wife's grandmother in Pall Mall. The assassins, having followed the coach on horseback, caught up with it, shot him five times and rode away. He was then taken to his house where, having summoned Monmouth, he died at about half-past ten. The Duke sent to Reresby to raise the hue and cry, and within forty-eight hours the murderers were taken; they confessed that they had been set on by Königsmarck, who had disappeared, leaving behind him his little brother, Philip, now lodged at Foubert's Academy of fencing in Soho. Count Philip —who, twelve years later, met a violent and mysterious death in Hanover—told the justices that Johann had hoped to marry Mrs Thynne. Reresby's officers pursued and finally arrested him at Gravesend. Charles II then called an extraordinary Council to examine the Count, who, says Sir John, 'appeared before the King with all the assurance imaginable'. In an age of shoulder-length wigs, Königsmarck made himself conspicuous by wearing his own hair, which fell below his waist—'the longest', noted Reresby, 'I ever see—and his parts were very quick'. He denied all knowledge of the murder, and accounted for his flight by 'the occasion of taking physic for a clap, with the intention to go away in a disguise'.

When all four prisoners came up for trial at the Old Bailey, the judges were told that Charles II and Louis XIV wished Königsmarck to be acquitted. (Their reasons for this demand have never been discovered.) The other three were sentenced to death, and hanged in the street where the murder had taken place. Sir John saw them go to the gallows, and describes how, when Vratz 'passed by in the cart, he bowed to me with a steady look, as he did to those he knew amongst the spectators before he was turned off. In fine, his whole carriage, from his first being apprehended to the last, relished more of gallantry than of religion'. Three months later, Thynne's red-headed widow married the Duke of Somerset, surviving to become the favourite of Queen Anne and to be celebrated as 'Carrots' by Swift in punning verse. It was then revealed that Königsmarck had given orders that nothing was to be attempted on Thynne while Monmouth was with him. Reresby complacently concludes his account of the affair as having 'made me generally known in the new employment of Justice of the Peace for Middlesex and Westminster'.

In the following March he and Halifax went together to Newmarket races. During the journey the Minister described his efforts to make the Duke of York change his faith, only to be told, 'My case is then more desperate than I understood it to be before, for I cannot alter my principles.' Reresby found Newmarket more than usually enjoyable, partly because Charles was so happy there. The sturdy little Yorkshireman and the tall, striding King walked about together, while the latter 'let himself down from Majesty to the very degree of country gentleman. He mixed himself amongst the crowd, allowed every man to speak to him that pleased, went a-hawking in the mornings, to cock matches in the afternoons (if there were no horse races) and to plays in the evenings, acted in a barn by very ordinary Bartholomew Fair comedians'.

Sir John was about to leave for Yorkshire when he had to deal with a family problem. His only surviving sister, Elizabeth, a spinster aged forty, had hitherto 'lived', he says, 'with the reputation of being a discreet woman', in lodgings. She was now about to marry an Irishman, Burke, who, formerly 'a common soldier', had no income but his captain's half pay. Reresby, horrified, 'did all I could to prevent a misfortune of this kind both to herself and her family, by threats [unspecified] of what I would do to her, and by disparagement of her gallant'. Poor Elizabeth, elderly and plain, saw this union as her last chance of an establishment, while her brother, not unreasonably, saw himself having to support her and Burke, as soon as the latter had spent her patrimony. She promised 'to think of him no more'—but a few days later Reresby discovered that she was corresponding with him, upon which he told Burke that he would never consent to the marriage, and persuaded Elizabeth to leave her lodgings for his house in Leicester Fields. He expected a challenge from the Irishman, but none came: and Elizabeth agreed to leave with him for Yorkshire. When asked if she and Burke were still writing to one another, she said that their relationship was at an end. On the morning of this assurance Burke, very drunk, was seen hanging about Reresby's house, 'and . . . gazing at the windows for a sight of his mistress'. Receiving no answer, he pulled down the railings leading up to the front door, and staggered away.

Sir John, returning from Whitehall, found his wife and sister 'in disorder', and all his neighbours agog; so he sent the ex-captain a summons 'to meet me with his sword and a friend behind Southampton House at two o'clock that afternoon'. Burke did not appear; he had been arrested for drunkenness and violence. A few days later, he called on Reresby and said, 'If I did it, I was drunk, not knowing what I did—and I ask your pardon.' Sir John accepted the apology; when he told Elizabeth what had happened, she appeared ready to abandon her suitor; but she was very resentful of her brother's interference. They then left for Yorkshire, to find the city charter suspended under a writ of *Quo Warranto*, and the laws against dissenters about to be more strictly enforced.

A meeting of eight local justices was then held in order to define the new restrictions. One of them, a Mr Jessop, thought by Sir John to be favouring dissent, refused to sign the resolutions agreed on by the others. 'All your proceedings and warrants,' he told them, 'are illegal.' 'It is something saucy,' replied Reresby, 'to arraign so many gentlemen of quality concerned in this commission for your single opinion.' 'You are very impudent,' said Jessop. Sir John, all his combative instincts aroused, seized a tray supporting inkstands, 'and threw it in his face, where, the edge lighting upon his cheek, cut it quite through. We after this drew our swords, and I went into the middle of the chamber, but the company prevented his following me, and afterwards reconciled of us,' while a clerk mopped up the ink. 'I was sorry for this accident,' Reresby mildly observes, 'it happening in a sessions of the peace—but the provocation could not be passed over.' Then the Assizes began, with a series of entertainments, and Sir John's inspection of the city garrisons, which he found in a very unsatisfactory state.

Having done what he could to replenish the stores and magazines, Reresby attended the sessions at Wakefield, and on his return had yet another escape from death caused by 'my horse falling with me upon the edge of a precipice; but I, throwing myself from my horse the other way, got no great harm, and gave my horse the opportunity to recover himself, though his hinder legs were already on the side of the bank.' He reached home to hear that his Governorship of Yorkshire had brought him into disfavour with his jealous rivals, and that his care for local concerns was displeasing the Court Party; 'chidden softly' by Halifax, he found it very difficult 'to steer an even course amongst so many several persons and interests'. Determined neither to yield nor to be put out by these criticisms, Reresby attended the Lord Mayor's banquet in York 'with all the good humour and civility to the citizens that was possible', and entertained them in return 'with a good dinner and plenty of wine'. He then kept Christmas at Thrybergh on a munificent scale. A hundred and ninety-seven tenants came to dinner, to the accompaniment of bagpipes, trumpets and drums. 'The expense of liquor,' he noted, '. . . was considerable, and my guests appeared well satisfied.'

When Reresby came up to London in February 1683, Halifax (now a Marquess and Lord Privy Seal) offered him the embassy to Sweden, which he refused, on the grounds that he would be 'ill paid. Being now in another station,' he explained, 'I have no mind to take an employment of that kind.' Halifax then described his successful interviews with the Duchess of Portsmouth. 'If I were as young as I have been,' he told Sir John, 'I could be as well with her as others.' 'You must have two P's, then,' his friend replied, 'the Purse, as well as the Other.' Having been rather coldly received by the Duke of York—his smile seemed forced—Reresby went on to attend the Middlesex sessions, where arrangements were made for putting down dissenting conventicles.

A few days later, much disturbed by the Government's threat to reduce the Yorkshire garrisons, Sir John pleaded with Charles II for their upkeep, and was told, 'I will not do it hastily—and if I do, I will be very kind to you in some other respect,' a characteristic half-promise which did not satisfy him. He complained to Halifax, who warned him to 'touch lightly the thing'. Undeterred, he then tackled the Duke of York. 'I have done nothing,' he said, 'but what has been for His Majesty's service.' 'I have endeavoured to serve you,' James replied, 'and I will continue to do so'—but he left for Newmarket without speaking to his brother on Reresby's behalf. Halifax then told Sir John that the Duchess of Portsmouth had betrayed the King with Philippe de Vendôme, Grand Prior of France, adding that His Majesty appeared perfectly indifferent about Vendôme's political intrigues. 'The King,' he said, 'is too passive in these things, and it is his greatest fault.' Reverting to his protégé's difficulties, he told him, 'You have enviers, as well as myself.' 'Their envy,' Sir John replied, 'is more, I hope, against my preferment than against my person.'

Reresby spent the spring and summer of 1683 in the north —not happily; wrestling with the garrison and other problems, he was recalled to Thrybergh by news of his son John's mortal illness. 'My poor boy,' he says, 'a very hopeful and witty youth', died of what seems to have been a series of haemorrhages. Finally, in the following September, Elizabeth Reresby, having repeatedly promised to have no more to do with her half-pay captain, married him secretly, 'which was a great trouble to me'. In mingled exasperation and grief, her brother attended morning service in York Minster, hoping to find consolation on a higher level.

It was not to be. 'I found the cushion which used to be in my seat removed to the next, where Sir John Brookes was to sit (a person that I had thought fit . . . to disarm, in our late search for arms). This gentleman,' Reresby goes on, 'rising at the Psalms, I took up the cushion, and replaced it in my seat.' As they were leaving the Minster, Brookes said, 'Have you the same commission to take my cushion that you have to take

my arms?' 'I took it as my own,' Reresby replied, 'as I shall
always do when I see it misplaced. You have made choice of
an ill place to quarrel in,' he added, 'and you dare not say those
things in any other.'

After waiting some days for a challenge, Sir John sent Brookes
the following message. 'If you have any resentment, either
for my taking your cushion or arms, I am ready to give you
satisfaction.' But Brookes had decided to yield. 'I am most
concerned,' he politely replied, 'at your taking away the cushion,
because it did prevent my giving it to you—which I intended,'
adding, 'I am willing to be quiet.' In Reresby's mind, this incident
illustrated one of his lifelong principles. 'When such disputes
offer themselves,' he noted, 'I have found that the best way
to prevent them for the future is not to seem too backward
in seeking reparation.'

Returning to London, he found Monmouth, formerly disgraced and sent away from Court, reconciled to the King and
the Duke of York, through Halifax's intervention. Charles,
taking Reresby's arm as they left the Duchess of Portsmouth's
apartments, raised the question of the Lord Mayor of York's
behaviour to James, adding, 'I fear he is but a bad man.' Sir
John, who knew that 'there was some private animosity in the
complaint', assured His Majesty of that official's loyalty, and
left Whitehall to dine with 'six gentlemen of quality' at a city
ordinary. Coming away from dinner to a coffee-house, two
of them, Major Orby and Mr Bellingham, started a quarrel
—'and though I did what I could to reconcile them,' Reresby
says, '[they] presently went out, and drew in the street . . . I
got into them, and broke one of their swords, and so they were
parted.' This annoyed the combatants, who, accompanied by
Sir John, called a coach, bought fresh swords, and drove to
Hyde Park. Reresby then offered himself as second to either
one or the other. Bellingham refused a second. 'I will decide
it by moonshine,' he said to Sir John, 'and I will confide in your
honour to see fair play done between us.' In brilliant moonlight
he and Orby then descended and engaged. 'Closing together,'
Reresby says, 'I came in to part them, and Mr Orby's footman
doing the same with me, we held their swords so that no mischief
was done, only Mr Orby had a slight prick in the thigh, and
Mr Bellingham a race [scratch] on the forehead, and I a slight

hurt as I came in to part them.' Then, honour satisfied, 'we all went to supper, and parted good friends'. Altogether, it seems to have been an enjoyable evening. Sir John, one of whose duties it was to keep order (his own affairs of honour were of course a different matter) was pleased to feel that he had asserted himself on behalf of the law, as became a good subject and a man of peace.

In January 1684 Halifax had a long talk with Reresby about his failure to make the King summon a Parliament. 'If Your Majesty does not have a good [i.e. a Tory] Parliament now,' he had said, 'the longer it is deferred, the worse it will be,' and reminded Charles that he had given his royal word to keep the law in this respect. The Minister then pointed out that, although the Whigs were 'very low and discouraged' (Shaftesbury, Essex, Armstrong, Sidney and Russell were dead, Buckingham was negligible and Monmouth exiled), 'an ill construction' would be put on His Majesty's reigning without one. Receiving an evasive response, Halifax had promised to stay in office, 'but', he told Reresby, 'there seems no possibility of a Parliament'. Neither he nor Sir John knew that Danby's financial reforms had begun to take effect, nor that Louis XIV's subsidies were being renewed.

In February Danby was released from the Tower. Reresby noted that Charles received him formally and in public, as did Halifax, who later sent him a friendly message by Sir John. Danby said, 'I shall go to my house out of town, and not meddle with public business,' adding that he was 'disgusted' with the Duke of York's behaviour. He gave no explanation for this, and Reresby, not much interested, left him to wait on the Duchess of Portsmouth, to remind her of her promise to make his son, Tamworth, page of honour to her boy, Richmond; for the little Duke was now Master of the Horse instead of Monmouth. Tamworth was only twelve, but, says his father, 'handsome, had good parts, and, I thank God, every way hopeful'. Reresby then began to hesitate about the appointment. 'I long disputed with myself,' he says, 'whether or not to put him in that way of education, which was more wicked and debauched at that time than in former ages.' Finally, he resolved to risk the boy's entry into Court circles, and a few weeks later Tamworth became page of honour to the King himself.

His father then accompanied Charles and the Duke of York to Newmarket. As he and the King were walking to the race course, Charles said, 'You have but thin shoes—get a stronger pair, to prevent getting cold'. Sir John was deeply touched. 'I here mention [this],' he says, 'as an example of that Prince his great goodness and care of all persons that came near him, however inconsiderable.' Charles's effect on Reresby was such that he could find no fault when the King sent the Duchess of Portsmouth to wait on Queen Catherine. That poor lady burst into tears, upon which the Duchess, according to Sir John, 'laughed, and turned it into a jest'.

Reresby remained in attendance on his master till June. When he came to take leave, Charles told him, 'Those that serve me so carefully and so well as you have done, will be in my thoughts —and so you will find it.' But he would not give this faithful servant any assurance about the Yorkshire garrisons, adding rather vaguely, 'I do not apprehend it a place fit to be continued, [but] I will not reduce it till I take care of you in some other capacity.' Reresby then attended the York Assizes in order to entertain the new Lord Chief Justice, Sir George Jeffreys, 'with all the respect I could . . . because he had ever been kind to me.'

In his thirty-seventh year, Jeffreys had not yet achieved the sinister reputation which has made him one of the best-known figures in English history. Already a toper ('You are going on circuit, therefore I desire you will not drink too much,' Charles told him when they met at Newmarket) this Judge was then handsome, witty and supereminent; his methods of cross-examination set a standard hitherto unknown in legal records. His kindness to Sir John had been shown during some disputes in the Middlesex sessions; and his 'quick parts and boldness, and zeal for the King's service' enhanced his value as a guest. Reresby therefore ordered a guard to receive him at the city gates, 'went to wait on him myself as soon as he lighted at his lodging . . . set him two sentries at his door [and] invited him to dinner the next day'. When the Assizes were over, 'my Lord himself came to me incognito one evening, and being a jolly, merry companion, stayed with us over a bottle till one o'clock in the morning'. Sir George pleased the city fathers by postponing the seizure of their charter, and 'upon their invitation' dined with them in state. Taking leave of Sir John, he said, 'I will acquaint the King and the Duke how good service you do them.' Reresby then celebrated Christmas at Thrybergh with more than usual splendour. And on New Year's Day, 'there dined,' he says, 'above three hundred, so that whole sheep were roasted and served up to feed them. For music, I had five violins, besides bagpipes, drums and trumpets.'

On 2nd February 1685 news came of the King's apoplexy. The next reports were more hopeful; but on the 6th, at midday, after the usual 'blooding, cupping and vomiting' treatments, and his great reception of the Sacrament according to Catholic rites, Reresby's 'gracious and great master departed out of this world'.

Sir John was then given orders to proclaim King James II, which was done on 10th February at nine in the morning, 'with all the signs of peace and satisfaction that could be . . . throughout the country, and indeed the whole kingdom'. It was the end of a disturbed and anxious era; and Reresby, as the long established supporter and friend of His Majesty, could look forward to greater powers. His doubts about the effects of James's Catholicism were entirely disposed of when he heard that the King had promised the Privy Council that 'he would defend the Government of England both in Church and State as by law established'. Clearly, the debauchery and wickedness of Court life would now be put down by James's severer methods. A new and better age had begun.

4

Sir John Reresby was fifty-one and James II a year older when that monarch succeeded his brother. Their friendship, one of some two decades' standing, was not entirely based on a combination of self-interest on the one side and patronage on the other; for they were temperamentally suited—with certain basic differences. The Yorkshire baronet was competent, energetic and clearheaded; the Stuart King, hitherto politically subordinated and always crassly limited, had long been a deluded fanatic, seeing himself as the future deliverer of his country from heresy, corruption and financial decline. Now, intoxicated by the abrupt cessation of his unpopularity and by his access to power, he seems to have been momentarily sincere in his promise to support the national faith. But in a few months a graver mood, an inflexible resolve, took charge, and he began to dedicate himself to saving the English soul. Sir John's loyalty, enhanced by ambition and absences from Court, made it impossible for him to take in this process; indeed, he never fully realized where James's doltish cruelty and arrogance were leading him, nor that his Catholic God—like the Israelites' golden calf, one of his own making—was turning him into a babbling imbecile in order to destroy him. Reresby followed his master to the edge of the precipice—and watched him plunge over it in helpless bewilderment.

The Lord Mayor of York now asked Sir John to stand for the new Parliament, which was to assemble in May. He had no sooner agreed to do so than he was approached by his former stepfather, Mr Moyser, who told him that he too might be chosen for that place by the local Council. 'I am very sorry,' he said, 'that we two are likely to be in competition, but it is not what I desire or seek, but I am put upon it by some people.' 'Nobody can compel you to a thing of that nature,' Reresby replied. 'It looks very unkind towards me,' adding that unnecessary 'disturbances and heats' would result from such a conflict. Moyser said that he would stand down, if he could do so without causing too much trouble to his backers; but he still, says Sir John, 'pursued what had been begun', and it was not until March that Reresby achieved his election, after which he came up to London to wait on the King and attend his coronation. A few days later, at James's *coucher*, he was assured of His Majesty's support. 'All things,' he then noted, 'seemed now to look very auspicious, the King not giving the least token to change the religion, but very much the contrary'—and this in spite of James's public attendance at Mass.

In May came news of Argyll's rebellion in Scotland (this had been agreed upon between him and Monmouth) and on the 29th of that month the King thanked both Houses for their 'cheerfulness and readiness' in defraying the expense of putting it down. 'I have a true English heart,' he told them, 'and I am jealous of the honour of the nation, pleasing myself with the thought, by God's blessing and your assistance, to carry it yet higher in the world than it was in the time of my ancestors.'

The failure of Argyll's rising followed Monmouth's landing at Lyme Regis on 11th June; this resulted in the attainder of the Duke, together with the announcement of £5,000 reward for his capture and his deliverance to his uncle, 'dead or alive'. Sir John then paused in his account of Monmouth's campaign to record his anxiety about his eldest son, William, who, with Tamworth, was at school in Kensington, and had got into trouble with the authorities. His father believed that he would improve, as Tamworth had. He did not do so.

With the increase of Monmouth's forces and his triumphal entry into Taunton, Reresby received the command of a troop of horse (Tamworth, now fourteen, was commissioned as his father's cornet) while remaining in London, in the event of a 'factious rising' in the City. On 7th July Monmouth was defeated at Sedgemoor, escaping to be captured in Dorset two days later. Sir John was informed (presumably by Lord Feversham, who had commanded the Royalist army) that 'from the beginning of this desperate attempt, [the Duke] had shown the conduct of a great captain, insomuch as the King himself had said that he had not made one false step. And thus this great storm,' he goes on, 'which began from a little cloud . . . was thus fortunately dispersed.' Reresby adds that if Monmouth had succeeded 'the disaffected were so numerous, that they would have risen

... to the very hazard of the Crown.' He saw no connection between this unrest and the King's policy, which was now based on the abolition of the Test Act, and his resolve to force on the country his brother's Declaration of Indulgence (cancelled in 1673) for Dissenters and Catholics.

Ostensibly, James appeared to be proposing freedom of worship for all his subjects. In fact, encouraged by Monmouth's defeat and execution, and the effects in the West Country of Jeffreys' Bloody Assize (for which the Judge received a peerage), he was in the process of breaking the law, and defying Parliament's decisions. His intention of converting England to Catholicism was gradually ceasing to be a secret, partly because of his employment of his co-religionists in the forces and the civil service.

Yet Sir John, while noting these changes with some disapproval, did not waver in his adherence to the master he had sworn to serve. Nor did it occur to him that his own rule, that of never being 'backward in seeking reparation', had now become a weapon in Parliament's hands, as one Member after another rose to point out to the King that he was breaking his promise (embodied in his coronation oath) to preserve the rights of the Church of England. In November, infuriated by these protests, James prorogued Parliament till February 1686. 'I hope when they next meet,' he wrote to William of Orange, 'they will be in a better temper.' By this time, Reresby, unperturbed, had returned to his duties in Yorkshire.

Here, riding home from the muster of his militia troop, he met with an ominous setback. Accustomed to carrying his sword unsheathed, he dismounted to find that it had slipped from his belt and was lost. This upset him very much, 'because it is reputed unlucky for a soldier to lose his sword'—and Sir John had long thought of himself as a soldier rather than as a courtier or a civil servant. Such a warning could not be disregarded; some disaster was on the way. Although his servant found the sword two days later, its loss remained in his mind, and was connected with the 'afflicting' news of Halifax's dismissal from the Privy Council, and also the fear, conveyed by the Archbishop of York, that 'the King might offer something in Parliament . . . in favour of popery'.

On his next visit to London Reresby took note of the conjectures about the prorogation, and came to the conclusion

that the only point of difference between King and Parliament
was that of his employment of Catholic officers; waiting on
His Majesty at supper, he was reassured by James about his
own powers. 'The popish party,' he adds, 'at this time behaved
themselves with an insolency that did them prejudice,' and in
his view their behaviour had been stimulated by Louis XIV's
Revocation of the Edict of Nantes, which resulted in the persecution and flight of some thousands of Huguenots. This holocaust did not so much concern Reresby as the changes in the
English ministry, which 'began', he says, 'to cool my ambition',
and he decided that 'every thinking man would choose to
retire and be content with his own . . . Could I have persuaded
myself to have com'd up to the point that some did, I had a
fairer opportunity of raising myself now than ever; but I was
convinced that safety was better than greatness.'

Before going home for Christmas, Sir John dined with Judge
Jeffreys, who had just been created Lord Chancellor, presumably
as a reward for his 'Campaign in the West', during which some
three hundred persons had been executed, and nearly a thousand
transported to the West Indies. In common with the majority
of his contemporaries, Reresby took these measures for granted.
Although he had not been afraid to tell Titus Oates that he was
a liar, he preferred not to comment on Jeffreys' execution of
a seventy-year-old widow, Alice Lisle, on the extremely doubtful
grounds that she had knowingly sheltered a Dissenter flying
from Sedgemoor; nor did he deprecate the burning to death
of Elizabeth Gaunt on the same charge. If he had openly criticized these judgements, he would have been arrested and sent
to the Tower for seditious libel; but it was not so much caution
that kept him silent, as his belief that high treason, however
questionably proved, must be punished by such sentences. At
no time does he refer to the Bloody Assize, by that or any other
name.

After thanking Jeffreys for his 'civilities' to himself, he privately
observes, 'I was not very much persuaded that he was my friend
to that degree—but the way to make friends at Court is to pretend
you think them so already.' Jeffreys said, 'I take it very kindly,
I have always esteemed you,' with other expressions of goodwill,
to which Sir John replied, 'I have always been firm to the Crown,
and shall so continue.' Dining again with the Lord Chancellor

in January 1686, Reresby reports that his host, having 'drunk
smartly (which was his custom)', sent for the actor, William
Mountford, to 'divert the company', which he did by pleading
before Jeffreys in the manner of an advocate. 'He acted,' says
Sir John, 'all the principal lawyers of the age . . . and thus
ridiculed, not only the lawyers, but the law itself.' This entertainment, amusing though it was, seemed to Reresby 'not so
prudent . . . for so eminent a man [as Jeffreys] in so great a
station of the law'.

Meanwhile Sir John, who had always accepted the King's
sexual promiscuity when he was Duke of York, began to adopt
a more censorious attitude about his relations with his principal
mistress, Catherine Sedley, daughter of the dramatist. James
had recently created her Countess of Dorchester, with a view,
it was thought, to her dismissal. He now renewed their affair,
to the great distress of his wife and her priests, who, according
to Reresby, 'set before him the sin and the discouragement
his amour . . . would give to the new gaining of converts to
their Church'. Catherine, a rather plain girl, was a wit, a Protestant, and also the mother of four children by the King. She
refused to leave England, remaining in her house in the most
fashionable quarter of London, St James's Square; and after
a short interval (spent by Catherine in Dublin) he continued
to visit her. His announcement that the immorality of his brother's
Court would no longer be tolerated did not of course apply
to himself. Having sent the Duchess of Portsmouth back to
Versailles, he received other ladies in his closets at St James's
and Whitehall, thus plunging the Queen into despair. In her
exasperation with her husband, she boxed the ears of Lady
Peterborough, and also those of an officer of the household;
she then threw a hairbrush at Princess Anne during a *lever*.
Although all three irritated her by refusing to become Catholics,
her anger sprang from a deeper cause, that of injured pride.
She made no attempt to conceal her grief and rage.

This scandal was followed by another of a more serious
nature. Judge Jeffreys 'had like to have died at this time', says
Reresby, 'by a fit of the stone, which he brought upon himself,
by a great debauch of wine'. Dining with Rochester (Laurence
Hyde, James's first wife's brother, and now Lord Treasurer)
Jeffreys and a City alderman undressed, and were only just

prevented climbing up a lamp-post in order, thus exposed, to drink the King's health, 'which', Sir John adds, 'gave reason of derision, not to say more of the matter'. A few days later, Reresby asked Lord Rochester for the moneys due to him 'for the charge I was at in raising my troop', and was told that the state was not responsible. 'I owe the favour [of recruiting the troop] to your lordship,' Reresby expostulated. 'No, do not say that—' Rochester began; Sir John interrupted with 'Yes—to your lordship, and my lord Halifax.' His protests were ignored, as were his efforts to put down riots in York, which he might have been able to deal with if he had gone there himself. Remaining in London, he noted the King's 'encouragement' of his Catholic subjects by 'putting more papists into office . . . [and] by causing . . . popish books to be printed and sold, and cried publicly'.

Worse was to follow. James now circulated the late King's statement—it had been found in his closet—on the reasons for his conversion to the old faith; he also caused to be published that of his first Duchess on the same subject. And yet, Reresby observes, 'there was no remarkable invasion upon the rights of the Church of England'—at least, he thought not: although he was somewhat disturbed when James ordered the clergy 'not to meddle with controversies in their sermons [and sent] my lord Castlemaine upon a solemn embassy to the Pope, and many other such things; which made all men expect that more would follow of a greater concern'.

Sir John disregarded these portents, for he was, as ever, deeply troubled about his Yorkshire garrisons. 'What does Your Majesty intend to do with the keys of the city?' he asked, adding, 'The only thing that gives it the face of a garrison is the small force that is there, and the keeping of the keys, and the shutting and opening of the gates by the soldiers.' The King prevaricated, flattered his old friend, and managed to soothe him by promising that more forces would be sent north. A little later he told him, 'It is for your sake only that I keep up York as a garrison.' 'Though it was a great compliment the King made me,' says Sir John, 'I was sorry to hear it—for those things seldom continue that consist for one man's sake.' He then asked Lord Feversham, now high in the King's favour, to support him on this point, and so became intimate with that nobleman, a widower and a French Protestant, who had received his title from Charles II.

By this time, Tamworth Reresby had replaced his elder brother in their father's esteem. Sir John removed both boys from their Kensington school to Eton, in the hope that William would improve in the company of older pupils. The result was so unsatisfactory that Reresby's account of him was scratched out shortly after he wrote it.

All these worries turned Sir John towards a different employment, that of furthering a marriage between Lord Feversham and the Duke of Newcastle's eldest daughter, Lady Margaret Cavendish. The Duke would have preferred a wealthier son-in-law; but he was not personally averse from Feversham, and so Reresby thought that he might be able to arrange the alliance on his new friend's behalf. It was not until October 1686 that he discovered the Duchess's determination to defeat this plan. He came to Welbeck to find the household in an uproar. The Duchess had decided against Feversham in favour of the Earl of Shrewsbury and had already promised Shrewsbury's trustees a larger portion for Lady Margaret than that arranged by her father. Not only so; the Duchess refused to allow her second daughter, Lady Arabella, to be married to the husband the Duke had chosen for her. This was the eldest of the King's sons by Arabella Churchill, James Fitzroy, later Duke of Berwick, a handsome and accomplished youth of sixteen. Her daughter, the Duchess declared, 'should never marry a papist and a bastard.' Both Margaret and her sister were allying themselves with their mother against the Duke, who begged Reresby to speak to all three, 'to make them friends' with him. 'I endeavoured all I could,' says Sir John, 'but to no purpose. I found them very foolishly obstinate, for the Duchess had had so great a share of government in that family, that she expected everything should go as she pleased'—a deplorable situation. Her wilfulness so enraged the Duke that 'he burnt his will, and made another settlement, not at all to the advantage of those daughters'. Then he informed Sir John that he and the Duchess were still at odds; and by the same post Reresby received a letter from Feversham saying, 'I now think myself more happy than married into that family.' It was all very distressing, in that 'so fatal to families are those differences occasioned by husband or wife, or both; and if the latter, though the man hath spirit (if he hath sense with it) he will suffer in some degree the insolency of a woman . . . Daughters,' Sir John concluded, 'are seldom desired out of such families.'

Reresby's involvement in this dispute kept him in Yorkshire, and thus out of touch with the effects of the King's latest manoeuvre, which took the form of his Ecclesiastical Commission; he put it before the clergy and the Universities as 'a prevention of indiscreet [i.e. Anglican] preaching'. As Parliament was once more prorogued—it did not meet again until after James had fled the kingdom—he was thereby enabled, or so he believed, to enforce Catholicism on the nation. To the French Ambassador he said, 'It will give me the right to exercize a power still greater than that of Catholic kings in other countries.' By this action, James was using his authority as Head of the Church of England, a position forbidden him by his religion—a characteristic mingling of mental confusion and inherent despotism. Archbishop Sancroft refused to sit on the Commission, which was then taken over by Jeffreys; he supported James's claim to supremacy, in spite of the fact that the Commission contradicted the Statute of 1661 forbidding royal interference with the established faith.

The significance of this procedure escaped Reresby, who was attending the York Assizes. The last case, he reports, 'was that of a poor old woman [who] had the hard fate to be condemned for a witch. Some, that were more apt to believe these things than me, thought the evidence strong against her.' Sir John remained sceptical, because, although the boy who accused her fell into fits when he faced her in court, 'on a sudden [was seen] coming to himself and relating very distinctly the several injuries she had done him'. Reresby came to the conclusion that the charge was a piece of superstitious nonsense—for the boy 'had no distortion nor foaming at the mouth'; and so the woman was reprieved.

Next day, however, Sir John began to doubt the verdict; for one of his soldiers reported that on the night of the woman's arrest he, being on guard at the Castle, and hearing 'a great noise . . . came to the porch, and being there see a scroll of paper creep from under the door, which . . . turned first into the shape of a monkey, and then of a turkey-cock, which moved to and fro'. The soldier called a comrade, and together 'they see the scroll

7*

dance up and down and creep under the door, where there was scarce the room of the thickness of half-a-crown'. Reresby found this account disturbing, especially as it came from both men; but, noting that the movements of the scroll had taken place by moonlight, he made no attempt to rearrest the old woman. The soldiers might have been deceived; yet in such cases one could never be sure. A witch's powers were unpredictable.

He was further alarmed when news came of the King's efforts to implement the authority of the Ecclesiastical Commission by summoning various Members of Parliament to his closet, and privately urging them to repeal the Test Act, as being 'an unreasonable law'. According to modern standards, it was; but the English people did not think so: and James either would not or could not take in the fear and hatred of Catholicism which prevailed throughout the kingdom. He had adopted it; therefore they must follow his example. So it was that those who refused to be converted were 'discharged', Sir John heard, 'of their employments', and he began to wonder what would happen to him if he were approached in this way, for he had determined to maintain the Act in all circumstances. Meanwhile, the local landowners were remaining firm in their faith, despite 'the King's frowns ... so far did honour help religion'—but it was all very worrying, although Reresby himself had not yet been affected.

In April 1687 he halted his narrative to note Buckingham's death at an inn in Kirkby Moorside, some thirty miles away. Although many years had passed since he had worked for the Duke, he still recalled him as 'the most witty man of his time, and the handsomest, as well as the best bred, but wholly addicted to his pleasures, and unsteady'. Sir John was relieved to hear that his former captain, whose reputation was that of an atheist, had received the Sacraments according to Anglican rites before he died, ruined, neglected and alone. Six weeks later he was buried in Westminster Abbey. The Duchess did not attend the funeral.

As if in pious mood, Reresby now 'repaired and beautified' the church at Thrybergh, and provided a new bell for the steeple. Then the proposed Feversham-Cavendish alliance moved into another stage, which was further complicated by King James's taking a hand in the negotiations.

Having persuaded the King to promote his suit, Feversham
asked Sir John to deliver a letter from His Majesty to the Duke
of Newcastle. 'Whatever favour you show his lordship,' James
wrote, 'I shall consider it as done to myself.' Reresby then succeeded, not only in temporarily reconciling the Newcastles,
but in obtaining the Duchess's verbal consent to the marriage;
yet she would not give it in writing, although she agreed that
Feversham should wait on her, on condition that her husband
settled £15,000 on Lady Margaret. In July 1687 Feversham
came to stay with the Reresbys, and together he and Sir John
dined at Welbeck. The Duke then told Feversham that he could
not allow the marriage until he had his wife's written consent
—'a strange fancy', Sir John thought. Feversham said that
£15,000 was an insufficient dowry; but he aked Reresby to
'intercede' for him with the Duchess, which he did. Sir John
observed that both she and her daughter were 'content' with
Feversham, whom they now saw for the first time. But, said the
Duchess, her husband must increase the settlement, to which
Feversham replied that the King would probably 'give him something', as Charles II had when he married his first wife. 'In the
meantime,' he added, 'I desire Your Grace and my lady Margaret
to take me into your good opinions.' 'Do not despair,' the Duke
told him. 'She will do it, the women approve of you very well.'
In August the Duchess supplied her written consent, and the
matter seemed settled, much to Sir John's relief.

He then left Thrybergh to stay with the Marquess of Winchester, who had borrowed Rufford from Halifax for a ten
days' stay, on his way to London. Reresby, although long used
to the eccentricities of great men, was considerably taken aback
by Winchester's manner of life. 'He travelled with four coaches,
and a hundred horse in his retinue. His custom was to dine at
six or seven at night [this feast generally took place in the early
afternoon] and his meals lasted till seven or eight in the morning.
Sometimes he drank, sometimes heard his music, sometimes
discoursed, sometimes took tobacco, sometimes ate, while the
company did what they pleased . . . continuing all the night.
In the morning he would hunt or hawk . . . if not, he would
dance, go to bed about eleven, and sleep till the evening.' And
yet, Reresby had to admit, 'the man all this time was not mad,
but had good sense'. On the whole, he enjoyed his visit, in spite

of its 'seeming disorder'. He returned home in September, to hear of the King's dispute with the Fellows of Magdalen College, Oxford.

Their President having just died, they met to elect a new one, to be faced with a royal mandate ordering them to install James's candidate, a Catholic who had been dismissed from Trinity College, Cambridge, for drunkenness, violence and debauchery. When the Fellows refused to vote for him, a series of scenes took place between them and the King, 'who put himself into so great passion that he changed colour and faltered in his speech'. After further discussions, which extended over several months, the Fellows were dismissed, to be replaced by James's co-religionists, and Magdalen became a Catholic seminary. Sir John did not follow or record all the ramifications of this controversy; once more, the full significance of James's attitude seems to have escaped him, as did the sensation caused by the arrival at St James's of the Papal Nuncio, whom the King greeted by falling on his knees. Neither event deeply disturbed Reresby, for he was involved in another quarrel between the Duke and Duchess of Newcastle, which took place in October 1687.

As the Newcastles were now living apart, Sir John had to go from one to the other. He persuaded Feversham to promise to invest Lady Margaret's jointure in land, which would accrue to her after his death. The Duchess, having agreed to this, wrote to her husband expressing her approval. Reresby, delighted, presented the Duke with her letter—and received a fearful shock. Newcastle, he says, 'flew into a passion', exclaiming, 'I never thought my wife such a fool as to do it! This is to beggar my daughter—she is lost for ever', adding that as he had agreed to the marriage, he would keep his word—but 'I shall leave the house when my lord comes to marry my daughter'. 'Much amazed at this transport', Sir John came to the conclusion that the Duke had decided that Lady Margaret, rather than Lady Arabella, should marry Berwick; and he had always known that Newcastle was 'of an unsteady fickle humour'. He left in a rage, and from Thrybergh sent the Duke an indignant letter, pointing out the folly and discourtesy of his behaviour at some length, and concluding, 'How will this sound in the wise part of the world? . . . If the trumpet give an uncertain sound, who can prepare themselves to the battle?'

This eloquence, which covered several pages, left the Duke unmoved. He then made a scene with his wife and Lady Margaret. 'You are led by your daughter,' he told the Duchess, upon which the girl burst out, 'I will live single till both father and mother agree on a husband for me!' Sir John, reporting this development to Lord Feversham, suggested that if he wished to pursue the alliance, it might be as well for him to offer to change his name to Cavendish; but that nobleman, who was a Duras, and the nephew of the Duc de Bouillon, would not consider giving up his French titles. The Duke's attitude, he added, was 'beyond imagination', and he could only pity his wife and daughter. Three years later, Lady Margaret married the Earl of Clare. Reresby's friendship with the Duke was then resumed, on the basis of their joint stand against the King's continuous attacks on the Church of England.

5

While Sir John wrestled with the Newcastle problem, James II received two warnings, one from a High Court judge, and the other from the wealthiest and most powerful nobleman in England. In the process known as 'closetting', the King told Sir Thomas Jones, Chief Justice of the Common Pleas, that he was determined to elect twelve judges who would support his prerogative, in other words, his supremacy in all matters of civil and religious administration. 'Your Majesty may find twelve judges of your own mind, but hardly twelve lawyers,' Sir Thomas replied—and was later dismissed from his post. The next setback came from the Duke of Somerset. When asked to introduce the Papal Nuncio in public audience—as Gentleman of the Bedchamber, this was one of his duties—that formidable patrician replied, 'I humbly desire of Your Majesty to be excused.' 'What is your reason?' James enquired. 'I consider it to be above the law,' was the answer. 'I will pardon you,' the King said. Somerset remained firm. 'I am no very good lawyer,' he explained, 'but I think I have heard it said that a pardon granted to a person offending under assurance of obtaining it, is void.' This refusal greatly impressed the French Ambassador, who told Louis XIV that the Declaration of Indulgence was still inoperative, and that the anti-Catholic laws had not been repealed. Then Innocent XI, who had received Castlemaine with extreme coldness—he used to break off their interviews by fits of coughing—told the Nuncio not to persist in public receptions, for fear of further antagonizing James's courtiers.

In December 1687 Sir John was ordered by the King to give up one of his manors to a priest, Father Lawson; he obeyed, noting that the loss of the rental amounted to some £40 a year. Then came the circulation of James's Three Questions, all of which had to be answered by Reresby, as Deputy-Lieutenant of Yorkshire. (1) Would he vote against the Test Act in the next Parliament? (2) Would he support those Members who voted against it? (3) Would he 'live peaceably' with those differing

from him in matters of religion? After privately setting down
his objections to these demands, Sir John evaded the issue by
replying that until the Houses met and debated the Questions,
he could not answer the first two, adding that he was perfectly
willing 'to live quietly with all men as good Christians and
loyal subjects'.

In February 1688 Reresby fell ill of what he describes as
'running gout or rheumatism', and thereafter his increased
lameness prevented him personally helping to put down the
rioting of his troops; nor could he go up to London to congratulate the King on the news of the Queen's pregnancy—
which actually dated from the previous November. In April
came the first rumours of the Seven Bishops' refusal to read the
Declaration of Indulgence, and in May, although still weak
and disabled, Sir John, with Lady Reresby and their family,
left for London, stopping at Cambridge. Here, he considered
—and no doubt consulted the authorities—as to where William
should be placed. Reresby was so worried about the boy that
he deleted all his entries on this point. No information survives
as to whether William was entered at one of the colleges, or
whether he remained in his father's care. At the age of nineteen,
he had become a problem.

Sir John now analysed and wrote down what he saw as the
rightful stand of the Bishops—they were led by Archbishop
Sancroft—about the Declaration of Indulgence. The fact that
the laws of England supported them was ignored by James, who
said to the Papal Nuncio, 'I will make no concession. My father
made concessions, and he was beheaded.' Meanwhile, his principal minister, the Earl of Sunderland, observed, 'There is no
leading the King but by a woman, or a priest, or both.' Reresby,
who was kindly received by James, and accompanied him to
inspect his troops on Hounslow Heath, did not share this view:
although he was much distressed when on 8th June the Bishops
were committed to the Tower on a charge of seditious libel.
The general indignation, amounting to panic, was increased
by the birth of a son to the Queen two days later; for now a
Protestant succession, as represented by the Princess Mary,
had been eliminated; and three weeks after that, the Bishops
were acquitted. James II, attended by Feversham, was again
inspecting his troops when he heard the sound of cheering in

the ranks, and asked what had happened. 'Oh, it is nothing,'
replied the Frenchman, and told him about the Bishops' triumphal
departure from the Tower. 'Do you call that nothing?' exclaimed
the King; and next day Reresby noticed that although he did
his best to maintain an outward impassivity, he was deeply
agitated.

Sir John did not know that the Whig party's representative,
Admiral Herbert, had been sent, disguised as a common seaman,
to discuss the situation with the Prince and Princess of Orange.
Reresby, still favourably received by James, seems to have decided
that his Catholic campaign must eventually fail; his loyalty to
his master remained constant, and was separated from his
dislike of James's actions. (This, the Church-and-King, High
Tory attitude, was shared by the majority of the English gentry,
until James's flight brought about a change of feeling, which
led to their accepting William.) And Sir John, as a Yorkshireman,
was inclined to discount, if not to despise, the turmoil made
by the Londoners, whose credulity and mounting hysteria were
catered for by the Whig party's carefully advertised doubts
about the authenticity of the Queen's delivery. That her son
had been born a month early strengthened their acceptance—
temporarily shared by Mary of Orange and the Princess Anne
—of the warming-pan story.

The King then arranged for the celebration of Mass in the
ships at anchor in the Thames. The sailors, firmly and traditionally
Protestant, threatened mutiny, upon which he hurried to placate
them. According to Sir John, he 'went from ship to ship, and
called the seamen his children, said that he had nothing to say
as to their religion, that he granted liberty of conscience to all,
but expected that they should behave themselves like men of
honour and courage when there was occasion for their service;
but all the popish priests were to be brought on shore'. James
had no sooner appeased the sailors when he heard of Admiral
Herbert's arrival at The Hague (Herbert had been deprived
of his post after refusing to vote against the Test Act) and a
number of seamen deserting to join him.

Reresby now approached the King in the hope that he would
give William a lieutenancy in a Yorkshire regiment, adding
that a sudden vacancy had made this possible. Such an appointment was usually automatic; but James said, 'I will consider of

it, and give you my answer some other time,' which seems
to indicate that he knew something of the young man's reputation. Sir John, who was about to return home, feared that he
might be asked to vote against the Test Act; but the King,
who had been greatly distressed by his own son's illness, merely
wished his old friend a good journey. When the little Prince
of Wales recovered, his parents were once more cast down,
this time by the rumours of a Dutch invasion. Neither they
nor Reresby knew that Herbert and his Whig confederates had
asked William of Orange to take over the kingdom.

Sir John reached Thrybergh to find that the Duke of Newcastle had been made Lord Lieutenant of Yorkshire. By this
time, their disagreement about the Duke's behaviour to Feversham had, he says, 'blown over . . . and I had that credit with
him that he scarce appointed an officer without my consent'.
So they worked happily together. In October 1688 news came
of the Prince of Orange making ready to sail with a fleet of six
hundred ships and a great army. Danby, dining with Newcastle
in York, told Reresby, 'We are in an ill condition now in this
nation in all ways, for if the King beat the Prince, popery will
return upon us with more violence than before; if the Prince
beat the King, the Crown and the nation may be in some danger.'

Sir John was horrified at the thought of the invasion, and
disgusted that 'neither the gentry nor the common people
seemed much afeared or concerned at it'. When he questioned
his neighbours, their response was cheerful and offhand. 'The
Prince,' he was told, 'comes only to maintain the Protestant
religion, he will do England no harm.' But his friends at Court
prophesied civil war, and he himself foresaw the loss of all
that he had acquired over the last thirty years. Nevertheless,
social life must go on, and on 18th October he gave a dinner-
party for Newcastle, the Lord Mayor and a number of other
friends at his house in York. 'I had music to improve the entertainment,' he says, 'and wine.'

Newcastle, not more of a toper than most of his contemporaries,
'tasted plentifully', according to his host, to the point indeed of
becoming affectionately maudlin. He sat next to Sir John; and
the feast was at its height when, regardless of the other guests,
he leaned over him, kissed him, and announced, 'You are
my mistress.' This gesture left Reresby rather gratified than

otherwise. It was kind of Newcastle, he thought, thus to seal
their alliance.

James II now fell into a panic about his son-in-law's invasion.
Counting on the adherence of the majority, he prepared for war,
and began, Sir John says, 'to find his error, but too late, in
carrying things so high upon popish councils and foundations
. . . and begins again to court the Church of England'. Reresby's
preparations for a civil war also went forward; but he had
little confidence in those of the King. 'The fleet,' he noted,
'was . . . much inferior to the Dutch, and did nothing to the
purpose.'

On 7th November news came that the Prince had landed at
Torbay. When Sir John consulted Newcastle, the Duke said
that it would be impossible for William to attack, because
the Dutch would receive 'not very good help in England'. By
the 16th York was secured—or so it seemed: but there was
disagreement among Newcastle's staff as to whether they should
now insist on a free Parliament. Sir John did not wish to enforce
this demand—it amounted to a threat—and would not sign
the petition. After a great deal of discussion, it became clear
that some of the militia were not going to support the Government; certain regiments refused to march or to obey orders.
'As I was preparing to go to the troops,' Reresby records, 'hoping
to regain them to the King's service if I appeared, Sir Henry
Bellasis [a Catholic] . . . drew up a party of thirty horsemen
before my door, and there prevented my going out, till my
lord of Danby, with his chief companions, came up to me.'

'To resist is to no purpose,' Danby began, 'I and these gentlemen are in arms for a free Parliament, and for the preservation
of the Protestant religion and the Government as by law established, which the King has very near destroyed, and which the
Prince of Orange has come to assist us to defend—and I hope
you will join us in so good a design.' 'I am for a Parliament
and the Protestant religion as well as you,' said Sir John, 'but
I am also for the King.' 'I hope,' Danby persisted, 'that as we
are agreed in principles, so we shall agree in action.' 'Though
we agree in the matter, I cannot agree with you in the manner,'
his friend replied, 'I do not conceive anything to be exerted
from the King by any manner of force, and, having His Majesty's
commission of Governor, and for his service, I cannot join

with those that act against his authority and the commission, let the consequence be what it may.' 'Then,' Danby announced, 'I must imprison you.' 'I am naked,' Sir John answered calmly. 'My friends have relinquished the King's service to me, and I am in your power.' There was a pause, while Danby consulted with his subordinates. Then he said, 'I know you to be a man of honour. Your engagement not to stir nor write is as good a restraint upon you as a guard or a prison.' Reresby agreed to these conditions, and was confined to his room. 'But,' Danby added, 'I recommend you to consider my offer.'

Within the next few hours Danby took over the city, and by 24th November all the principal inhabitants had declared for the Prince of Orange. Danby then asked Sir John to dine with him, and said that he was free to leave York whenever he pleased. Reresby departed to Thrybergh 'there to live peaceably, and not to act in any hostile manner' against Danby's authority. He remained firm in his resolve not to sign the petition; it was not for him to give orders to his sovereign. His part in the Revolution now became that of a spectator. Appalled, he saw events rush past him; and day by day felt his own position deteriorating. Yet in no circumstances would he desert his master; he did not know, and never would have believed, that James was about to desert him.

Indeed, stories of desertions now prevailed over all other news, even that of the Prince's march from Torbay. While James II, with his army, was trying to work out some kind of a campaign from Salisbury, he was deserted, Sir John says, 'by several great men . . . and peculiar confidants'. This contingent included Churchill, Grafton, Ormonde, Prince George of Denmark and Lord Drumlanrig, together with their subordinates, and some troops. Meanwhile the Princess Anne, escorted by Sarah Churchill and Bishop Compton, left Whitehall to join the Orangists in the Midlands.

In the first week of December Reresby noted that in his neighbourhood 'very few gentlemen continued firm to the King, nor indeed, in any part of England', adding, 'There was scarce an hour but His Majesty received, like Job, some message of some revolt, or misfortune or other'. It then dawned on him that James had arranged to fly; his first attempt to do so was made on 11th December. On the 13th he was detained and arrested near Sheerness; from there he wrote to William, asking to be released, so that he might return to London. By this time, at his command, Feversham had disbanded the army. James then proceeded to Whitehall. As he drove through the City he was greeted by cheers and bonfires—'but', the French Ambassador reported, 'the majority of the people are for the Prince of Orange'. In the early morning of 18th December the King left for Rochester, and at dusk of the same day William entered London. On Christmas Day James crossed to Ambleteuse.

Meanwhile, Sir John had offered to stand for the next Parliament, and had been politely denied by Danby. 'If I can serve you in anything,' that nobleman told him, 'I shall be very ready.' On the 26th Reresby heard that James had reached France, and was on his way to join his wife and son at St Germains. So his lifelong principle, to fear God and honour the King, was partially in abeyance. He could continue to fear God; but there was now no King to honour—for James's flight amounted in his view, as in that of many others, to abdication.

'Under which king, Bezonian? Speak, or die!' Reresby, crippled with gout and in failing health, had long ceased to be belligerent, or even as active as became a man in his position; he had no intention of rushing into a conflict that, as the days went by, seemed less likely to end in civil war than he had at first believed. Meanwhile, his views on religion and politics remained unchanged. Despising the Dissenters as vulgar and rebellious fanatics, he detested the Catholics (he would not have cared to admit that he also feared them); also, not unreasonably, he mistrusted the Whig party. His prevailing wish was to maintain his power in the northern kingdom his ancestors had helped to rule for nearly four hundred years. He now saw that he could only continue to do so—and, more important still, bequeath that same power to his descendants—by submitting to the authority succeeding that of the monarch who had let the sceptre fall into the hands of his adversaries. But he could not even guess at their plans, because they were already disagreeing among themselves. He must therefore watch and wait, while his dislike of the general uncertainty increased. Finally, he decided to place himself in the power of the man he most admired and respected—Halifax, that supple and ingenious specialist in political intrigue.

Amongst those who later followed James II into exile, Reresby had a number of friends: but he would no more have become a Jacobite than a traitor to the English Government; the only trouble was that he could not determine, any more than the majority of his contemporaries, what that Government was going to be. He had little knowledge of, and not much interest in, the intentions of the Prince of Orange; and Princess Mary, as a woman, did not count, even though her claim to the throne now seemed to precede that of her half-brother; for a Catholic dynasty was as unacceptable to Sir John as to the mass of the English people. To sum up, the situation was fluid; and he would have no part in it till he had been shown the way by the only man he could trust. For Newcastle did nothing but abuse Danby, and reiterate his loyalty to the King who had abandoned the bewildered and angry Tories without even consulting them. Reresby's one consolation was 'that in these confusions no more mischiefs had been committed', and that although 'in the West Riding there was few or no Justices of the Peace sworn but papists, [they] all absconded . . . and yet [there had been] very few robberies, felonies, and not one murder'. Also, the Prince had promised to retain the Test Act, and to 'hazard himself for the laws and liberties and the preservation of the Protestant religion at all times in these kingdoms, it being the end for which he came'. Therefore, that enigmatic young man might not be so unwelcome or so dangerous as had first appeared.

A circular letter from William of Orange reached Sir John, the Duke of Newcastle and other Yorkshire notables on 17th January 1689, summoning them to sit in the Convention Parliament on the 22nd. Newcastle refused to attend. He told Reresby that he would not accept any employment from the Prince's hands. Sir John decided to go, thus circumventing Danby's embargo; he arrived in London on the day appointed, and found everything sadly changed. The King's guards, 'which both in their persons and gallantry were an ornament', had been replaced by a Dutch contingent, 'ill looking and ill habited'. And yet, he goes on, 'the city were so pleased with their deliverers, that they did not or would not perceive their deformity'.

On the 28th Sir John recorded the arguments and disputes in both Houses as to whether the little Prince of Wales (later known as the Old Pretender) should be made 'unacceptable to succeed' because he had been baptized according to Catholic rites. 'The Prince of Orange all this while,' he adds, 'seemed not much to concern himself.' 31st January was a day of thanks-giving, celebrated with bonfires and bell-ringing, for the deliver-ance of England 'from popery and tyranny'. All this fuss disgusted Reresby. 'So unstable are the minds of Englishmen,' he observes, 'that they are not very long fond of anything.'

Next day he interviewed Halifax, but was rather put out to find with him the ex-Speaker of the House of Commons, Sir Edward Seymour, and, worse still, Dr Burnet, a staunch Whig and one of William's most ardent supporters, whom he describes as 'the great Creature' of that Prince. Burnet further displeased Reresby by saying that England 'could never be happily settled' till William was crowned, and 'placed in the head of the Govern-ment in strict conjunction with Holland'. Seymour did not agree about this, and the discussion continued until, at last, Halifax and Sir John were left alone. 'Now that the Prince is here,' Halifax said, 'and upon so good an occasion, we are obliged to defend him,' and went on to outline his own solution, which was to submit to William's government. Reresby does not record his answer—it was perhaps angry and confused—and Halifax con-tinued, 'I think it advisable for you to go ambassador to some prince or state, by which means you might be out of the way till the clouds that appear are dispersed, by being so fit for that employment,' adding further 'kind things' as to his friend's ability. Finally, he offered to present him to the Prince the very next day, after warning him 'to be careful of my company' —in other words, not to join any movement for restoring James II.

Poor Sir John now faced a fearful problem. Ageing, in bad health, with a wife and eight children to care for, he must either refuse to take the oaths to the man who was about to supplant the exiled King, and thus give up everything he had worked for—position, authority, perhaps England itself—or break his solemn word to his rightful, if mistaken, sovereign. Clearly, Halifax wanted him to remain. He could only do so by indulging in the kind of time serving he had always despised, and openly censured. Newcastle, a great aristocrat, living on his vast estates, and tolerated by the Whigs as long as he did not assert himself on behalf of James, could afford to remain neutral. Sir John, a soldier and an administrator, must take one side or the other, bearing in mind the fate of his family and some three hundred tenants, all of whom depended on him. In his *Memoirs* he makes no mention of his own feelings. He simply records that, with Halifax, he went to wait on William at Whitehall. A few days later, he took the oaths. Ironically, his first gesture was wasted. The Prince of Orange was too busy to receive him.

On 7th February Parliament voted for the joint rule of King William and Queen Mary. He then agreed to administrate the kingdom, and that she should become regent in his absence, and Queen Regnant if—as seemed more than likely—he pre-deceased her. In the week preceding these decisions a number of people, enraged by Parliament's assumption that James had abdicated, approached Halifax in the hope that he would be able to use his influence against this resolution. One of them, a Court lady, whom Sir John does not name, employed him as an intermediary between herself and that nobleman. Gratified by her confidence in his powers, Reresby recorded in full her confused and inaccurate account of her attempts to bring about the re-establishment of James's authority by arranging a meeting at her house between the King and Halifax in the last week of November 1688. She told Sir John that Halifax had thrown James into a panic by warning him that his life was in danger. To another courtier the King had said, 'If I do not retire, I shall certainly be sent to the Tower, and no king ever went out of that place but to his grave.' (This was, of course, nonsense. William had no intention of penalizing his uncle, quite apart from the fact that a sojourn in the Tower was more often than not a temporary measure, as had been shown by the recent incarceration of the Seven Bishops.) In fact, Halifax, far from threatening James, had urged him to let Parliament settle every-thing, and thus avoid all danger to himself. This the King had refused to do.

Now, the lady told Reresby, she must see Halifax, in order to persuade him to vote for a regency—she did not mention by whom—rather than for an abdication. Sir John did his best: but Halifax could not see her till 9th February, two days after the settlement of the crown on William and Mary. She began their interview by blaming him for James's flight, and thus for Parliament's announcement that he had abdicated. Halifax

heard her patiently, and told her of his efforts to reconcile James
with Parliament by recalling the Houses, adding that the King,
having sent him to ask William to negotiate, had left London
for Sheerness before he returned with the Prince's answer. The
lady went on to berate Halifax, dealing with him, according
to Reresby, 'more boldly than any other could venture to do
with so great a man'. Sir John was shocked by her temerity;
but Halifax, who seems to have pacified her by allowing her
a visit of two hours, told him, 'It is not amiss to hear what
everybody has to say.' He said that although there seemed 'no
great hopes for peace', the present agreement 'was the best
that could be made at this time'.

Reresby did not think so. 'There was truly great discontents
at this day,' he says. He did not believe that William had had
no desire to become King of England; and was horrified by
the number of Catholics—he rated it at 2,000—in his army.
Also he felt that Princess Anne's succession, which was to follow
that of her sister and brother-in-law, in the event of their remaining childless, had been wrongfully 'postponed'. His disapproval
did not prevent his attendance at the Banqueting House on
13th February, when William and Mary accepted the crowns
of England, Scotland, Ireland and France—the English claim
to the French crown dated from the battle of Crécy—and were
proclaimed King and Queen throughout the city, with 'expressions of joy—though many', he adds, 'looked sadly at it.'

Danby was then made President of the Council, and Halifax
Speaker of the House of Lords, and—for the second time—
Lord Privy Seal. On 28th February Sir John, dining with Danby,
was treated 'with more intimacy and freedom than I expected',
but found his host, who had been, and was still, very ill, in a
gloomy mood. If only, he told Reresby, King James would
'quit his papists', his restoration must follow. Then he criticized
Halifax. 'I wondered,' says Sir John, 'he durst trust me so far
as to be so open before me, but he knew I would not betray
him—not so much as to my lord Halifax.'

That same afternoon, Halifax presented Reresby to King
William. 'Having kissed his hand,' Sir John records, 'I told him
that I had a trust upon me from the late King to the last. I was
not made privy to Your Majesty's designs,' he went on, 'till
I saw them in execution, and I could not then, in honour or

justice, comply with them. But I am a firm Protestant, and have suffered in my estate for being of that religion—and I shall be faithful in my duty wherever I serve.' Halifax then asked the King to let Sir John retain his company of militia, and Reresby put in, 'Sir—if you have resolved to take away my two governments of York and Bridlington, I hope you should not expect I should wait on [command] a single company.' 'No,' said William, 'I do not expect any attendance [militia support] from you,' and dismissed him. In view of this rather disappointing answer, Reresby decided to give up his governorship of York, because 'I did not think it safe or honest'.

He was then asked by a second unnamed lady to warn Halifax that James was planning an invasion. 'I believe,' the Minister replied, 'that there are great designs on foot,' adding, 'I speak always very respectfully of King James, for fear it might come to blows.' He told Reresby that any attempt of this kind would be halted by a newly raised army, and that 'all suspicious persons would be secured'.

Sir John's next interview was with Lord Bellasis (father of Sir Henry), also a Catholic, and formerly Lord Treasurer to James II. That nobleman had been appalled by his master's attempts to force Catholicism on his subjects, and by his disregard of the Pope's advice to him to desist. Many English Catholics of Bellasis's standing, remembering their sufferings during the Popish Plot, had wished James to retain the Test Act: for his refusal to do so must increase the general hatred of his co-religionists. Bellasis was thankful that King William had declared that all his subjects should be allowed to worship as they wished—the Catholics privately, as in Holland. 'As to yourself,' he told Sir John, 'I understand from all hands that you have acquitted yourself like a man of honour.' He concluded that James's religion alone prevented his restoration; and a few days later Halifax said to Reresby, 'If King James were a Protestant, he could not be kept out four months.'

Throughout the turmoil and suspense of the Interregnum, which lasted from 11th December 1688 to 12th February 1689, Sir John, that acute and observant chronicler, does not make a single comment on the looks of the principal figures. He had not seen William III since the banquet he and Buckingham had given for him in 1670; yet he says nothing about the fact that, after eighteen years of conflict, illness and overwork, the lively and elegant youth of twenty was now an emaciated, stooping, hollow-eyed invalid, whose dry and infrequent remarks were interspersed with fearful bouts of coughing; while his pretty, girlish wife had become a majestic and voluptuous beauty. Such contrasts, however startling, had no interest for a north-country squire intent on the security of the family fortunes. Also, Reresby's native caution forbade him to give a detailed account of the manner and tone of his closest associates. Bellasis was a loyal Catholic: Danby's throat infection made him gloomy and cross: Halifax's serene courtesy never failed. No more need be said. And yet the very bareness of Sir John's increasingly succinct record is both more individual and more vivid than the letters and diaries of many of his contemporaries. That the new King, from the first moment of his arrival in London chilled and snubbed all those who waited on him (he treated both Whigs and Tories in the same manner) did not affect Reresby; he accepted William as the substitute for James, resigning himself to the inevitable. The times were bad; he could not hope that they would improve. A strange indifference, a detachment from both national events and personal affairs had begun to creep over him.

So he briefly noted the landing of James at Kinsale on 12th March 1689, subjoining a list of Louis XIV's 'assistance' of ships, tents, arms, mercenaries, and £200,000 in cash. He adds that James had refused his cousin's offer of 15,000 French soldiers. 'I will succeed by my own subjects,' the poor old fellow declared, 'or perish in the attempt.' That he did neither, epitomizes his whole existence.

When Halifax and Danby were attacked by the Commons, Sir John, reporting their threats to the former, said, 'It looks very foolish for men that are about building a new fabric at the same time to pull down the pillar that supports it.' 'I do not value [them],' Halifax replied, 'though if they succeed, I shall not be sorry to lose my place.' A few days later he remarked, 'This King uses no arts.' 'Some arts,' Reresby replied sharply, 'are necessary in our English Government, in my opinion.' 'Come, Sir John,' Halifax said, 'we have wives and children, and we must consider them, and not venture too far.' Foretelling the possibility of James's return, he then spoke of a general pardon, from which, in that event, he himself would be excepted. 'But as you know,' he continued, 'I gave you some little hints of this change before you went down [to Yorkshire]. So you must tell me what you hear on the other side.' 'And indeed,' Reresby says, 'I loved him so well that I was ready enough to inform him of what related to the public service, provided it was ... not to the prejudice of any particular person, or of a confidence reposed in me.'

Once more he succumbed to gout and a feverish cold, recovering to hear that his youngest son, Leonard, had had smallpox, but was now out of danger; then George Reresby caught the disease, dying of it in the first week of April. 'It was a great affliction to me,' his father wrote, describing this son as 'a very beautiful, apt, understanding child. But God gives and God takes, blessed be the name of the Lord (especially of those that are left).'

On the day that Sir John received this news, Halifax told him that he did not think King William could survive much longer. Nevertheless, he managed to support the fatigue of the coronation on 11th April, described by Reresby as a ceremony 'of great splendour', concluding with a magnificent feast in Westminster Hall. As before, he makes no comment on the contrasting looks of William and Mary. He, bent, hobbling along beside his tall and graceful Queen, did indeed give the impression that his days were numbered. And presently, finding the London atmosphere unendurable, he abandoned Whitehall for Hampton Court, to the great inconvenience of his ministers. Only Halifax dared to remonstrate with his recalcitrant master.

'His inaccessibility,' the Minister told Reresby, 'ruins all business. Could Your Majesty,' he had asked, 'not lie sometimes in town?' to which the King coldly replied, 'It cannot be done, unless you wish to see me dead.' 'It is my opinion,' Halifax concluded, 'that if the King lives this summer—which I think he might, notwithstanding his consumptive distemper, [and] if he is not killed by the papists, the Government will scarce be shaken, though it should devolve on the Queen singly.' (For William was now considering whether he should cross to Ireland.) 'However,' he resumed, 'concern of my family must make me act with as much moderation as possible, and therefore take no great or additional places, no honours or blue ribbons—as others have done.' (Evidently, Danby's acquisition of a marquessate had both amused and irritated him.) He then told Sir John, who, still ailing, was about to leave for Yorkshire, that next day they must both wait on the King at Hampton Court, adding, 'I will do for you what I can—but let two or three months pass, to see what becomes of things.'

This is Reresby's last entry. He did not have long to wait for his situation to change. Returning to Yorkshire in the first week of May 1689, he died there on the 12th of that month, and was buried in the little church of Thrybergh. He had just passed his fifty-fifth birthday, thanking God, when he did so, 'for preserving me through so many dangers . . . and humbly begging Him to lead the remainder of my life better than I had hitherto done'.

Sir John Reresby was as fortunate in the timing of his death as he had been during his varied, arduous and eventful life; for he was spared the knowledge of his eldest son's total disregard of the family honour. Lady Reresby may have had some control over William's profligacy: but when she died in 1699, he set about squandering his inheritance, whether by gambling, drunkenness, or both, is not known. Having got rid of everything his father had so laboriously accumulated—places, income, properties —he ended a misspent career as a tapster in the Fleet prison. As John and George Reresby were dead, and Tamworth did not marry, Leonard eventually inherited the title, but nothing else (he could not of course afford a wife), and it then descended to a cousin. Of Sir John's five daughters, only the once beautiful Frances survived, following William to the Fleet, where she married one of the wardens. Nothing more is known of her. In 1748 the seven-hundred-year-old baronetcy became extinct. Gradually, the manor-house of Thrybergh fell into ruins; and in the nineteenth century the park, of which Sir John had been so proud, was turned into a golf club.

Charles Talbot
twelfth Earl and first Duke of Shrewsbury
(1660—1718)

If thou hast run with the footmen, and they
have wearied thee, then how canst thou contend
with horses?

Woe is me, my mother, that thou hast borne
a man of strife, and a man of contention!

Jeremiah xii, 5, and xv, 10

Charles Talbot, Duke of Shrewsbury
after Kneller

The talbot, a large white dog of a breed now extinct, was used for hunting and tracking. It resembled those Spartan hounds whose 'gallant chiding' so entranced Hippolyta when, with Hercules and Cadmus, she 'bay'd the boar' in Crete. Two of these creatures support the crest (a lion statant) of the Earls of Shrewsbury, turning their heads to snarl at the spectator; their feet rest on the family motto—*Prest d'Accomplir*.

This design was produced by the royal heralds in 1442, when Sir John Talbot received the earldom of Shrewsbury from Henry VI. Dying eleven years later, at the age of eighty, he is described in the play of that name as 'the Achilles of England, valiant Talbot of the grisly countenance, the Frenchmen's terror and their bloody scourge'. 'Is Talbot slain?' exclaims Bedford. 'Then I will slay myself,' and a soldier adds, 'The cry of "Talbot!" serves me for a sword.' (That Sir John was taken prisoner by La Pucelle was no disgrace; he could not be expected to escape the clutches of a witch.) In fact this warrior, rather than his unfortunate King, is Shakespeare's hero.

There is a certain irony in his seventeenth-century descendant's association with these medieval triumphs, as illustrated by the ferocity of his ancestor's armorial beasts of chase, and the motto that supports them. Charles Talbot, twelfth Earl of Shrewsbury, ready to accomplish distinction and fame, found himself defeated by his success in doing so. His pedigree, crowded with noble names dating from Domesday Book onwards—Beauchamp, Ormonde, Arundel, Glendower, Hastings, Pembroke, Manners— weighed upon him less heavily than the tragedy that shadowed his childhood and adolescence. Eventually, this seems to have increased his need to take refuge in invalidism. Achieving immense public fame, he failed in his private life, no one quite understood why. His story is a strange one, well documented, yet with a number of gaps.

In 1658 Francis, eleventh Earl of Shrewsbury and a widower, who had a daughter, Mary, but no surviving son by his first wife, married Anna Maria Brudenell, daughter of Lord Cardigan. In August 1660 she gave birth to Charles, first godson of the newly restored King. Five years later, she produced another son, John. As their parents were Catholics, both boys, who were handsome and intelligent, Charles particularly so, were brought up in the old faith. They stood to inherit vast properties in Kent, Staffordshire, Ireland, Suffolk and Essex. The Earl's country seats were situated in the neighbourhood of Isleworth, Worcester and Oxford, and his principal London house, one of four, overlooked the Thames on the site of what is now Cheyne Walk.

The daily routine of children whose parents had managed to retain an aristocratic standard of living throughout the Civil War and the Protectorate varied very little from that of the sixteenth century. Until they left the care of their nurses and the study of their horn-books, they seldom saw either father or mother, who visited them ceremoniously and at rare intervals. At the age of seven or eight they ceased, as it were, to be unpresentable, and took part in the family meals as waiters, kneeling to offer certain dishes, and standing behind the chairs of hosts and guests in silent subservience. They attended prayers and followed the hunt without expecting to be noticed or spoken to, and were in their turn served by pages or waiting-women; so their lives became increasingly processional as they grew older. Then, trained by a group of tutors in languages, music, dancing and fencing, such boys as Charles and John Talbot emerged into adolescence, and entered the social scene. By the time they were grown up, the extreme formality, the rigid orderliness of this existence had made them into public figures. They sat, stood, walked or rode as if their portraits were being painted. In many families, especially large ones, these customs might be disregarded. This does not seem to have been the case with the young Talbots, whose half-sister Mary remained in the background. Until she reached the age of marriage she was negligible.

Meanwhile Charles, as the heir, received much more attention than his brother did. The Shrewsburys were in constant attendance at the Court of Charles II; and their elder son's deep attachment to his mother may be partly accounted for by his occasional frequentation of a circle in which she became notorious. Vaguely, uncomprehendingly, he saw her surrounded by admirers; what gossip he heard about her will never be known:

but the fact remains that her behaviour caused more talk than that of anyone but the King himself; and so he became aware of her reputation before he reached maturity.

When he was still in the nursery, the train of her lovers began with Colonel Thomas Howard, who was followed by Lord Arran, Henry Jermyn the younger, and Harry Killigrew. Jermyn and Howard fought a duel for her, in which Jermyn's second was killed. It was at about this time that the Comte de Gramont exclaimed, 'You would think that she received plenary absolution for everything she did! There are three or four gentlemen who wear each of them a yard of her tresses by way of bracelet—and nobody cares a pin.' He adds, rather contemptuously, that Lord Shrewsbury was 'too well bred to reproach his wife'. In fact, the rapidity with which one affair succeeded another seems to have forced him to accept the role of cuckold, until she became the mistress of the Duke of Buckingham, whose 'fatal amour' for her was so publicized as to destroy the remnants of her husband's tolerance. The scenes and quarrels described by Reresby during the Shrewsburys' stay in York reached a climax in London, when she decided to dismiss Killigrew for the Duke, to whom she, rather surprisingly, remained attached for nearly seven years. But Killigrew, a fire-eater, was not so easily eliminated. Sitting near her and Buckingham at the play, he shouted abuse at them, and struck Villiers on the head with the flat of his sword—upon which the Duke jumped out of his box, chased Killigrew across the theatre, and threw him down the steps on to the cobblestones. Killigrew was then imprisoned in the Fleet for brawling, emerging to apologize to his rival. Lady Shrewsbury, unappeased, ordered her lackeys to waylay and dispatch him, while she leant out of her coach to watch, urging them to 'kill the villain', whose valet they murdered. Left for dead, Killigrew recovered to bring an action against her, which he lost. According to the French Ambassador this incident caused Buckingham much 'worry and anxiety', and was followed by Francis Shrewsbury's sending the Duke the long-delayed challenge. This famous duel, in which the principals, their seconds and thirds engaged simultaneously, resulted in the slaughter of Buckingham's second, Jenkins, 'upon the place', according to Pepys, and finally the death of the Earl from his wounds on 16th March 1668. Eleven days later, Buckingham received a pardon.

8

The talk caused by this encounter lasted for years, and reached the new Earl in various forms, one being that his mother, dressed as a page, had watched the duel, and then spent the night with Buckingham, who pleasured her by wearing the shirt spattered with her husband's blood. In fact, the lovers' arrangements for the disposal of his father were less lurid and rather more sinister than these inventions. Having decided to get rid of Francis Shrewsbury, his wife goaded him into making the challenge on the assumption that Buckingham, a brilliant swordsman, would put an end to him. She then retired to France, where she remained for two months, before rejoining the Duke, with whom she set up house, and whose son she bore in the spring of 1671. Buckingham had him baptized as Earl of Coventry, and persuaded Charles II and Lord Shaftesbury to be his godfathers. (The King was always amused by impertinence, however tasteless, while Shaftesbury and the Duke were temporarily allied.) Five months later the child died, and was buried in the Villiers vault in Westminster Abbey.

By this time Charles Shrewsbury had been adopted by his uncle, Sir John Talbot, and put in the care of his grandfather, Lord Cardigan. But the story of his father's death, and the continued relationship of his mother and Buckingham, could not possibly have been hidden from him; it was further advertised by the Duke installing Lady Shrewsbury in the riverside palace of Cliveden, which he built for her at about this time; it was described by Evelyn as 'a romantic object . . . somewhat like Frascati', and only a little less magnificent than Windsor Castle. In the same year, the diarist noted that Buckingham continued 'in mighty favour' with the King, who allowed him to bring 'that impudent woman' to Newmarket, with a number of 'jolly blades, racing, dancing, feasting and revelling'. Lady Shrewsbury, as the established mistress of Charles II's chief minister, was then granted a yearly pension of 10,000 livres by Louis XIV.

Meanwhile, according to Gramont, 'Lady Shrewsbury and the Duke of Buckingham remained happy and undisturbed; never had she been so constant; never had he proved himself so tender and considerate a lover'. As her sons' guardians had separated them from her, she made no attempt to see them. Charles and John lived in the country, with either Lord Cardigan or Sir John Talbot, who were awaiting an opportunity to attack Buckingham, and conclude his relationship with their mother. This did not occur till the Cabal ministry ceased to exist, and the House of Commons asked Charles II to dismiss the Duke from his councils. In January 1674 the Lords were asked by Talbot and Cardigan to grant their petition against Buckingham on their elder ward's behalf. They charged him with 'the public debauchery of Lady Shrewsbury', the murder of her husband, and the christening and burial of their illegitimate child in the Abbey, adding that they would not have accused Villiers and his mistress 'if the offenders had employed the usual care to cover their guilt and shame'—a significant comment on current morality.

Supported by Shaftesbury from behind the scenes, Buckingham admitted his guilt, throwing himself on the mercy of the Lords, acknowledging 'the miserable and lewed life' he had led with his mistress, and describing his 'grief' for the 'accidental' death of her husband. He escaped impeachment by promising 'never more to cohabit with my Lady Shrewsbury', and he and she were ordered to sign a bond of £10,000 to that effect. This, and the fact that his expenditure had brought him to the verge of ruin, ended their relationship. She had no further use for a lover who had lost both fortune and position. Talbot and Cardigan then asked leave to send the fourteen-year-old Earl abroad to complete his education, and in May he came up to London, having obtained a pass 'to travel beyond the seas for seven years'. He outlined his preparations in a letter to Sir John Talbot.

Having become head of his house in his ninth year, the young man was well aware of his eminence as Earl of Shrewsbury, Wexford and Waterford, Baron Talbot and Hereditary High Steward of Ireland. His appearance on the continent must be sartorially faultless; he therefore wrote to his tailor in London for 'a handsome riding suit', and told his uncle, 'I have bespoke a periwig of my own periwig-maker, who lives within ten doors of you of the same side of the street.' (Sir John's house was in Long Acre.) '. . . Pray send for him to you, and let him know that I am grown above a handful since he saw me, and give him what other directions you please, for if he does not make me a very good one, I will not have it.' His letter ends with a disturbing and ominous sentence. 'I am very sorry that my mother has changed her resolution.'

For Lady Shrewsbury was now about to begin a new course of

life. She had had enough of bloodshed, adultery and ill fame, and was determined on respectability. This could only be achieved by showing herself as a perfect mother and a devout Catholic. At some point between Buckingham's disgrace and Shrewsbury's guardians' arrangements for his tour, she had managed to re-enter his life, and conjure up his devotion and loyalty to herself. This may not have been a difficult or lengthy process; a woman who had charmed so many would have found it easy to entrance an affectionate and chivalrous boy in his teens, and even to convince him that she had been the victim of other people's violence, as also of the jealous censure unjustly meted out by gossip and scandal-mongers.

She was still, at this time, very beautiful; and the resemblance between her and Shrewsbury is striking. Both have a dreamy, voluptuous air, large eyes, delicate colouring and full mouths; the difference lies in his gentle serenity of expression and her look of contemptuous insolence. Her hold over him, and its later, disastrous effects are best illustrated by Buckingham's scribbled comments on her moods. The entries about her in his Common-place Book are curiously revealing. She tortured him; but his remarks also show that when she wished, she could be—as in her son's case—irresistible; and her portrait in one of her famous rose-coloured gowns demonstrates this rather specialized allure.

'You are in everything a goddess,' Villiers wrote, 'but that you will not be moved by prayer,' presumably when his court-ship of her began. After the duel, when Lady Shrewsbury chose to go through the motions of a broken-hearted widow, he observes, 'She weeps and beats herself; aye, she need strike the rock to get water out of it.' And yet—'Her sadness became her so well that it bred delight in everybody else.' His comment on her desertion shows the uselessness of his pleading. ' 'Tis not your tears will keep you from love, fishes that live in water feel that fire.' And finally—'You must water your life well, if you would have it grow again . . . Such a woman was made to punish man, and the Devil to punish such a woman.' Lady Shrewsbury did not mean to punish her elder son; she crippled him, never-theless. Shrewsbury seems to have counted on her joining him in Paris; her decision not to do so was a great disappointment.

Accompanied by two footmen, a valet, and a tutor, Mr James

Morgan, he reached Paris by way of Margate, Dieppe and Rouen in June 1674. Morgan reported on his progress in a manner that fully reveals his own status and the relationship between them. In the eighteenth century, the tutor would have been allowed to join his employers at their meals, provided he left the table before the pudding was served; in the seventeenth, such persons ate below stairs, with the house steward and the chaplain. Now, in sole charge of a youth accustomed to subservience from all but his guardians, Morgan's position was that of an equerry, or an aide-de-camp. He could suggest—even, if tactfully, direct; he had no power to command: and in no circumstances must he criticize, however mildly. So today his letters seem sycophantic to the point of self-abasement; it could not be otherwise. He endured a rough crossing; but his account of it centres on Shrewsbury's immunity from seasickness—and on his first voyage too: 'His Lordship was so well in health,' he tells Sir John Talbot, 'that one may believe he was rather designed to become an admiral at sea than to be esteemed a passenger.' At Rouen, 'His Lordship spent two days in visiting what that town could afford worth his curiosity.' And when they reached Paris, and inspected Navarre College, where Shrewsbury had been entered as a resident pupil, the boy had only to say, 'I do not want to be shut up in the walls of it', for Morgan to set about finding lodgings in the Faubourg St Germains.

As the resultant expenditure had not been allowed for, Morgan found himself short of funds. 'Had his Lordship . . . brought a letter of credit along with him,' he writes, 'we should not then have been at that inconvenience for money.' Otherwise, everything was going according to plan. The English Ambassador had hurried to wait on the Earl, together with a number of other expatriate notables. But 'we shall scarcely compass all things under less than a hundred pounds.'

The money arrived, and Shrewsbury began on his studies. In October he caught smallpox. Morgan then hastened to assure his employers that the attack was so mild that 'Mr Arden [Shrewsbury's bodyservant] and I are far from being alarmed.' A doctor and a male nurse had been engaged, and their patient continued 'merry and well', owing, Morgan thought, 'to the weather and the declining of the moon', and also the spots coming out 'so kindly'.

In May of the following year Lady Shrewsbury insisted on joining her son, in the face of his uncle's objections. Her claims as a mother having overriden his efforts to separate them, she, Lord Cardigan and her step-daughter carried Shrewsbury off to Pontoise, where they remained for several weeks. This reunion caused something of a sensation in England. 'In Shrewsbury we find,' wrote a ballad-monger, 'A generous mind, So kindly to live with his mother'—while the Earl found it necessary to reassure Sir John. Her ladyship, he wrote, had altogether changed her way of life, which gave 'very good content to my friends'. Not only so; she had visited the convent of Maubuisson, of which Princess Louise, Prince Rupert's sister, was the Abbess, 'where she did see that virtuous lady's austere way of living, which did work very much upon her'.

In fact Lady Shrewsbury had made her plans, of which the basis was readmittance to the Court of Charles II. As one responsible for the deaths of four men—Killigrew's valet, Buckingham's and Jermyn's seconds, and her own husband—she faced what looked like a hard task; but it was by no means insurmountable. With cool efficiency, and the growing reputation of a kind step-mother and a devoted mother, she set about the first move in her campaign. Sir John Talbot may have been enraged; but in view of Lord Cardigan's chaperonage of his daughter, there was nothing he could do.

Lady Shrewsbury returned to Paris with her son, sharing his lodgings for a week. She could not of course be received by Louis XIV—as Shrewsbury noted—but she provided distraction by arranging a visit to Versailles for them both. They were taken round by an old friend of the Stuart family, the Abbé Walter Montagu (known as 'Wat Mot' by Charles II) who, Shrewsbury reported, showed them 'the house and the waterworks there, which, by his interest, he got to play for us'. She then returned to the very mild austerities of Maubuisson, 'and I do not,' Shrewsbury added, 'hear anything of her leaving it, or her return for England.' In short, Sir John was not to worry.

Yet he did. 'You complain,' his nephew wrote, ' "why might I not know of your journey out of Paris?" I do assure you . . . I designed waiting upon my mother no further than Pontoise.' It was not until January 1676 that Lady Shrewsbury made her next move; all this time, she had remained at Maubuisson (her father

having gone back to England) attended by her stepdaughter and
her waiting-women, much as a lady in the nineteenth century
would have stayed at a quiet country hotel. If Shrewsbury
visited her regularly, he said nothing of it to his uncle; he did
mention his presence at a *prise d'habit*, which was attended by a
number of English guests.

His next letter indicates the opening of his mother's offensive.
This must be inaugurated by Charles II's leave for her to appear
at Court, and by her being allowed to kiss Queen Catherine's
hand. The Abbé Montagu, allying himself with Shrewsbury, was
now her adviser on tactics. As the latter was not of age, the whole
Talbot family must support his request for his mother's return.
The Queen, informed of her approach, refused to consider it.
She would never, no matter what pressure was used, permit such
a creature to come near her. At her husband's command, she had
had to put up with Lady Castlemaine, Louise de Kéroualle, and
several others. The reception of a murderess was unthinkable.

Shrewsbury was better informed about the obstacles facing his
mother than Montagu, whose ignorance of English affairs made
him almost useless. The Earl first got in touch with Arlington, to
whom he wrote that he was 'highly satisfied' with Lady Shrewsbury's conduct during her stay at Maubuisson, adding that his
uncles and his grandfather would be 'highly obliged' by the
Secretary's help—for they also, in view of the family honour,
wanted to see her reinstated. 'She is the only lady of quality that
is restrained from paying her duty to Her Majesty,' he went on,
subjoining his mother's promise that, having obtained her
entrée, she would not offend Queen Catherine by frequent
appearances at Court; all she desired was to 'wash out the
particular blot that lay upon her'. Montagu then halted Shrewsbury's negotiations by giving him a letter to Arlington, which
he must copy 'against next post—and I', he said, 'will come and
call for it'. This 'good man', as Shrewsbury rather contemptuously called him, believed that 'there was no other difficulty',
until he was disillusioned by Lady Shrewsbury herself, now in
almost daily communication with the Talbot family, while they
worked on the Queen through Arlington. Finally, Charles II's
'absolute command' to his wife to receive her ladyship concluded
the struggle, and in the spring of 1676 she and her stepdaughter
returned to England. Her next plan, that of consolidating her

position as a respectable person, was concealed both from the Talbots and from her son.

Meanwhile Sir John had been making arrangements for his nephew's marriage. An alliance with the eldest daughter of Lord Northampton was put before him in March 1676, and he was ordered to arrive in England in twelve days' time, to become acquainted with, and ask for the hand of, this eminently suitable young lady. He was to stay a month, having first fitted himself out with new suits, linen, periwigs, hats, gloves and boots; and his footmen must be provided with new liveries. Then, agreement having been reached between his guardians and the Northamptons, he could resume his studies in Paris.

These peremptory orders threw Shrewsbury into a frenzy of irritation. His long letter of protest is one of the most revealing he ever wrote. At sixteen, he was settled in a way of life—luxurious, interesting, pleasurable—which perfectly suited him. To be told to abandon it for a month's visit, during which he must submit to an undesired betrothal, was intolerable. He began by objecting to 'the drudgery of a troublesome journey to and fro', (and in Lent too!) and angrily continued, 'Although it is necessary I should have a view of the young lady, yet I cannot see the necessity of this particular time . . . It is an easy thing to give orders; those that comply only find the inconveniences', i.e. 'a nasty packet-boat' instead of 'a commodious yacht'. And then, having arrived, 'a month's time is very short to enjoying my mother and my sister', quite apart from the interruption to his studies.

Nevertheless, Shrewsbury was preparing to obey his uncle. Of his two principal complaints one, the difficulty of obtaining a periwig from Chedreux (and no other wig-maker could be considered) was fully described. 'Under ten or twelve [days] Chedreux will not undertake to make a periwig—and it is a great favour if he keeps his word.' His innermost shrinking was from the prospect of marriage. If he had to inspect the dreaded object, he told Sir John, it should be privately, and Lord Northampton 'must be ready to contrive things' to that end. In no circumstances would he be committed, or consent to appear as a suitor. So began Shrewsbury's long battle against matrimony—of which the cause is only too obvious. He sustained it for twenty-nine years, yielding, suddenly and mysteriously, at the age of forty-five.

His next extant letter, written in October 1676, came from Paris, and concerned the hiring of a coach, bearing his crown and arms ('and the coachman wears my livery') about which he desired Sir John's advice. Should he buy a new one? 'I would rather undergo the charge, than do a thing below myself.' Eventually, he bought both coach and horses, and, thus equipped, started on a round of calls, the first being on Lord Berkeley, Ambassador to the Court of Louis XIV.

On his way into the Embassy Shrewsbury met the Duke of Somerset, who had been deeply affronted, he said, by the manner of Berkeley's reception; for the Ambassador had not only remained seated, but kept on his hat during their interview. Somerset, known as 'the proud Duke', and later famous for his public defiance of James II, reinforced Shrewsbury's awareness of his own position by this complaint. As soon as he entered, the young man took a chair, and kept on his hat in the face of Berkeley's indignation. His discourtesy was justified, he pointed out, by the fact that in England his titles gave him precedence over the Ambassador.

This seemingly unattractive gesture was not then censurable, but rather the reverse. In the eyes of Shrewsbury's contemporaries, maintenance of the hierarchic tradition had always been a duty—one of the responsibilities of rank. Berkeley had betrayed that tradition by improper behaviour; and Shrewsbury's demonstration showed that, young though he was, he knew his place, and had been taught to set an example. (In the same way, Somerset found fault with his Duchess's manners when she ventured to tap him on the arm with her fan at a reception. 'Madam,' he said, 'my first wife was a Percy, and she would never have dared to take such a liberty.') These formalities were the basis of the social order in the seventeenth century; to ignore them was as shocking as to observe them would be today. In maturity Shrewsbury was noted for a gentleness that grew from his early self-assertion. He could then afford to give way, because he did so from an impregnable height. So the picture of a boy of sixteen being insolent to a man nearly three times his age is historically incorrect.

The consequences of his mother's reception at Court were unexpectedly wounding. 'I cannot choose but wonder,' he wrote to Sir John Talbot, 'it was so secretly carried on, that I should not hear of it till 'twas done.' In fact Lady Shrewsbury, having

8*

achieved her object, ceased to concern herself about the son who had helped her to do so. During the next two years she wrote to him only once: and then, it was, 'in three words, to tell me she was married, and that not till six weeks after she owned it in Town'. Her choice of husband, a Mr Rodney Bridges, enraged her family, partly because she bought him a place as Gentleman of the Bedchamber for £4,500, without asking her father's leave.

Shrewsbury's reception of this news, and of her split with the Talbots, was surprisingly cool; for now, in March 1678, he had the prospect of joining Charles II's threatened invasion of the Low Countries, with the Dutch, against France. The Duke of York had sent for him, 'which', he told Sir John, '. . . I embrace with as much joy and content as can be'—but he was rather disappointed that war had not yet been declared. Meanwhile, he went forward with his preparations.

He was in the highest spirits, not only because of his hopes of military glory; for Sir John's second attempt at arranging a marriage for him had fallen through. Shrewsbury's joking reference to the wearing of 'a willow garland for the loss of a mistress' is followed by his plans for new liveries, which Sir John was to choose for him in London. 'I most incline to blue', he wrote, 'because red is too near the King . . . Pink is not so common, but it does not wear well, nor last long handsome.' The trappings of the led horses must also be blue, lined with orange. He added, 'The colours for the embroidery I leave to your fancy'—and again, more emphatically, 'I do not fancy pink.'

Such trivialities as these may provide a certain significance— one that can only be conjectured, and then, perhaps, discarded. The rose-pink of the gown worn by Lady Shrewsbury in Lely's marriage portrait that must have been very familiar to her son was, gossip reported, her favourite colour, as attar of roses was her preferred scent. And another, unauthenticated story describes Shrewsbury's inability, in later life, to endure the smell of roses, which brought on faintness and nausea. But as he often suffered from various incapacitating symptoms, the connection cannot be proved; if it existed at all, it may have been a sign of the sensitivity disregarded by the faculty of his day. Yet the circulation of such a legend is worth recording because it lights up, although uncertainly, the current view of Lady Shrewsbury's effect on him, and of the relationship which helped to mould his character, with its otherwise inexplicable deviations. Shrewsbury became what is now called a neurotic; his reiterated dislike of a fashionable colour—rose-pink was constantly worn by both sexes at the Court of Charles II—deserves a brief consideration, in spite of his rejecting it on practical grounds.

Shrewsbury's most immediate concern was with his grandfather's attitude towards his becoming a soldier. 'I believe,' he told Sir John, 'he designed me an idle life in England, as secure from danger as from honour.' When leave came for him to go, he hurried to London, and thence to Flanders; but in June 1678 he was still waiting to be actively employed. He then joined Marshal Schomberg's staff, only to find that peace between Louis XIV and Charles II was being arranged, and so returned to England, remaining in one of his country houses till the autumn.

He was now eighteen. His education had come to an end, and he had nothing to do but enjoy himself; for his estates were administered by agents and stewards. So he decided to settle in London, and enter the world of fashion. As a reputation for gallantry had preceded him, his uncle sent him a letter of warning, to which he replied, 'I know not what you mean . . . where you mention my sitting up nights and playing hide and seek. [This last is presumably a euphemism for some more exciting activity.] I have often done both . . . but I suppose, whatever it is, it has lost nothing in the telling. I am glad I pass among the women for a silent young man, it being . . . more advantageous than what commonly their sex can challenge.'

Silent or otherwise, Shrewsbury's success at Court was undeniable. His fluency in French and Italian, his knowledge of literature, his engaging manners, and his range of accomplishments were all that could be desired. But he himself was not satisfied: for his hopes were set on a career. He then found that his religion disqualified him from any kind of post, the more especially because both Court and city were now immersed in the violent intricacies of the Popish Plot. No Catholic, however talented and highly placed, had a chance to compete. Shrewsbury could neither sit in the House of Lords, nor obtain a commission in the army, nor became the protégé of a minister. The only alternative was a life of pleasure, on which he embarked readily enough; but it was not what he really wanted. While accepting the old faith without question, he had not the religious temperament; and his years in a Catholic country had created a certain detachment from such matters. Between 1678 and 1679 he began to take in the ₁English attitude towards 'popery', and to consider the rights and wrongs of the present situation. He was—ancestrally, as it were—a patriot; and the perfect patriot must now, it seemed, help to protect the Church of England from her enemies; only so could he serve his country according to the traditions of his family.

To apostasize was a very serious matter; and as soon as it was rumoured that this highly desirable young man had been debating the question, Bishop Tillotson approached him. Their discussions were deep and prolonged, for Shrewsbury would not lightly abjure the beliefs in which he had been educated. He must hear both sides; and so, having absorbed the Bishop's explanations, he put the case to his grandfather—who was horrified, and replied as became a Catholic of the old régime. Shrewsbury then reported back to Tillotson, and after further consideration decided on Protestantism. But the Bishop did not think that he was in a fit state to be received; for he had become something of a libertine, and was keeping a mistress when he should have been getting married. As this lady, whose name has not survived, was not in Court circles, Tillotson simply referred to her as a 'connection', which Shrewsbury must abandon. 'I am more concerned,' he wrote, 'that you should be a good and virtuous man than a good Protestant,' and added that certain stories about his pupil's habits had much distressed him. Finally, he consented to receive the Earl into the Anglican Church in May 1679. Yet Shrewsbury's popularity with women—and presumably his use of it—so continued that he was known as the King of Hearts, a soubriquet he retained for the rest of his life. Bishop Burnet, who became devoted to him a few years later, summed up the situation with his usual shrewdness. 'He had been bred a papist,' he says, 'but had forsaken that religion upon a very critical and anxious enquiry into matters of controversy . . . Though he had forsaken popery, he was too sceptical, and too little fixed in the points of religion . . . It is not so easy for me to affirm that he became a hearty Protestant . . . As to all other things, he is the worthiest man I know.'

Having achieved the right to enter the political scene, Shrewsbury inclined towards the Court Party; for he could not affiliate himself with the Country Party, which was partially directed by the murderer of his father. Then all his hopes of distinction in this field were destroyed by a crippling disaster, the worst he ever endured. In January 1680 he contracted a disease of the eyes, losing the sight of the left one altogether, while that on the right was threatened with the same infection. The left eye was removed; the other recovered. Eventually he found that he could read and write as well with one eye as with two; but for some time the shock incapacitated him. He sat in the Parliaments of October 1680 and May 1681, was nominated Gentleman of the Bedchamber, and made Lord-Lieutenant of Staffordshire; yet he took no part in national affairs.

By February 1685 he had regained his health, and was ready for action, when the death of Charles II and the accession of a Catholic monarch destroyed all his prospects; for Shrewsbury was not only a Protestant, but also—far worse—an apostate. Everything he had hoped to do now vanished: or so it seemed. Rank, riches, talents, popularity, were of no avail. A future of endless monotony, interspersed with a few minor duties, lay ahead. At the outset of his career he was condemned to the idle life he had always despised.

2

If James II had not succeeded in driving the English people into the panic-stricken revolt that became known as the Glorious Revolution, Shrewsbury's executive genius might have been wasted on local business, and he would have remained a courtier of no great importance. As it was, the King's policy pitchforked this young man into fame; and so, over a period of some thirty years, an accumulation of honours came to him, sometimes against his will; for while many of his contemporaries intrigued, and even paid, for powers and places, Shrewsbury received them without having to compete: and more than once he sank under the burdens thus imposed. During four reigns he became, at different times, Lord-Lieutenant of twelve counties, Principal Secretary of State, Lord Justice of England, Lord Chamberlain, Privy Councillor, Ambassador to the Court of Versailles, Viceroy of Ireland, High Treasurer of Great Britain, Groom of the Stole, Lord Privy Purse, Marquess of Alton, Knight of the Garter and Duke of Shrewsbury. He sustained these positions and the work they entailed conscientiously and well, complaining often, and, some felt, unjustifiably. That aspect of his administration is not easily defined. His weaknesses were as mysterious as his strengths, and the two were inextricably intermingled. His withdrawals irritated and bewildered both his employers and their dependants; yet he never lost the esteem or the trust of those he inconvenienced by attacks of ill-health that defied diagnosis.

Shrewsbury carried the sword of mercy in the coronation procession, and in the spring of 1685 received a second Lord-Lieutenancy, that of Worcestershire. His position as a servant of the Crown was further improved by Monmouth's invasion, when he raised a troop of horse for the King, although it was not used during the rising. Once more, he fell back into inactivity, while observing James's first efforts to invalidate the laws penalizing Catholics by his illegal Declaration of Indulgence. Although this included freedom of worship for Dissenters, that

sect could neither trust nor rally to a sovereign who had perse-
cuted them both before and after the Western rebellion.

In February 1686 personal tragedy overtook Shrewsbury,
as if to recall his father's murder. His brother John was killed
in a duel by the Duke of Grafton, eldest son of Lady Castlemaine
and Charles II. No details as to the challenge or its cause survive;
and nothing is known of John Talbot's character. In a single
reference to this event he is described as Jack, or Jake, Talbot
—perhaps in denigration—while a street ballad criticizes Shrewsbury for not revenging him by challenging Grafton, irrespective
of the fact that a one-eyed man is barred from duelling. In any
case, to challenge the late King's bastard might have got Shrewsbury into serious trouble; for James II looked on Grafton—
a coarse, violent youth—as one of his chief supporters in his
pro-Catholic campaign. (Here, as so often, he was completely
deceived; for the Duke made no secret of his total indifference
to the religious issue.) So now Shrewsbury stood alone; it was
high time, people said, that he got married and founded a family.
His half-sister Mary had married; but she had no children.

In the following year Shrewsbury, with other Lord-Lieutenants,
was commanded by James to tour his counties, in order to promote Catholic civil and military powers, and to report on the
results of his progress. He refused to break the law. Two months
later, he was deprived of his lieutenancies and of his commission
in the army.

These penalties, and the general resentment, rising to fury,
caused by the King's determination to institute a Catholic
régime independent of Parliament (inadequately masked by his
subscribing to the support of the Huguenot refugees) turned
Shrewsbury towards the Whigs. He became a valuable member
of that party, sat on their committees, and convinced the most
sceptical, not only of his loyalty, but also of his effectiveness,
first as an organizer, and then as a conspirator. He was soon to
become a hero; meanwhile, he watched James's increasingly
rapid progress to disaster in growing disgust and alarm. He
may not have wanted to be a rebel; but he was not going to
be bullied or bribed into subservience. His innate horror of
tyranny sprang less from concern for the national faith than
from the proud independence that in his teens had caused him
to disobey his guardians and defy the pretension of older men.

Also, his great wealth combined with his ancient name to protect him from the King's vengeance. Deprivation of places and favours did not seriously affect him; for he was not, in a material sense, ambitious.

Four major events—the Revocation of the Edict of Nantes, the expulsion of the Fellows of Magdalen, the trial of the Seven Bishops, and the birth of the Prince of Wales—had now resulted in the determination of Whigs and Tories to unite in calling on William of Orange to help them establish a new Government, and to rescue, as they put it, the Protestant religion. That they were already in communication with William and Mary is shown by Shrewsbury's letter of May 1687 to the Prince; this had been caused by the Whig party's conferences with Dykveldt, the Dutch diplomat sent over to report on the English situation. As Shrewsbury had not then met William, he began by apologizing for his approach. 'Though I hope you have a great many servants and friends in this place,' he went on, 'yet there is not one more entirely and faithfully so than myself . . . The great and only consolation that we have left is, that you are so generous to countenance us in our misfortune . . . Your commands is the rule I have set myself to conduct the rest of my life . . . They shall be obeyed with that duty that becomes, Sir, Your Highness's most humble and most obedient servant.' Three months later, Shrewsbury visited The Hague with a letter of introduction from Halifax, who wrote of him as 'the most considerable man of quality that is growing up amongst us'.

William was deeply impressed by Shrewsbury; their first meeting formed the basis of a friendship that endured for the next thirteen years. Dr Burnet, who had been living at The Hague since 1684, was equally taken with him. 'He seemed to be a man of great probity, and to have a high sense of honour. He had no ordinary measure of learning,' Burnet went on, and then described one of the principal reasons for Shrewsbury's success, which was, 'a sweetness of temper that charmed all who knew him.' Later, he added that the Earl's 'silent and reserved answers' were sometimes disappointing. Nevertheless, Shrewsbury's 'modest deportment gave him such an interest in the Prince that he [William] never seemed so fond of any of his ministers as he was of him'.

'Personal charm' is now a phrase so loosely used as to have

become meaningless. In Shrewsbury's case, the difference between his approach and that of his contemporaries partly accounts for the fascination he exercised over nearly everyone he met; he was known as the King of Hearts, not only for his effect on women, but also because his manners were not those of his day, nor of the group to which he belonged.

The brutal freedom of speech, the coarse insensitivity of most seventeenth-century patricians, was taken for granted by all but a few; and of those few William of Orange was one. He himself could be blunt and uncompromising when the occasion required; but he disliked the bold yet insinuating address of the English aristocracy, because he rightly suspected that it concealed a self-seeking, arrogant attitude that was basically hostile. Only with such statesmen as Sir William Temple, whose social standards were those of an earlier, pre-Restoration day, could he be at ease; and Shrewsbury's instinctive—and very rare—consideration for other people's feelings was combined with a reserve that was equally appealing to anyone of a highly strung temperament.

Shrewsbury's gentleness, allied to his resolution, intelligence and daring—for as the messenger of the conspirators, he risked a charge of high treason—had an immediate effect on the Prince, the more especially because the Earl's self-confidence, once so arbitrarily demonstrated, was immensely reassuring. In short, he seemed to represent all that was best in the English ruling class. The outstanding characteristics of his coadjutors—Halifax's satirical brilliance, Danby's harsh forcefulness, the slightly synthetic ferocity of Admiral Russell, the pomposity of Nottingham—were to strike a jarring note at William's Councils, to which Shrewsbury did not contribute. The natural modesty observed by Burnet underlay all the suggestions, and informed his advice; and yet both sprang from a quick response to the changing aspect, not only of the English, but of the European scene. For in the summer of 1688 one complication succeeded another so rapidly as to require an adaptability of which the older nobles were not always capable. Shrewsbury's grasp of events was not invariably faultless; but it remained that of a shrewd and honest young man, who pleased without using flattery, and knew when to keep his mouth shut. (The other conspirators, like most English people, then and now, were exhaustingly verbose.) Shrewsbury's sympathetic response to those confiding in him exercised a spell which isolated him from the men he worked with; later on, he had to pay a high price for that isolation.

During the secret negotiations that lasted from the spring of 1687 to the summer of 1688, William of Orange made it clear that the support of a number of leading men must be guaranteed before he went on with his preparations. This produced the formal request for his help from those later known as the Immortal Seven, of whom five were Whigs; Shrewsbury, Devonshire, Admiral Russell (cousin of Lord William Russell, executed in 1683), Lord Lumley (formerly a Catholic) and Henry Sidney. The Tories were represented by Danby, while Bishop Compton signed for the Church of England. Efforts had been made to recruit Halifax and Nottingham, but without success. On 31st June the conspirators, having signed this document in code, assured the Prince that his forces would be joined by the greater part of the English army and navy, together with the principal landowners, who, with their tenants, would hurry to his side wherever he chose to appear.

Shrewsbury, who, with other peers, had offered to stand bail for the Seven Bishops and attended their trial, then informed William, 'If the violence of my wishes do not deceive me, I flatter myself you never had more friends in England than now.' In September 1688 he and Russell arrived at The Hague with further suggestions; Shrewsbury brought with him £12,000 in cash, which he placed in the Bank of Amsterdam. He then, with Burnet's help, revised the Declaration which William was to issue on his appearance in England, and remained at The Hague till, with Russell and Burnet, he sailed in the Prince's ship on 31st October. During those last weeks his influence over William had increased; the Prince began to rely on him as on no other Englishman.

William's fleet landed at Torbay on 5th November—Guy Fawkes' Day, the day after his thirty-eighth birthday—after several setbacks, including the loss of five hundred horses. Indeed, at one point, storms and contrary winds had threatened the total failure of the expedition, and Russell was heard saying to Burnet, 'You may go to prayers, Doctor—all is over.' William's triumphant progress from Brixham to Newton Abbot was halted so that his Declaration might be read to the people; in this, he announced that he had not come to conquer England; all he intended was the establishment of a free and legal Parliament, whose decisions he promised to support. As soon as the disturbance had died down, his troops would be sent home.

William entered Exeter in state on 11th November. Here he halted again, expecting to be joined by the local magnates. None came. Meanwhile, James II, at the head of a large army (30,000, as opposed to his nephew's 10,000 men) was preparing to advance from Salisbury.

Disgusted, enraged, the Prince summoned his staff, and told them that he was going to return to Torbay and re-embark. 'I have been betrayed,' he said. He seems to have disregarded the assurances and pleadings of Russell and Burnet. Then Shrewsbury intervened. 'The great difficulty,' he began, 'is, who shall run the hazard of being the first. If the ice is once broken, they will be as much afraid of being the last.' Eventually he persuaded William, much against his inclination, to wait a little longer. Twenty-four hours later, a squire from Crediton appeared; he was followed by several other landowners—including the Marquess of Bath—with troops of horse. Shrewsbury then formed them into a special association.

So the situation was saved by the youngest of the Immortal Seven. Only he could have prevailed on William—who was not a man to make empty threats—to change his mind. Thenceforward, their relationship became closer than ever, and Shrewsbury's responsibilities weighed on him more heavily; for he did not feel himself equal to all he was expected to do; nor was he in agreement with the extremist section of the Whig party, who chose to forget what his persuasions had done for their cause. None of them, then or later, remembered that they would have been left to James's vengeance if Shrewsbury had not prevented William's withdrawal; and their Glorious Revolution might have resulted in another Civil War.

As Bristol was the second most important English city, William decided that Shrewsbury should declare for him there, while he himself proceeded towards Sherborne. With a small body of troops, Shrewsbury entered, was acclaimed and made Governor. On 7th December he received orders from William to join him at Hungerford.

By the time he arrived, the whole pattern of the administration had changed. James, deserted by the principal members of his staff, had gone back to London, and from there had sent three Commissioners, Halifax, Nottingham and Godolphin, to negotiate with William, who withdrew to a manor-house near by, so that Whigs and Tories could make their arrangements independently of his jurisdiction. He had determined to remain neutral—while preserving a silence that surprised and daunted both parties —till the time came for their decisions to be submitted to his. And his, long worked out, would be paramount and unalterable. He knew, although the English did not, that James II could be relied on to betray them.

The meeting in the hall of the principal inn had a surface amiability; both sides seemed ready to work together. Only Shrewsbury was aware of the hatred recently arisen between the two chief Tories, Danby and Nottingham, which had been caused by Nottingham's vacillation about joining the Immortal Seven. He had agreed to sign, and then drawn back. This so alarmed Danby—for he feared that Nottingham would betray them to the King—that he had said to Shrewsbury, 'Things are brought to a short point—either Lord Nottingham or we must die. He can be shot on the Kensington road, which I will undertake to do in such a manner that it will appear to have been done by highwaymen.' Shrewsbury made no recorded reply to this proposal, which he repeated to Burnet; now, he hoped to mediate between Whigs and Tories by supporting the latter, who were in a minority.

Halifax, speaking for the Commissioners, then said that James had agreed to free Parliament, the dismissal of all Catholics from office, retention of the Test Act, and a pardon to those who had gone over to his nephew. The King had, of course, no intention of keeping these promises; but the Commissioners believed that he would be forced to do so.

These concessions, which would have transformed James's position into that of a constitutional ruler, did not please the Whigs, for they could no longer trust him. They said that he should abdicate in favour of the Princess Mary; when the vote was taken, Shrewsbury sided with the Tories. Meanwhile, James was confiding in the French Ambassador. 'This negotiation,' he said, 'is a mere feint. I must send Commissioners to my nephew that I may gain time to ship off the Queen and the Prince of Wales,' adding that Parliament, if called, 'would impose on me conditions that I could not endure.'

On 9th December the Commissioners, dining with the Prince of Orange, were empowered by him to accept his uncle's concessions. To Burnet, Halifax suggested, 'If the King were to go away?' 'There is nothing so much to be wished,' was the answer. William then repeated that he was leaving all arrangements to Parliament, and agreed on an armistice, to the great disappointment of the Whigs. On the 10th James received, by courier, the terms of the armistice, approved them, and publicly announced, on the word of a king, that he would remain to govern England according to the new decrees. At one o'clock in the morning of the next day he left for France, but was held up, manhandled and robbed by a group of fishermen. Rescued by some local noblemen, he returned to London on the 16th, to the intense annoyance of his nephew, who was now established at Windsor. Here again, William retired from the discussions, headed by Halifax, as to what should be done with the King, whose palace was surrounded by the Prince's troops and mobs bawling out Wharton's *Lillibulero*. ('I have sung him out of three kingdoms,' that nobleman used to say.) It was then agreed that James should go to Ham House, and William ordered Halifax, Shrewsbury and Lord Delamere to take this message to him. They reached Whitehall at midnight, to be told that His Majesty was asleep. 'He must be woken,' said Halifax, and they were shown into his bed-chamber. After some further discussion, it was settled that James, who objected to Ham House as being too damp, should be escorted to Rochester. From there, it was hoped and believed that he would escape. He himself was in tears. Halifax and Delamere remained coolly detached, while Shrewsbury tried to soothe and comfort him. 'He always,' James said afterwards, 'treated me gentlemanlike.' A few days later, to the relief of all but a few, he left his kingdom for the last time.

Shrewsbury did not contribute to the lengthy and complicated discussions in Parliament as to whether James had abdicated or deserted, or to the question of his successor, or to that of a regency—by William, for Mary as Queen Regnant. These continued till 31st January 1689. And then, at last, William broke the most disconcerting of his silences.

Sending for Shrewsbury, Danby and Halifax, he outlined his intentions in the characteristically 'cold and unconcerned manner' that always baffled the older men—now, more than ever; for they had counted on ruling the country through his wife. 'It is for Parliament,' he began, 'to decide for a regency. But I will not be that regent. Nor will I administer the kingdom under the Princess. I esteem her as much as it is possible for a man to esteem a woman, but I cannot submit to be tied to the apron-strings of the best of wives. If the Estates offer me the crown for life, I will accept it. If not, I will, without repining, return to Holland, and meddle no more in your affairs.'

The three Lords, withdrawing for further consultation with their compeers, finally agreed on the joint rule of William and Mary. On 11th February the Princess arrived in England, and on the 13th she and the Prince were offered and accepted their crowns.

A month later, Shrewsbury carried the curtana at the coronation, for the second time in four years. He had already been made a member of the Privy Council, and Secretary of State for the North (this included Ireland) and was partnered by Nottingham, as Secretary of State for the South. The combination was not a happy one for Shrewsbury, because Nottingham, a high Tory and a strict Anglican, was not attuned to the new régime, and also out of sympathy with his junior; yet he remained loyal to William and Mary, and distrusted (with some reason) the other Ministers. Of these, Danby became Marquess of Caermarthen, Mordaunt (a firebrand and an exhibitionist) Earl of Monmouth, and Bentinck Earl of Portland. Churchill, with whom Shrewsbury formed a close attachment, was already Earl of Marlborough, Admiral Herbert, a highly unreliable character, was created Lord Torrington, and Henry Sidney became Lord Romney.*

Both Nottingham and the Spanish Ambassador thought that Shrewsbury was too young and inexperienced to be thus promoted; and very soon he himself began to feel that he was not suited to the responsibilities laid upon him. At this time, he seems not to have been fully aware of the vast range of William's schemes for a European settlement, in which England's role

* To avoid confusion, all these persons but Marlborough will henceforth be referred to by their original titles.

was to be the principal but by no means the only factor. He needed his new kingdom, because he intended to use it against what he rightly saw as Louis XIV's determination to dominate Spain, the Low Countries, the United Provinces, Germany and Austria—and, if need be, to dictate terms to the Vatican. William's resistance to French aggression had begun twenty years ago, when Shrewsbury, a boy in his teens, was far removed from continental politics. Some time passed before he was able to see the plan as the King saw it, or to understand that it was in the nature of a crusade, aiming at the destruction of an archaic and monstrous tyranny. Now, Shrewsbury found himself faced with problems he had never really visualized; and the first symptoms of the disease that afflicted him for nearly thirty years—from which William also suffered—were creeping up on him and shadowing his daily life.

When Halifax spoke to Sir John Reresby of the King's 'consumptive distemper', he had of course no idea either of the nature or of the early effects of tuberculous infection. In Shrewsbury's case, these took the form of what seemed to his contemporaries a neurotic obsession over trifles, and a feverish shrinking from duty, both described, as late as the mid-nineteenth century, as 'unmanly', and therefore contemptible. He could not accept the fact that he was bound to make mistakes, and assumed that, if he did, they would be fatal. Never having had to endure the gruelling routine of office work, of issuing orders, or of dealing with a huge correspondence, he told William that he was unfit, in every sense, for the post of Secretary, and asked to be released. The King replied sympathetically, and in such reassuring terms as temporarily to soothe Shrewsbury's nervous agitation.

It was at about this time that a friend of the Earl's, Lord Ailesbury, whose Jacobitism eventually resulted in his permanent exile, came to call for him for a trip into the country, just as a bursting letter-bag was delivered. Ailesbury, assuming that their expedition must now be cancelled, prepared to withdraw. 'What is to hinder us?' Shrewsbury said, and explained that his clerks made précis of his correspondence, 'on which I draw what answers are requisite, and set my hand to them—and that is all I do'. Ailesbury, reporting this incident some forty years later, wilfully misunderstood Shrewbury's methods, which in fact were those used by all the ministers of his day, as is shown by Sir William Temple's advice to his son, when that young man took office. Far from being negligent or lazy, Shrewsbury was over-conscientious, and therefore exhausted himself; and his fear of fatigue brought on further needless suffering. Now, encouraged by William, he continued in his post, fighting the difficulties which increased with every month. The chief of these was the enmity between Whigs and Tories, which resulted in a general dissatisfaction with the régime they themselves had instituted. Fortunately for Shrewsbury, both parties continued to value his qualities. He 'was the best beloved of the whole ministry,' Burnet wrote, 'and deserved to be so; there lay no prejudice against him, but that of his youth, which was soon overcome by his great application and wonderful temper.'

Shrewsbury's instinctive amiability did not mitigate his dislike of the minister with whom he now had to work; for Nottingham's resentment of the younger man's friendship with the King made him more than usually difficult. He was apt to get on most people's nerves (Mary's letters to William during his absence in Ireland are full of complaints of 'Lord Nott's' mannerisms) and Shrewsbury was tormented, not only by the Tory Secretary's hostility, but by his gloomy outlook and cold loquacity. Shrewsbury 'had not strength,' says Burnet, 'to resist the Earl of Nottingham's pompous and tragical declarations.' In March 1689 the news of James II, with his forces, landing at Kinsale was another worry; and the proclamation of William and Mary as King and Queen of Scotland and Ireland did not prevent war breaking out in both kingdoms; also, William's refusal to persecute any of his subjects on religious grounds became a grievance.

William had foretold his own unpopularity; but he seems not to have been prepared for its growth, nor for the increasingly violent hostility between Whigs and Tories, nor for their bitter criticisms of himself. Neither party, and very few ministers except Shrewsbury, understood the effect of his state of health on the King's behaviour; this, combined with his consciousness of their dislike, make it impossible for him to produce the surface geniality expected of a public figure. Talking made him cough: so he spoke briefly, and never on trivial matters. Showing himself to the people exhausted him; and his devoting all his energies to his work gave most of his courtiers the impression that he was an unwilling and disagreeable ruler. 'Well, they use me very ill,' he said to a Dutch friend, 'but my head will be in a short while underground,' adding, 'I am a Protestant, but if I were popish, I would leave this people to themselves.'

Shrewsbury shared William's disappointment at his failure to unite the rival parties; and he was further disillusioned by his master's partial relegation of the Whigs, the majority of whom considered that he owed them his crown, and should therefore have become their leader, while subordinating the Tories. Shrewsbury was not one of these; but he did think William harsh and unkind in refusing to accept his resignation. In August 1689 he implored His Majesty to let him go; he was now in bed, and incapacitated. 'There are,' he wrote, 'a thousand faults I see in myself, and more . . . that others see [was he thinking of Nottingham?] which make me sensible of my own unfitness.' His mind was 'on the rack', and his life 'one continual disquiet'. This, he urged, was 'not the melancholy whimsy of a sick man', but 'the instant prayer of a faithful servant'.

William sent Bentinck to reason with Shrewsbury, who begged the latter to intercede for him with the King. William, entreating Shrewsbury to remain at his post, promised to make it 'as little troublesome . . . as possible. No man,' he added, 'can feel more friendship for you than I do.' So Shrewsbury, still in great distress, consented to stay, in spite of the fact that both Danby and Nottingham were now working against him; they were thought to be corresponding with James II, as indeed were others in positions of trust. The Tory view was that James, having been given a good fright by his son-in-law's invasion, might return to rule as a constitutional monarch, while William and Mary went back to Holland. Or, better still, William might die; and then the Tories, having defeated the Whigs at the elections, would rule the kingdom, using Mary as a figurehead.

Shrewsbury now became involved in the quarrel between the King and Queen and Princess Anne about the latter's settlement as heiress-presumptive. Urged on by Sarah Marlborough, the Princess was privately negotiating with the Commons for a much larger allowance than the £50,000 originally voted her. Hoping that Shrewsbury's friendship with the Marlboroughs would have effect, William sent him to ask Marlborough to influence the Princess to accept that sum, the payment of her debts and his assurance that her allowance would be continued. Marlborough, counting on his own share of the Princess's increased income (£90,000 was the amount agreed on by him and Sarah), fell back on the role of the hen-pecked husband. Abandoning all pretence of Anne herself having any say in the matter, he said that his wife was adamant. 'She will by no means hear of it,' he told Shrewsbury, 'but is like a mad-woman.' When Shrewsbury approached Sarah, she first accused him of accepting bribes, and went on to say that William was very unlikely to keep his word to her mistress. Shrewsbury then asked to be received by Anne, who told him, 'I have met with so little encouragement from the King, that I can expect no kindness from him, and therefore I shall stick to my friends.' In the end, she had to put up with the £50,000: a miserable sum, Sarah told her.

This dispute, combined with the fierce hostility of the rival parties, made it clear to William that Parliament must be dissolved; and once more, Shrewsbury, now leader of the Whigs, protested, on the grounds that the Tories would set about bringing back James II as soon as the Houses were recalled. In December 1689 William summoned him, with other ministers, and told them that, having been unable to effect any kind of working agreement with either party, he had decided to leave the governance of the country to the Queen, while he returned to Holland. 'Though I cannot please you,' he said, 'I am sure that she will.' He was later suspected of 'artifice and contrivance' on this point; but his letters to Bentinck, who was now at The Hague, show him to have been perfectly sincere.

After a horrified silence, there was an outburst of remonstrance; but William remained firm. Several ministers then began to cry. A long argument ensued, which ended in the King agreeing not to abdicate; but it was essential, he said, that he should shortly leave for Ireland, to conduct the campaign against James II's forces; and to this his councillors consented.

In January 1690, Shrewsbury, although deeply chagrined by what seemed to him William's desertion of the Whigs, remained in office. He gave a dinner-party at his lodgings in Whitehall for William, Mary, Princess Anne, her husband Prince George, and a selection of courtiers. As soon as the ladies retired, serious toping began. Everyone, the King included, a French guest reported, became incapably drunk—even Nottingham succumbed. Eventually, William managed to reach his own rooms, to find Marlborough stretched out, unconscious, on a sofa in the antechamber. Shrewsbury's entertainment of Their Majesties was considered a success; there is no other record of his getting drunk, either in public, or in the presence of his employers. Next day, Huygens, William's private secretary, was distressed to find that his master 'had no inclination to do business'.

When Parliament met again in March 1690, the Tories, now in a majority, threw out a measure on which Shrewsbury had set his heart—the Abjuration Bill. This required all holders of office to swear that in no circumstances would they readmit James II as their King. To Shrewsbury this seemed the definitive blow against Jacobitism; its rejection so discouraged him that, once more, he decided to resign his Secretaryship. This time, he told Burnet, he would not be persuaded to continue against his will. Nothing would induce him to serve a Government and a King so careless of their cause.

The King and Queen were now established at Kensington Palace; and Shrewsbury, carrying his seals of office, was about to wait on them there, when he met Burnet. 'I am resolved to deliver them up,' he said, speaking, according to the Bishop, 'with some heat.' Burnet persuaded him to pause, and think over his decision. 'I had no mind,' he says, 'that the King should be surprised by a thing of that kind,' and warned William of Shrewsbury's intention. Several people, including Bishop Tillotson, were then sent to mediate with the Earl, 'but all', Burnet goes on, 'to no purpose', adding, 'the agitation that this gave him threw him into a fever which almost cost him his life'. Still William hoped that when Shrewsbury recovered he could be won over, and promised not to call upon him till after he returned from the Irish campaign. But Shrewsbury, now in bed in his house at Newmarket, sent back the seals by Russell. 'It troubled [the King] more than I thought a thing of that kind could have done,' Burnet concluded. 'He loved the Earl of Shrewsbury; and apprehended that his leaving him at that time might alienate the Whigs more entirely from him.' 'He does not consider,' said William bitterly, 'how kind I have been to him.'

It was at this point that Lady Shrewsbury—as was then the custom, she retained her title—intervened. She had become a Jacobite agent; and she now saw how best to earn her salary.

It appears that Shrewsbury, having accepted his mother's second marriage, remained in touch with her after the Revolution. And now, the fact that he was, as he himself said, 'disgusted' with the administration of the kingdom, seems to have encouraged her to approach him on behalf of James II. Although Shrewsbury had everything to lose by changing sides, and was not the kind of man to break an oath, Lady Shrewsbury's power over him, permanently ingrained, could yet have prevailed over his principles and interests, if only for a time. It was thought that during this interruption in his career he was corresponding, through her, with James—to what extent, is not clear. Portions of this interchange are suspect, and some letters known to have been forged; but one statement, made two years later, by James to Louis XIV's ministers, is in the French archives, and has never been questioned. It runs as follows: 'Il y a le Comte de Shrusbery, qui, étant Sécretaire d'Etat du Prince d'Orange, s'est défait de sa charge par mon ordre.'

This piece of evidence does not conclusively prove Shrewsbury's betrayal of William III, in that James might have used the Earl's abandonment of his post in order to show Louis the prevalence of Jacobitism in ministerial circles; and the majority of Shrewsbury's fellow-workers had, as we should now put it, taken out insurance policies against a counter-Revolution by keeping in touch (as Halifax had hinted to Reresby) with the exiled King. William, knowing this to be so, had decided to accept a form of treachery which was eventually defeated by his uncle's inability to use it.

Meanwhile, Shrewsbury's temporary double-dealing might partly have accounted for his physical collapse. His yielding to his mother's persuasion would have shown him to himself as a traitor; and therefore he could only maintain his refusal to work for William on the grounds—genuine enough—of ill-health. This phase did not last. By July 1690 his feeling for Queen Mary had re-established his loyalty.

Before setting out for Ireland, William had formed a Council of nine—four Whigs and five Tories—to advise the Queen during her regency. Shrewsbury was to have equalized the numbers ('You may trust him entirely,' William told Mary) as the tenth. His refusal greatly distressed her; for she thought of him as a faithful friend; and their relationship had been happy and serene, partly because they were rather alike. Her gentle sweetness of character, combined with acute intelligence, great courage and high principles, much resembled his; and so his behaviour 'greatly surprised me,' she wrote in her diary, 'and gave me a very melancholy prospect of things'. Shrewsbury had treated the husband she adored and reverenced most ungratefully—and after such a desertion, 'What could I expect from others?'

The answer was—practically nothing. Shortly before William's victory over the Franco–Irish Jacobites at the Boyne, the Dutch and English navies were defeated by the French at Beachy Head through Admiral Herbert's inefficiency and cowardice, with the result that he was sent to the Tower, and England thrown open to invasion. The danger was extreme, and the preparations for dealing with it were woefully inadequate. So it was that Shrewsbury, now convalescent, impulsively offered his services to the Queen in any capacity she desired. They were not accepted, presumably because she could not overlook his desertion of William; and she continued to wrestle alone with the problems and quarrels of a Council she could neither trust nor respect. Yet Shrewsbury continued to wait on her; and some courtiers came to the conclusion, not only that he had fallen in love with her, but that she reciprocated this feeling. Both showed some agitation when they met; and Lord Howe, the Queen's Vice-Chamberlain, declared that she would probably marry the King of Hearts if and when William died. Also a fortune-teller, so people said, had told Shrewsbury that he would be 'lucky in love' after the death of a king. In fact, gossip, most of it spiteful, was turning the perfectly innocent relationship of two rather susceptible persons into a romantic drama. Mary's marriage was shadowed by her fears for William; and his behaviour sometimes made her very unhappy. Meanwhile, Louis's armies had defeated the Allies in Flanders. William returned to England in the autumn of 1690, leaving for the continent in January 1691. In May 1692 the English defeat of the French fleet at La Hogue removed the immediate fear of invasion.

Shrewsbury's political star was now in eclipse, with the result that his health ceased to trouble him. In February 1692 Marlborough's dealings with St Germains became known to William, who deprived him of his command, and later sent him to the Tower. Shrewsbury's friendship with Marlborough remained unaffected; this caused further suspicions about his Jacobitism, and he was dismissed from the Privy Council. In February 1693 he was approached by a Whig friend, Philip Lord Wharton (father of Thomas Wharton, author of *Lillibulero*) who asked him to consider marriage with one of his granddaughters, and Shrewsbury visited Wharton at his house in Glamorganshire in order to discuss the alliance. He then decided that the girl was too young to be married, and the scheme—that he had ever seriously considered it seems unlikely—fell through. Shrewsbury now applied himself to the question of Triennial Parliaments, a measure disliked by William as an encroachment on his prerogative; the disputes about it coincided with the return of the Whigs to power. While resisting the Bill for the Triennial sessions, William accepted the Whig domination (and, later, the Bill) on condition that Shrewsbury resumed the Secretaryship of State. But the Earl would not do so unless William agreed to the Bill. In November 1693 the King, refusing to bargain, determined to reinstate Shrewsbury. Their disagreement produced a correspondence which throws a sudden light on Shrewsbury's private life—and also on the reasons for William's trusting him above all his other Ministers.

3

In November 1677 Elizabeth Villiers, eldest daughter of Sir Edward and Lady Frances Villiers, became one of Mary's ladies-in-waiting on her marriage to William of Orange. A year or so later, Elizabeth was established as the Prince's mistress; and in 1688 she followed him into England. Here, officially, she remained in the background; but their relationship, discreetly sustained, was accepted by William's entourage; they tended to approach him through her, rather than through Bentinck, whose first wife, Anne, was Elizabeth's sister. Anne, dying in 1688, had shared her husband's disapproval of the affair; it continued to distress the Queen. Mary could not combat Elizabeth's power over William. Plain, elegant and witty, this young woman, who had been known in Holland as 'squinting Betty' (according to Swift, one of her many admirers in later life, she squinted 'like a dragon') knew how best to help the King, and subordinated any ambitions she might have had for her own future to his interests. So William, confronted with Shrewsbury's second refusal to take office, called upon her to intervene.

Clever Mrs Villiers was perhaps a little too clever in Shrewsbury's case. She decided to influence him through a friend, Mrs Lundee, daughter of the late Governor of Londonderry, who was now Shrewsbury's mistress, and entirely devoted to him. Elizabeth began by imploring the Earl to reconsider his decision, and when he denied her, sent Mrs Lundee to his house in Oxfordshire, the better to plead with him on the King's behalf. But Shrewsbury remained politely adamant, and Mrs Lundee returned to London. In December 1693 she wrote to him describing Elizabeth's irritated chagrin, and added that if only he would be persuaded, 'a dukedom was to have been given you immediately'. She also reminded him of the fortune-teller's having said that he was 'one that would often stand in [his] own light'. As this and other letters had no effect, William instructed several Whig friends, including Admiral Russell, to add their persuasions to those of the ladies. Shrewsbury then explained that the King's antagonism to the Triennial Bill made it impossible for him to take office. To Elizabeth he wrote, 'When you, Madam, have attempted to persuade, and have failed, you may conclude the thing is impossible.' A private meeting with William was then suggested by Mrs Lundee ('You are an ill-natured devil,' she told Shrewsbury) and refused; still she and Elizabeth, urged on by the King, persisted. Shrewsbury simply replied that being 'unfit for the world', he was thinking of travelling to Spain. (At least William would not be able to get at him there.)

In February 1694 the Triennial Bill was accepted by the King. But Shrewsbury had moved to Gloucestershire, where he was hunting and entertaining his neighbours. Then, much to his embarrassment, he was visited by Sir James Montgomery, who had deserted the Whigs to become a Jacobite, and was under the impression that Lady Shrewsbury had succeeded in persuading her son to change sides. Shrewsbury received him coldly, refused to discuss politics, and finally made it clear that he would have nothing to do with the Jacobite cause. In March William summoned the Earl to a private audience, and after reproaching him for his former ungracious behaviour, once more offered him the Secretaryship.

Once more, Shrewsbury excused himself on the grounds of ill-health. 'That,' said the King, 'is not the only reason.' Shrewsbury, deciding to speak out, replied, 'No, Sir, it is not,' and added that William's rejection of the Triennial Bill had made his refusal inevitable. William said, 'When did you see Montgomery last?' Shrewsbury, appalled, made no reply. William then repeated some of Montgomery's remarks. Shrewsbury, pulling himself together, said, 'Sir—since Your Majesty has been so correctly informed, you must be aware that I gave no encouragement to that man's attempts to seduce me from my allegiance.' William pointed out that Shrewsbury's acceptance of the seals would conclusively prove his loyalty and silence his enemies. 'I know,' he went on, 'that you are a man of honour, and that if you undertake to serve me, you will serve me faithfully.' So Shrewsbury, to the delighted relief of his party, became Secretary of State. In April 1694 he was created Marquess of Alton, Duke of Shrewsbury, Knight of the Garter and Governor of the Charterhouse. These honours brought with them an intolerable burden, which very nearly made an end of him. He never found out who had spied on and reported his meeting with Montgomery to the King.

Lady Shrewsbury now assured the exiled King that her son had accepted the Secretaryship in order to continue working for him; with characteristic ingenuity, she explained that he had put off doing so in the hope of a Jacobite invasion, and that he had been persuading Admiral Russell to hand over the fleet to James; a letter from Marlborough to St Germains confirmed these statements. Shrewsbury seems to have been unaware of his mother's persistence in the Jacobite cause at his expense; her efforts, whether William knew of them or not, did not affect his relationship with Shrewsbury, whom he left in charge when he went to the continent in May 1694, after refusing to restore Marlborough's commands. Meanwhile, Shrewsbury was inundated with letters of congratulation. 'No friend or servant you have in the world,' wrote Admiral Russell, 'is more sincerely delighted . . . I may live to see some of the race of a man I from my heart love . . . and . . . I hope you will enter into the honourable state of matrimony.' Indeed, none of Shrewsbury's friends understood why he did not now select a wife; Russell told him that he was in a position to marry an heiress.

From his office in Whitehall Shrewsbury corresponded almost daily with William, Russell, Bentinck, and the Irish and Scottish statesmen. Although he became increasingly dependent on his under-Secretary, James Vernon, he made himself personally responsible for every department of the administration; and within a very short time his grasp of national affairs so developed as to defeat all criticisms. Indeed, his abilities might be described as Churchillian. Nothing escaped his attention; no problem daunted him; his tact and courtesy never failed; and during his first year of duty this vast interchange was sustained without difficulty—or so it seemed—while his popularity remained unaffected. He even made time to stand for Kneller in his Garter robes (in which that courtly artist showed him with both eyes) and here again, the resemblance between himself and his mother is strikingly apparent. Whether he continued to see her, or tried to prevent her plotting, has not transpired. That side of his life was hidden; there is no hint of it in his correspondence. He waited on and received orders from, the Queen several times a week; she and William relied on him as on no one else.

9

Shrewsbury's constancy as a friend survived many setbacks, including that caused by the attempted invasion of Brest, which involved the loss of four hundred sailors and seven hundred soldiers, and for which Marlborough and Godolphin were partially responsible, by betraying William's plans to Louis XIV. (In fact, that monarch knew of them long before the attack took place.) To Shrewsbury's renewed plea for Marlborough's reinstatement, the King curtly replied, 'I do not think it for the good of my service to entrust him with the command of my troops.'

In July 1694 was founded the Bank of England, to which Shrewsbury subscribed £10,000. He also had to deal with a series of Jacobite plots, and a threatened rising in Lancashire. Shortly after William's return in November the Triennial Bill was confirmed. And then, in the last week of December, came a fearful blow, both to Shrewsbury personally, and to the whole kingdom. After a few days' illness, Queen Mary died of smallpox.

The King's misery and despair—enhanced, it may be, by remorse—were so terrible, so agonizing, that those about him feared he might not survive. He would see no one, transact no business; nor did he seem to concern himself as to whether the Revolution settlement would be disrupted by Mary's death. At last, after a series of collapses, he regained enough strength to receive a few intimates, of whom Shrewsbury was one. When his master left for the continent, the Duke fell ill; he had gout and fever, and was beginning to spit blood; yet he struggled on, tied, he told Russell, 'to this hateful, unnatural, sedentary life'.

When his eyesight began to trouble him, he was ordered by his doctors to retire to the country, where he remained for a month, returning to London to deal with the reformation of the currency, a long, anxious and complicated business. In March 1695 he managed to get Marlborough reinstated, and to heal the estrangement between the King and the Princess Anne, who as heiress-apparent had to be received by her brother-in-law both publicly and in private. A few months later, Shrewsbury committed an indiscretion that might have had fatal consequences, and was to be used against him in an attempt to destroy both his reputation and his career. It was the more unfortunate, in that it coincided with one of several plots to assassinate the King.

Some twenty years earlier, Lady Shrewsbury's sister, Catherine, had married the Earl of Middleton; both husband and wife were corresponding with St Germains. It is possible that the sisters belonged to the same group—there were many—of Jacobite plotters, although no written evidence of such a connection exists. Now Shrewsbury, whether influenced by his mother or not, decided to visit his uncle by marriage when, in 1695, that nobleman was sent to the Tower on suspicion of intriguing against the Government—a rash and strangely naif gesture, arising, it seems, out of family feeling. 'I visited him,' the Duke said afterwards, 'as often as I thought decent, for the nearness of our alliance.' Then Shrewsbury, dining with Middleton after his release, 'when he was pretty well in drink', was told, 'I am about to go beyond seas—will you command me no service?' 'By the course you are taking,' Shrewsbury replied, 'it will never be in your power to do yourself or your friends service,' adding, 'If the time should come that you expect [i.e. a counter-Revolution], I look upon myself as an offender not to be forgiven, and therefore you will never find me asking it.' Shortly after Middleton's departure for France, his wife told the Duke that her husband 'has left me trustee for the small concerns he had in England'. Shrewsbury, having made his own loyalty clear, merely bowed, replied, 'I shall always be ready to serve you, or him, or your children,' and thought no more of the matter.

At about this time, a Jacobite invasion had been planned, which was to be preceded by the murder of William III, and followed by the arrival of James II from Calais. The commander of the troops, Sir John Fenwick, was arrested on 13th June 1696, and sent to the Tower to await his trial for high treason. It seemed to him that his best hope of mercy lay in the betrayal, not of the real conspirators, but of those ministers who had been in correspondence with St Germains. He therefore informed Devonshire, now Lord Steward, that Shrewsbury, Marlborough, Russell and Godolphin were privy to the invasion scheme, adding that Shrewsbury had been in touch with Middleton for the same purpose since 1694. Fenwick's trial was then postponed, and his confession forwarded to William, who, with Bentinck, was in Holland. Both men wrote to Shrewsbury, assuring him of their trust in his loyalty, and ordered Devonshire to tell Fenwick that unless he could prove his accusations his trial would take place at once. Shrewsbury, writing at length to William, described Fenwick's statements as 'impudent and unaccountable . . . and as wonderful to me as if I had been accused of coining'. He went on to give an account of his visits to the Middletons, and concluded, 'I am sure, when I consider with what reason, justice and generosity Your Majesty has weighed this man's information, I have little cause to apprehend your ill opinion upon his malice.' William then declared himself 'perfectly satisfied' with Shrewsbury's explanation; but Fenwick's trial was postponed until the autumn, although he had not been able to substantiate his accusations, against either Shrewsbury, or any of the other ministers. In October William, assuming that the Duke had been reassured, came back to England to find that he had quitted London for Eyford, his seat in Gloucestershire, leaving no message with his secretary as to the date of his return. A few days later, the King heard that Shrewsbury had had a fall out hunting, was again spitting blood and unable to move.

In a long letter to William Shrewsbury described his symptoms ('I cannot yet endure the coach') referred to the 'animosity' of his enemies, and indicated that retirement was the only solution to these problems. A few days later, he wrote, 'I humbly and earnestly entreat Your Majesty will allow me to return the seals.' The King refused to accept them ('I cannot consent to what is so contrary to my inclination and interest'), adding that Shrewsbury should remain in the country till he could resume his post, while Bentinck pointed out that his retirement would merely substantiate Fenwick's charges. 'It would look very odd,' Shrewsbury expostulated, 'to keep the seals while my health prevented me excuting the office,' and went on, 'I tried on Sunday to take the air in a coach, and in less than half an hour was seized with such a sickness in my stomach that I was forced to return, and was indisposed all the day after it.'

William was adamant. He would not release the Duke, not only because a bill of attainder was about to be laid against Fenwick, but also because peace terms between France and England were being considered: and for this, Shrewsbury's advice was absolutely necessary. In November 1696 Fenwick's accusations were pronounced 'false, malicious and scandalous', and he was executed in January 1697. In March Shrewsbury came to London, and had a long talk with the King; then, finding himself 'in a condition as weak, and more desperate than I have yet been', he again implored William's leave to retire, and was again denied.

Shrewsbury had nearly always detested his responsibilities ('I never yet was a month in business without wishing thirty times to be out of it') and was never well in London. Now, it seemed to him that he might not survive if he was forced to remain there. And so certain questions arise—were his symptoms, those of tuberculosis, partially self-induced, or at least enhanced by his wish to retire?

Shrewsbury was one of those on whom illness has a frightening effect. His early life, although disturbed, had been devoid of physical setbacks; and so his resistance was quickly undermined. Also his sense of duty brought on paroxysms of guilt when his master urged him to retain a position requiring efforts he was unable to make. William did not mean to be inconsiderate; he himself, afraid of nothing but the desertion of one of the few Englishmen he trusted, had always disregarded his own illnesses (he sustained nineteen hours on horseback at the Battle of the Boyne) and may have thought that, given a respite, Shrewsbury could do so too. So it was that the leisure he promised the Duke, together with his refusal to let him retire, increased Shrewsbury's tendency to give way to invalidism; also, the attacks made on him by Fenwick's supporters—these continued throughout the summer of 1697—threw him into a state of despair which may have had some connection with Lady Shrewsbury's attempts on his loyalty. In fact, his eminence and the King's dependence on his abilities made him the favourite target of those working against the régime. It seemed to them that if Shrewsbury could be brought down, then William's overthrow must follow; and so they continued to persecute the minister whose dearest wish was to abjure his position, and live as a private gentleman.

To describe Shrewsbury as a hypochondriac is to over-simplify; he was in a dilemma from which he could not escape, and which was rapidly weakening such strength as remained to him. The situation was complicated by the fact that the Whig party proposed to substitute Thomas Wharton for Shrewsbury. The King, detesting Wharton, was determined to avoid this situation, and so continued to assure the Duke that he would wait for him to resume his duties, repeating that his retirement was out of the question.

In November 1697 Shrewsbury waited on the King at Kensington (when the French Ambassador noted that he looked like a dying man) in order to give him the seals. William refused to accept them, and advised the Duke to leave for Eyford. Here he remained for three months, rejoining William at Windsor in March 1698. This visit eventually resulted in further haemorrhages, and once he retired to Gloucestershire. In some bewilderment, William wrote to Bentinck, 'Nobody here considers him dangerously ill, because, during the four days he spent with me at Windsor, he seemed tolerably well, and went out hunting with me three times . . . I do not know what to make of it.' In December 1698 William agreed to Shrewsbury's relinquishing the seals, on condition that he became Lord Chamberlain to the Household, which post he retained for eighteen months. In May 1700 William offered the Duke the Lord Lieutenancy of Ireland, together with the sinecure of Groom of the Stole. Shrewsbury, refusing both, again succumbed to illness, and gave up the Chamberlainship. And then, at last, William accepted the inevitable. 'I will not press you in anything,' he wrote, 'but will leave you entirely at liberty . . . May God soon perfectly restore you.'

So ended Shrewsbury's final struggle for freedom; it had lasted three years. His physicians advised him to go abroad, but he was not well enough to travel till the autumn. He could now look back on an administration of such range and variety as to be phenomenal and unequalled. Not all of his correspondence has survived; completed, it would fill many volumes. His interchange with envoys at The Hague, Vienna, Madrid, Brussels and a number of other cities is amplified by instructions and advice on naval and military strategy, finance, and local and Parliamentary government. The complications are endless, the difficulties almost insuperable; yet the tone of the letters is always one of understanding and ingenuity, elegantly and succinctly expressed. No one appealed to Shrewsbury in vain, even when he felt himself hopelessly constricted. The conditions in which he worked had been so appalling that, shortly after his release, he recalled them with amazement, wondering 'that a man can be found in England who has bread, that will be concerned in public business. Had I a son,' he goes on, 'I would sooner breed him a cobbler than a courtier, and a hangman than a statesman.'

The Whigs were enraged by Shrewsbury's departure; and the triumph of the Treaty of Ryswick—in which Louis XIV acknowledged William III as rightful King of England, and which resulted in the apparently satisfactory first Partition Treaty of 1699—did not quite make up to William for the loss of his favourite minister. He himself had now acquired a certain popularity with the English people; but they still resented the honours and riches he had given his Dutch entourage; and his last years were embittered by Parliament's insistence that he should send back to Holland his private troop of guards, whose blue and white uniforms disfigured, so they declared, the rather squalid splendours of Whitehall. And now those splendours were no more; in the fire of 1698 all but Inigo Jones's Banqueting Hall had been destroyed. So Shrewsbury may well have felt that he had come to the end of a chapter when he left for Paris, after a last meeting with William at Hampton Court.

At this point, he began his travel diary, which reveals him in an entirely new and somewhat startling aspect as an indefatigable sightseer and patron of the arts. The next five years were to be a happy time—perhaps the happiest of all his life. They concluded with a climax that was totally unexpected, and is still unaccountable. To his contemporaries it appeared utterly bewildering.

4

Shrewsbury was in his forty-first year when he set out for the continent with the comparatively modest equipage of a carriage and four, two footmen, a valet and a coachman, having parted for ever from three persons, two of whom—William III and Lady Shrewsbury—had made his life a misery; his relationship with the third, Mrs Lundee, had come to an end some time ago. Although he had no travelling companion, he could yet count on a large circle of friends wherever he chose to stay.

News of his arrival in Paris had preceded him, and when he visited Versailles on the morning of 23rd November, he was thought to have come 'on a negotiation' from the Court of St James's. After he had been received—'tolerably civilly'—by Louis XIV, some of the Jacobite exiles began to present themselves, followed by a number of shopkeepers hoping to place their goods with this famous English milord. He was then approached by an old acquaintance, the Duc de Lauzun, whom Louis XIV had sent to escort Mary of Modena and the Prince of Wales to France in 1688. 'How kindly,' Lauzun began, 'King James has always taken the distinguished civility Your Grace showed him when you were sent on the message—' referring to their last interview at Whitehall. He was about to continue, when Shrewsbury put in, 'I had great compassion at that time for his circumstances,' and desired his visitor to change the subject. Lauzun withdrew, reappearing to speak of the twelve-year-old Prince of Wales. 'I wish,' he said, 'that you might have the opportunity to see so fine a youth.' 'I do not question his merit,' Shrewsbury answered, 'but if I must see him—and I have no great curiosity—I would rather it were here than in England.' 'This reply,' he notes, 'dashed all further discourse of this kind, although [Lauzun] continued extreme civil, walking with me all the time.' Returning to Paris via St Germains, where he took care to avoid the Middletons and other Jacobites, he then left for Montpellier and a tour of the Midi.

His sightseeing now began on an exhaustive scale. Passing

through a number of cities, he visited churches, monasteries, galleries, *châteaux forts* and public gardens, setting down his experience of the inns, where 'you have often ill beds, always ill linen, generally ill chambers, and dirty and few attendants; but then the meat and the cookery is far beyond England.' He delighted in the social life of Montpellier, which he did not leave till January 1701, for Geneva, where his haemorrhages recurred; for these he was dosed with a mixture of vitriol and opium. September found him in Turin, and then in Genoa, Viareggio and Lucca. Here his sightseeing was equally thorough: but he balked at some of the relics, one of which—a piece of Thomas à Becket's hair-shirt—was, he observed, 'an imposture'. From Pisa, where he inspected 'a garden of simples and . . . the Tower awry', he went on to Leghorn, reaching Florence in October. Here he was fêted by all the principal English residents, and by the Grand Duke; he also attended the opera, where 'the scenes were poor, the theatre little, no dancing, and not above two or three good voices; but the music pleased me much better than the French'.

At some point in his travels news reached Shrewsbury of James II's death from a stroke at the age of seventy-one. The chief occupation of his last years had been characteristic of his tendency to go to extremes. Piety, replacing, or rather, compensating for, lust, had taken the form of flagellation; for the embraces of Catherine Sedley, Arabella Churchill, and his other mistresses, the more suitable 'discipline', or scourge, was substituted, in the privacy of his closet. 'He was a saint!' his wife exclaimed, when the monks of St-German-en-Laye discovered and handed on to her this useful instrument, which she deposited with the nuns of Chaillot, as a sacred relic.*

After staying in Siena and Viterbo, Shrewsbury arrived in Rome at the end of November. Then, unexpectedly, a relationship which became the principal feature of his daily life was inaugurated by a Monsieur Flamarin, who escorted him to the house of a celebrated hostess, the Princess Carpegna. This visit took place shortly after Shrewsbury moved into his own residence, a

---

* The author once took part in a 'Brains Trust', sponsored by the B.B.C., when one of the team, a Roman Catholic historian, described his participation in the scheme for canonizing James II. Another member, also a Catholic, was enraged by the notion, and a fearful scene ensued. So far, the Vatican has done nothing to encourage this movement, which is still, it seems, under consideration.

palace next to the church of Ara Coeli, on the Capitol. He intended to stay a long time in Rome; the range of its social and aesthetic amenities was just what he needed.

He and Monsieur Flamarin were disappointed to find that the Princess Carpegna was away: but her closest friend, the Contessa Adalhaida Paleotti, was deputizing for her, it seems satisfactorily; and that same afternoon a friendship between her and Shrewsbury began, continuing throughout—and beyond—his stay in the city.

The Contessa, a widow in her forties, had been married to a Swedish nobleman, by whom she had a daughter, but had now resumed her maiden name. On her mother's side, she was descended from John Dudley, Duke of Northumberland, father-in-law of Lady Jane Grey. Her appearance, according to the indispensable and pitiless Saint-Simon, who saw her a few years later, was unusual to the point of fantasy. 'A large person,' he says, 'tall, fat and mannish—both before and behind—she had been beautiful, and still claimed to be so. She wore very low cut dresses, and tucked her hair behind her ears in bunches, tying them up with ribbons, she rouged heavily, with many patches, and was rather mannered, talking loudly in bad French, and speaking familiarly with everyone. Her behaviour was that of a lunatic; but her gambling, her magnificence and her informality made her the fashion.' In fact, the Contessa Paleotti was a very peculiar lady indeed, quite unlike anyone Shrewsbury had ever known. Far from being stupid, she was acute enough to exploit her eccentricities, and so maintained a reputation which pleased and diverted Roman society. From the first moment of their meeting, Shrewsbury was greatly taken with her.

In his diary he does not record his impressions of her, merely noting his visits (these took place several times a week), while devoting the greater part of his rather brief entries to his tours of the city and its environs, and the calls he paid and received. Every now and then he described a picture or a statue at length; and this interest presently gave him the reputation of a connoisseur, not only in Rome, but in his own country; he was asked to buy works of art for his English friends; they trusted his judgement, and followed his advice about prices. He also inspected and reported on the manuscripts in the Vatican Library, where he was a frequent visitor.

It was characteristic of Shrewsbury that he made a point of being kind to young and humble tourists; one of these was Dryden's son, William, whom he entertained and took to concerts and artists' studios, in the intervals of calling at various embassies. Meanwhile, he steadily refused to have anything to do with the Anglo-French disputes caused by Louis XIV's accepting the crown of Spain for his grandson, proclaiming the Prince of Wales as James III, and thus breaking the promises made in the Partition Treaties. As William III prepared for war, and Louis to invade Holland and the Low Countries, Shrewsbury became increasingly attached to the Princess Carpegna and the Contessa Paleotti: so much so, that in his diary they are simply referred to as 'Prin. Carp.' and 'Con. Ad.'

On 12th April 1702 news came of the death of William at Kensington Palace. 'Much afflicted', Shrewsbury retired to bed, dined alone, and a few days later ordered a mourning coach and liveries. Then, on 31st May, he received a more startling piece of news, which he dismissed as follows: 'Received letters from England that on the 19th of April my mother died. I said nothing of it in my family [i.e. to his servants] till I enquired how I ought to mourn.' So he discarded the past. Lady Shrewsbury was buried in the church of St-Giles-in-the-Fields.

Two days later, Shrewsbury and young Dryden went to look at a collection of pictures, and ten days after that the Duke heard that England had declared war on France and Spain. He was then offered the post of Master of the Horse to Queen Anne, which he refused. His frequentation of his faithful Con. Ad. and Prin. Carp. prevailing over all other pleasures, he found himself sympathizing with the Princess, who was quarrelling with her husband, and, with her and the Contessa, watched the fireworks on St Peter's Eve. Having seen the latter off on a trip to Bologna, he visited the Princess at Frascati, where she asked 'my opinion in many things of her private concerns'.

As Shrewsbury became a prominent and much sought-after figure in Roman society, a scheme was set in hand for his conversion to the old faith, and one of his friends, Father Forbas, approached him. 'Having made a short, nonsensical discourse of controversy,' Shrewsbury says, 'he assured me, if I would abjure, nobody but he and Cardinal Sacripanti should know it.' 'What ground,' the Duke demanded, 'have I given you to make me such a proposal? When once I think your belief to be the true one, I shall not be ashamed or afraid to own it—but at present I am far from thinking that. I desire you will hold no more such discourses to me.' His contempt for Catholic practices increased when, on 13th January 1703, a slight earthquake sent the Roman citizens 'running to confession, imagining that mumbling a few words to a priest, and the priest to them, their consciences are safe, without any real or firm purpose to amend their lives'. But Father Forbas had not yet lost hope; he may have been encouraged by Shrewsbury's attending the Contessa Paleotti's daughter's *prise d'habit* at an Ursuline convent—after which, her mother abandoned the girl, and never visited her. She then told Shrewsbury of various cures effected by conversion to Catholicism, as one advising him about his health. Father Forbas followed this up by urging the Duke 'to think of another world', to the same end, and got a violent reception. 'You are all in a mistake about me!' Shrewsbury burst out. 'I appeal to God, and damn myself if I do not think you in error! I protest to God I think the Roman Church full of ignorance, tricks and error!' Unperturbed, Forbas referred to the proposed canonization of James II. 'Several persons,' he told the Duke, 'have recovered their limbs and health through his intercession—' and departed.

Shrewsbury's attitude towards the Contessa now began to change. As if preparing to return to England, he started a correspondence about Anglo-French affairs with Queen Anne's envoy at Vienna; and so, when his devoted Con. Ad. consulted him about a proposal of marriage from a French nobleman, he said, 'I advise you, as a friend, not to decline it.' She however remained single—and available. Shrewsbury then began sittings for his portrait to a German artist.

He saw her as frequently as usual; but in his diary—which is obviously destined for his descendants' use as a guide to continental travel—he takes care to note the times of his return from her parties. He never stayed later than six o'clock; often he left at four. In such gatherings there were plenty of opportunities for discreet têtes-à-têtes—on the balcony, in an alcove under cover of music, in the embrasure of a window. On such occasions, her grotesque appearance and harsh, rattling tone of voice must have contrasted oddly with Shrewsbury's splendid elegance, and what Lord Ailesbury once described as his 'soft, genteel' way of speaking. He received her attempts to proselytize him with the courtesy for which he was famous; presently, he began to evolve a plan for converting her to Protestantism; this scheme matured slowly and in secret. Life was too full, too pleasant for controversy; and Shrewsbury's interest in English affairs was on the increase. By the spring of 1704 he was corresponding with Marlborough, Godolphin, Somers (now Lord Chancellor) and several other Whig noblemen, who were all urging him to come home.

In July news came of Marlborough's victory at Blenheim; already a duke, he was now Prince of Mindelheim. Writing to congratulate him, Shrewsbury begins, 'My lord . . . I must tell you that in this holy, ignorant city your name is so terrible that they have an idea of you as Tamerlane.' Marlborough replied, 'My lord . . . I hope God Almighty has further blessings in store for us before the end of the campaign,' and in his next letter begged his friend 'to set on foot a negotiation with the Venetians for bringing them in to the Grand Alliance [against France and Spain]'. So Shrewsbury was being gradually drawn back into the public business he had formerly abandoned. But there were those in England whose jealousy of his prestige was temporarily exerted; they suggested that his refusal to leave Rome was caused by his intended conversion to Catholicism. When his friends raised this point, he defended himself at length. 'I have constantly here endeavoured to convince everybody of my steadiness,' he wrote to the Bishop of Oxford. 'I never go to any of their churches unless it be to look at a picture . . . I have never omitted to express the folly and superstition of this religion,' with a great deal more to the same effect.

This attitude to the old faith, and his conversion of a Cardigan cousin to Protestantism so alarmed Pope Clement XI that he set spies to watch and report on the Duke; but with the news of Blenheim his behaviour changed, much to Shrewsbury's amusement. 'A year ago,' he noted, 'I was so ill in the opinion of the Pope that it was thought a crime to go near me; now that they fear the D. of M. and his redcoats should come to Italy, His Holiness does nothing but commend me.' Some time ago, he had lent the Contessa Adalhaida a Bible 'in the vulgar [presumably French] tongue, in which', he says, 'she was infinitely surprised to find so little of her old religion'. Then his efforts at her conversion were halted by her falling ill. 'She was like to die in the night by a mistake of the physician . . . in a prescription of opium.' As soon as she recovered, she told Shrewsbury that she had had to ask the cousin he had converted and introduced to her not to call so frequently, as she was being accused by an English Catholic bishop of 'trepanning him into a match'. 'I have already observed,' Shrewsbury noted, 'how great a liar this prelate is, and here he shows his malice.'

This awkwardness drew him and the Contessa closer together; but Shrewsbury had forgotten that the offer from her French admirer had been only 'something like' a proposal of marriage. He does not seem to have realized that she was trying to give him the impression that she was in great demand. Having disposed of her dowerless daughter, she wanted, naturally, to acquire another husband; but without wealth, youth or looks, her chances in the Roman marriage market (or in any other, for that matter) were poor indeed.

Throughout 1704 Shrewsbury was as attentive as ever, and met several of her relatives; but she was careful not to produce her only brother, Ferdinando Paleotti, a most undesirable character, who some years later was hanged for murdering his valet. In December she, Shrewsbury and the Prince and Princess Carpegna went to an exhibition provided by a famous 'strong man' who, among other feats, lifted a board with his teeth.

He saw slightly less of the Contessa till, in the spring, he began to make plans for departure from Rome for Venice, with a view to returning home through the Tyrol, Germany and Holland. On 24th April 1705 he saw her alone. Then follows an entry which marks a turning-point in their relationship. It is both startling and mysterious. The second half of Shrewsbury's record of it is in an apparently unbreakable code; yet the first half makes his meaning clear. 'Went to the Con. Ad.; *first in my whole life* talked to her of—' and then follows a series of numbers—'191 081210. 31. 27.'

The rest of the diary shows that on this date Shrewsbury proposed marriage to the Contessa (as he observes, this was the first time he had offered his hand to anyone) and was accepted. Three days later, he left Rome. During the rest of his stay in Italy, which lasted two months, he wrote to her twice. In his diary, her code name is '9000'.

So Shrewsbury, one of the greatest matches in Europe, allied himself, in his forty-sixth year, with a woman his contemporaries,

as their comments show, considered not only undesirable from
every point of view, but unpresentable: at best, comic, at worst,
disastrous. Why did he do so?

To this question there is no answer but that provided by con-
jecture. Such a gap in the story of a life can only be bridged by
guesswork. Yet this shaky plank must be thrown across the abyss
of his motives.

Some of Shrewsbury's biographers have assumed that he fell in
love with the Contessa. Obviously, he needed her; but neither
men nor women always fall in love with those they need. There is
a very faint possibility that she, hearing of his departure, accused
him of compromising her, and so forced him into an engagement;
but the phrase, 'first in my whole life', seems to contradict this
theory, as do his later entries concerning her. The fact remains
that his use of a code was meant to conceal the circumstances of
his proposal from his descendants. Comments on the marriage
from two of his friends, Speaker Onslow and Lord Dartmouth,
supply some information about the results of the Contessa's
pursuit and capture—if that is how they should be described—of
her second husband.

Onslow says, 'He had the skill and temper to preserve ever
afterwards all appearances to the world of respect and affection to
her . . . She . . . was in truth vain, impertinent, without virtue or
sense . . . The Duke's management [of her] . . . seemed to take up
more of his time and thought than all his other . . . concerns did;
and all this from the hopes he had of concealing what all the
world did really know.' And Dartmouth adds, 'With all [his]
advantages [he] was a very unhappy man . . . His Duchess . . . was
the constant plague of his life, and the real cause of his death.'

These remarks, collated with Saint-Simon's description of the
lady, are of course prejudiced, in that Shrewsbury had defied all
the customs of his day by this inexplicable and extraordinary
choice; but in such cases very few men, and certainly not one as
proud as Shrewsbury, would admit to a mistake of so grave a
nature. He remained loyal to, and seems, at one point, to have
grown fond of, the woman who had nothing, humanly speaking,
to give him, and who ended by causing him great unhappiness.

Shrewsbury did not reach Venice till 3rd May; he travelled
from there to Padua and back again during the next four weeks,
entertaining many English and Italian friends, and though he

was troubled by gout and haemorrhages, he inspected a number of pictures, gardens and buildings. On 27th June he wrote to '9000'; in his diary he uses a different code—'my 17102216. 62425222 72516'. Subsequent entries show that her conversion to Protestantism had been agreed on, but must be effected before they were married, and that her change of faith was, in Shrewsbury's eyes, a very serious matter. He need not have concerned himself. His Con. Ad. consented to apostasize without a moment's hesitation; it was a negligible price to pay for a large income and the status of an English Duchess.

Meanwhile Shrewsbury, who dreaded leaving Italy, came to the conclusion that Venice was 'the only great city I ever was in where I declare I could not live, for there is no place to walk and take the air, and I think the air moist and unwholesome.' Reaching Augsburg in Bavaria on 16th July, he again fell ill, but recovered in time to call on Prince Maximilian of Hanover (brother of the future George I), 'a hearty, free [i.e. Protestant] German', and on the 28th sent to his betrothed to join him. He then informed a Lutheran minister of his intentions, and that cleric consented to marry him and the Contessa as soon as he had her promise to become a Protestant.

On 18th September she arrived and took rooms at an inn, where Shrewsbury waited on her, taking care to return to his lodgings by nine o'clock in the evening. Next day, chaperoned by a Mr van Stetin (a local dignitary, or Senator) he escorted her to a goldsmith's, to buy the ring and a wedding-present. All three then had dinner together, and after the meal, 'she declared herself to the Senator in a manner that gave him full satisfaction as to religion. We went again,' Shrewsbury continues, 'to other shops. I supped with her at the inn, as I had dined; came home before ten.'

On 20th September 1705 they were married, at nine-thirty in the morning, 'in the presence of Mr. van Stetin, his brother-in-law Mr. Hervart, two patricians [unnamed], the master of the house [i.e of Shrewsbury's lodgings], her servants and mine. After, we took the air; to the woods, and home about six'. Next day, bride and groom gave a dinner-party for all the witnesses; and then Shrewsbury, as if taking pleasure in his new status, writes, almost proudly, 'My wife and I went abroad, and came home after six.' They now prepared to leave Augsburg for

Frankfort, which they reached on 17th October. But as Shrewsbury was not perfectly satisfied about his Duchess's conversion, he summoned a French Calvinist minister to interview and instruct her before they went to church on the following Sunday. She passed these tests with the greatest of ease.

Before leaving Augsburg, Shrewsbury had written to Sir John Talbot about his marriage in a slightly self-exculpatory manner. 'I believe you will be surprised,' he began, 'with what I am about to tell you, that yesterday morning I was married to an Italian widow lady I knew at Rome. Her being without fortune and a foreigner will make my choice censured by everybody, but I am persuaded she will prove so good a wife and so good a Protestant that I shall not have just cause to repent what I have done.' Sir John seems to have protested: for his nephew wrote to him again, emphasizing the wisdom of his choice. His letter to Marlborough on the same subject has not survived. That Duke, staggered but courteous, replied, 'My lord: I have received the honour of Your Grace's letter, and must confess, I was not a little surprised at what you are pleased to tell me, though I agree entirely with you that we ought to marry to please ourselves, and not others. I am infinitely obliged to you for the early intimation . . . which I take as a particular mark of your friendship.' In a letter announcing his marriage to Robert Harley, Shrewsbury, foreseeing an outcry, hopes 'that people will not be contented to judge till they may do it upon grounds that are reasonable'.

This hope was not to be realized; for already, English travellers, returning home, had begun to report on Shrewsbury's bride, and gossip of the wildest nature soon grew up round the circumstances of their marriage. She was credited with two brothers, who, it was said, had followed the Duke to Augsburg, and forced him, at the sword's point, to make her his wife—how else could he have brought himself to take up with an ugly, penniless 'strumpet', long past the age of childbearing, who had lured him back into popery?

Meanwhile Shrewsbury, bent on treating his Duchess as became her station, bought her 'jewels and rich stuffs', and presented her to a number of 'Protestant potentates' in and around Frankfort. He seems to have been preparing her for the arrival of Marlborough, who was expected to enter the city on 31st October.

Reaching Frankfort at four o'clock, Marlborough supped alone with Shrewsbury, visited him again next day, 'and stayed above an hour', with a view to persuading his friend 'to come into business' as soon as he came home. Shrewsbury was non-committal; he then asked Marlborough to meet his wife, and they gave a dinner-party for him. On 2nd November Marlborough called on her—she had tea ready for him, quite in the English fashion—and made his farewells. The Shrewsburys now prepared to leave Frankfort for Cologne, which they reached on the 15th—and there they were joined by Ferdinando Paleotti, who attached himself to them, dining and supping at their inn—'The Holy Ghost, a very bad one', Shrewsbury noted. It was agreed that he should accompany them to London, via Rotterdam, Leyden and Amsterdam, where they caught up with Marlborough, who, Shrewsbury observed, 'is beloved by the people of that city'.

Throughout their stay there, Shrewsbury precedes many of his entries with 'My wife and I were invited to dinner', or, 'My wife and I dined with the Duke of Marlborough', or, 'The Duke of Marlborough persuaded me to go with my wife to dinner', thus stressing his married state. It was then more usual for a man of his standing either to write of himself and her as 'the Duchess and I', or simply 'we'. This repetition seems to indicate that he was enjoying her company. He makes no comment on her response.

He bought her more jewels, and some pictures from a Jewish merchant in Amsterdam, took her to the seaside, and on 7th January 1706 prepared to cross to England from The Brill in one of the royal yachts, the *Henrietta*. Marlborough, now aboard the *Peregrine*, visited them, and the squadron sailed next day. The sea was so calm, Shrewsbury noted, that 'I hoped to sup well, as I did'. In the evening of 8th January the *Henrietta* put in at Dept-ford. Shrewsbury had been away five years and two months. His happiest time was over.

5

When Shrewsbury re-entered the political arena he so much disliked, Queen Anne, a physical wreck at the age of forty-one,
had eight more years to reign. During this period he was granted
distinctions and powers even greater than those he had forsworn
under William III; but he achieved neither peace of mind nor the
support of his contemporaries; for he was shadowed by ill-health,
and his efforts to organize a policy of moderation were frustrated
by the hatefully familiar rivalry between Whigs and Tories. Both
parties accused him of weakness and vacillation; and all the time,
Duchess Adelaide, as she was now known, humiliated and grieved
him by her total disregard of her own dignity and his wishes.
Seemly behaviour was something she could neither practise nor
understand. So it may be that Dartmouth did not exaggerate when
he came to the conclusion that her self-absorbed exhibitionism
shortened her oversensitive husband's life. She seems to have
enjoyed setting him and his friends by the ears; and to have been
fully aware of, although perfectly indifferent to, the mockery that
greeted her calculated defiance of the conventions. Yet she was
chaste, and, in her odd way, respectable, while unashamedly
revelling in her own absurdities.

At this time, there were two Queens in England—the crowned
and anointed 'poor unfortunate faithful Morley', and her adored
and cruel Mrs Freeman, on whom Dean Swift may as well have
the last word. 'Three Furies,' he says of Sarah Marlborough,
'reigned in her breast . . . sordid Avarice, disdainful Pride, and
ungovernable Rage.' Although her husband was Shrewsbury's
closest friend, her venom poisoned a relationship that should have
been happy for both men. Her comments on the Shrewsburys are
characteristic. She allows the Duke 'a sort of an appearance of
wisdom', and continues, 'He . . . brought over with him on his
return a very old woman for his wife, an Italian papist, who upon
this marriage had professed herself a Protestant. . . . His covetous-
ness [Shrewsbury was noted for his generosity], which was the
prevailing bias in his constitution . . . had increased upon him with

the years.' She then censures the Duke for refusing the Mastership of the Horse, which would have brought him a large salary. She concludes by accusing him of betraying the principles of the Revolution, and his Duchess—with some truth—of a 'foreign assurance to ask, as well as to say, anything, though never so improper.'

For some time after his return, Shrewsbury remained at Heythrop in Oxfordshire, where he began to build a mansion in the Italian style. 'He excused himself,' according to Sarah Marlborough, 'either from want of health, or some other frivolous pretence,' from the post in the Government his friends were urging upon him. During this time of retirement he may have hoped to train his wife in English ways. Her command of that language became fluent enough; her accent was of the kind still derisively imitated by those who look on all foreigners as ridiculous and contemptible. The curiosity she aroused caused her and Shrewsbury to be much frequented. 'A Mrs Key,' wrote one lady to another, 'told me a great deal of Lady Shrewsbury, and such stories as made me sick of Her Grace—' and this before they even met. Lady Cowper declared that the Duchess, 'with all her prate and noise', must be 'the most cunning, designing woman alive'—how else could such a creature have entrapped the Duke? The men were equally censorious. 'Sure, my lord,' wrote Henry St John to Lord Cutts, ' 'tis a matter of great merit to make an ancient Roman beauty a convert, at the expense of making her a wife.'

Meanwhile, Shrewsbury's refusal to take office ('I beg my friends will permit me to be an insignificant cipher,' he wrote to Charles Montague, second Lord Halifax) produced a polite remonstrance. 'I always thought,' that nobleman replied, 'that there was too much fine silver in Your Grace's temperament; had you been made of a coarser alloy, you had been better fitted for public use.' It was quite true. When Shrewsbury took a house in St James's Street, and was received by the Queen, with whom he had always been very popular, both Whigs and Tories suspected him of planning to play a double game. No one believed that he was neither grasping nor ambitious. In fact, his affiliation with the Whig party remained firm; for he was now strongly in favour —as they were—of continuing the war with France, a conviction justified by Marlborough's next victory, that of Ramillies, in May 1706.

Shrewsbury retained his privacy by asking Marlborough to be his proxy in the Lords throughout the session of 1706–7. 'I cannot recollect,' he said, 'that we have ever differed.' Marlborough, disappointed but resigned, wrote to Sarah, 'I do not think he can ever be of much use, but it is much better to have mankind pleased than angry.' It was then suggested to Shrewsbury by Mulgrave, Duke of Buckinghamshire, that an alliance between Whigs and Tories should be arranged. Shrewsbury replied that he was now settled in a retirement which perfectly satisfied him; and after the election of May 1707 he was not asked to join the Ministry. He then changed his mind—his wife was urging him to get her a place as Lady of the Bedchamber—left Heythrop for London, and joined Robert Harley, who had lost his position as Secretary of State. When Harley asked him to renew his attendance on the Queen, so as 'to give Mrs Morley right impressions', Shrewsbury, accepting, gradually became involved in the group organized by Harley and Mrs Masham, who were undermining Sarah's domination; they intended ultimately to eliminate both her and her husband. They were helped by Sarah's heartless treatment of the agonized Queen on the death of Prince George in 1708, which caused the first serious breach between the two women. Sarah now began to see her defeat at Mrs Masham's hands as a possibility; a little later, Shrewsbury's acceptance of the Lord Chamberlainship set him, officially at least, in opposition to her husband and the Whig party. This seemed to her unforgivable. Furiously raging, she observed Shrewsbury's daily meetings with Harley and her sly, odious cousin. Then, once more, to Sarah's infinite disgust, the Italian Duchess became conspicuous. Waiting on the Queen, she said something—unrecorded—which made that poor lady burst out laughing. It was the first time, Anne told the Duchess of Somerset, that she had laughed since her husband died: a minor triumph, no doubt; but not one Shrewsbury was likely to appreciate.

His motives for allying himself with Harley and the curiously indistinct yet pervasive figure of Abigail Masham were based on the conviction (evolved over a year's correspondence with Tories and moderate Whigs) that after two great victories, Marlborough and the Allies would be able to bring about a general peace, while putting an end to France's power in Europe. So his patriotism warred against his need of a healthy and tranquil life in his new palace. His friendship with Marlborough cooled; and Sarah's anger with him increased, as did her awareness of the transference of Anne's affection for herself to the hitherto despised relative originally installed by her in the royal household. The Harley-Masham siege—slow, subtle, and at first imperceptible—was prolonged by the invalid Queen's inability to reveal her shrinking from Sarah, to whom she continued to write almost as devotedly as in their young days. Shrewsbury's connection with this intrigue was intermittent, partly because his wife's impact on London society had, it seems, begun to affect his attitude towards herself. He may have tried to curb her; if he did, his efforts failed.

In the early summer of 1708 Sarah Marlborough gave a party, at which two singers, Mrs Tofts and Signor Nicolini, were to perform. At the last minute Nicolini sent a message to say he could not appear—and the Duchess of Shrewsbury at once sprang to the rescue. 'A sister Italian, and of a sprightly disposition,' another lady reported, 'she made him come, and brought him in her coach.' The picture of the bedizened Duchess, escorted by her elegant and stately husband, gaily hobnobbing with a lowbred foreigner, and chattering away to him in his own tongue, convulsed the fashionable world. Shrewsbury was conventional enough to dislike such a situation; but, as Onslow later pointed out, he made no comment on, and no complaint of, his wife's behaviour. He may have realized that delight in her position had gone to her head, and that she could not be restrained. So, enduring in silence, he took refuge in public life.

Within a year, the split between Sarah and the Queen became public knowledge. It had been preceded by the Pretender's first attempt to land in Scotland. That high-minded, rather uninteresting young man, developing measles as the ship approached the shore, had had to return to France. Seven years were to pass before he tried again.

Meanwhile, Marlborough's victories at Oudenarde (July 1708) and Malplaquet (September 1709) enraptured the English people, but did not affect the Queen's withdrawal from Sarah, who lost the posts of Groom of the Stole, Mistress of the Robes, Keeper of the Privy Purse and Ranger of Windsor Park. When Anne implored the national hero to influence his wife, Marlborough made one of his few protests in a letter to Sarah from Flanders.

'Upon my word,' he wrote, 'when you are out of humour and dissatisfied with me, I had rather die than live.' So it was that when Shrewsbury moved over to the Tories and the peace party, he had to take into account Marlborough's devotion to Sarah; it endured till the day of his death, as did hers to him. Marlborough was genuinely uxorious; Shrewsbury had determined to appear so.

Shrewsbury was now sure, he told Harley, that 'the generality of the nation long for peace', and also that Louis XIV would, at last, co-operate. He therefore ceased calling on Sarah, while his wife, she says, 'made court visibly to Mrs Masham . . . with high civility and compliment, which . . . the Duke had taught her, in order to hide the part they both were acting'. In fact, Shrewsbury's change of attitude arose from his reasoned conclusion that England could no longer afford the fearful expenditure of lives and money, and that France was in the same position. The Queen delighted in his company; she depended on him, much as William III had, and was less demanding than her brother-in-law. When the Duke read out to her an address from the City of London, she expressed disapproval of the clause about her Divine Right. 'Having thought often of it, I can by no means like it,' she told him, and thenceforward it was omitted.

Shrewsbury's next duty as Lord Chamberlain—one to which he was eminently suited—had been preceded by a long report from a Mr Nelson, then employed as agent in the American colonies. This gentleman was especially concerned with the English treatment of 'our' Red Indians, as compared with that of the French, in their Canadian colony. The French, Mr Nelson wrote, took much more trouble with their tribes than did the English. This was a sad mistake; when a group of native chiefs crossed the Atlantic to be received by Her Majesty, particular attentions should be paid them—and who better to do so than His Grace of Shrewsbury?

They arrived, in all their splendour of feathers, blankets, war-paint and beribboned boots. Presented by Shrewsbury, they addressed their Great White Queen through an interpreter, and produced gifts of wampum and shell necklaces, receiving in return her portrait, two hundred guineas, looking-glasses, laced hats, kettles, razors and guns. Shrewsbury then escorted them to Windsor, Greenwich and Hampton Court, and to a special performance of *Macbeth*—surely a rather taxing ordeal for the

interpreter? They were compared to the Magi, and wildly
cheered by the crowds. Anne's next order to Shrewsbury was less
pleasant. He was told to retrieve her early letters to Sarah—
'strange scrawls', of which she was now ashamed. Sarah refused
to part with them. In August 1710 Shrewsbury and Harley,
backed by the Queen, began to consider putting forward
unofficial peace proposals to France.

The Whigs protested that Shrewsbury had betrayed them, to
which he replied, 'I will never depart from my principles as an
Englishman, and an assertion of the rights and liberties of my
country.' This declaration embodied, not only his efforts for
peace, but also his adherence to the Hanoverian succession; in no
circumstances could the Pretender's claims be considered. When
Shrewsbury's alliance with Harley was criticized, as opening the
door to a Tory ministry, he said, 'I open no door but what I can
shut when I please.' While retaining the post of Lord Chamberlain,
he continued to refuse all other places, and in October of this
year was reported by Dean Swift to have gone over to the Tories.
That cleric, now at the height of his power, was presented on
11th April 1711 to the Duke, to whom, he told Stella, he made
'two or three silly compliments, suitable to the season'. When he
met the Duchess, she commented on his name. Swift—that was
presto in Italian; and the Dean, delighted, thereafter referred to
himself as Presto in his *Journal*. He became intimate with both the
Shrewsburys, and encouraged her advances. On one occasion he
described how, at a party, she 'came running up to me, and
clapped her fan, to hide us from the company'.

The Duchess then set up a *salon*, which was a great success,
partly because her guests never knew what she was going to say
next. 'She is more ridiculous in her talk than ever,' said Lady
Strafford, who had been bewildered by her hostess's announcement that she was suffering from 'things growing upon my toes
that are like thumbs. I am very much out of humour,' added Her
Grace, 'they make me so lame that I cannot stir.' Thumbs?
Further enquiry revealed that the Duchess had developed
bunions, which she described at length to all who would listen.
Worse was to follow. 'She became very coquet with Lord
Ashburnham', and even more so with another nobleman, whom
she 'pulled about so in the Queen's lodging that it was a shame to
see her'. And when an old friend of the Duke's appeared un-

expectedly at a levée, she called out, 'Oh! here is Colonel Murray, the town says I have an intrigue with him, so I would not give him any of my pretty kind eyes—but I will smile upon him too.' So she made sure of her audience, and added to it by complacently reporting the stories told of her. To Harley's wife—he was now Lord Oxford—she said, 'Madam, I and my lord are so weary of talking politics, what are you and your lord?' 'I know no lord,' that lady replied austerely, 'but the Lord Jehovah.' 'Oh dear, Madam!' the Duchess exclaimed, 'Who is that? I believe 'tis one of the new titles, for I never heard of him before.' This, with other anecdotes, went the rounds. The general view was that Her Grace of Shrewsbury 'had a wonderful art of entertaining and diverting people', but that she 'would sometimes excel the bounds of decency' (as in the matter of her bunions) although 'she had a great memory, had read a good deal, and spoke three languages to perfection'. Doubtless it was this that had attracted the Duke to her parties in Rome. Now, the display of her accomplishments only caused him humiliation. Swift, sitting by her dressing-table, railled her about the rumours of Shrewsbury being sent to Versailles without her knowledge. 'I know nothing of that,' she said, adding, 'I am resolved not to stay behind.'

Nor did she. In the autumn of 1712 Shrewsbury, ordered to France to discuss the peace terms, was accompanied by the Duchess, whose reputation as a figure of fun had preceded her. They made their state entry into Paris (where he had taken a house) on 11th June 1713, and were received at Versailles by Louis XIV two days later. Here, Saint-Simon enters the scene, as being chiefly concerned with the effect on the other ladies of the Duchess's strange coiffure. He had long deprecated the fashion of black or white muslin *fontanges*, which of late years had become so high as to make the wearers' faces look as if they were 'in the middle of their bodies', and were 'inconvenient to the last degree'. Not even the King had been able to restrain these absurdities. Now, Saint-Simon observed, so startling was the Duchess of Shrewsbury's appearance, that where a great monarch had failed, 'an old, mad foreigner brought about a change in an amazingly rapid manner. From an extremity of height, the ladies' headdresses descended to the utmost flatness'—and so continued.

The Duchess's entry into Paris created a less satisfactory sensation. When she drove out to a fair, her coach was mobbed, and cries of 'Oh! la vilaine bête!' pursued her through the streets. It was at this point that the goaded Duke, who was not altogether satisfied with the terms of the peace treaty, gave her health as an excuse, and asked leave to return to England. He and the Duchess were 'very graciously received' by the Queen at Windsor on 26th August 1713.

To the fury of the Whig extremists, Shrewsbury's moderate policy had triumphed, peace was signed, and the Marlboroughs had to retire to Holland. Shrewsbury was then offered the Lord-Lieutenancy of Ireland. He was thankful to go; it may well be that his wife had made life in England unendurable. He had 'long aspired', one of his friends said, to this new post, having confessed himself 'very much fatigued with the compliments, ceremony and feasting' given him in France, which had of course drawn further attention to the jewelled scarecrow at his side. In a half-savage country her eccentricities might be less noticeable.

The friendship between Shrewsbury and the bland, invincible genius described by his countrymen as the saviour of Europe—exiled through the machinations of a backstairs cabal—had now lapsed. Marlborough's days of glory were over; he was sixty-three, and his health had begun to fail. He and Shrewsbury no longer corresponded; Sarah's enmity and Shrewsbury's pre-occupation with Irish problems made that impossible. The first difficulty that the Duke had to deal with was the Jacobite influence of Sir Constantine Phipps, Chief Justice and Lord Chancellor of Ireland.

Shrewsbury publicly defined his own beliefs on 4th November, the anniversary of his late master's birth, by drinking to his 'glorious memory' at a banquet in Dublin. He had some trouble in supporting the Hanoverian succession, and was sharply criticized by the Irish Privy Council. Catholics and Jacobites then instigated a series of riots during the parliamentary elections, and Shrewsbury was forced to close down several Catholic chapels. 'I have been very ill since I came,' he wrote to an English friend, 'and the vexation of this usage has made me worse.'

The Irish Whigs, triumphing in the elections, then introduced a bill attainting the Pretender of high treason, attacked Phipps, and begged Queen Anne to remove him, which she refused to do. The general turmoil found Shrewsbury powerless in what he described as 'this tempestuous station'. His efforts were not supported by the English Government, and as he perceived that he was about to be recalled, he noted his resemblance to 'the figure of a Viceroy in a play', adding, 'It signifies little what opinion I am of, since little regard will be had to it in England.' So the spring of 1714 went by, and in June he returned home, to find the Queen seriously ill, and the Protestant succession endangered. A Jacobite Restoration seemed imminent, partly because Anne's refusal to let George of Hanover visit her was ascribed to a secret wish to let her half-brother succeed.

The dying Queen was divided between her loathing of her German cousin and her determination to avoid a Catholic successor. One hope remained—the conversion of the Pretender. Then, from Lorraine, he announced that 'to his last breath' he would maintain his religion. The French Ambassador was told that England 'would rather welcome the Grand Turk' than a papist; and Marlborough, now in Antwerp, persuaded the Elector of Hanover to reinstate him as Captain-General of the forces as soon as the Queen died.

This event was expected almost hourly; but still the wretched woman lingered on, forcing herself to attend a Council meeting, to which she was supported by Shrewsbury. 'She has not been able to walk so far for some weeks,' he was told. A few days later, she received the Hanoverian Ambassador. She then said to one of her doctors that she trusted no one—Harley had been dismissed, as he was thought to be making advances to the Pretender—and on 30th July the Queen was put to bed in Kensington Palace, attended by seven doctors, the Duchesses of Somerset and Ormonde, Abigail (now Lady) Masham, and a number of bishops and ministers. She sank into a coma, rousing herself to give Shrewsbury the Treasurer's staff; her hands were so weak that they had to be guided to his. On 1st August 1714 she died at seven-thirty in the morning, and at nine George I was proclaimed King of England, Scotland, Ireland and France. Next day, the Marlboroughs landed at Dover, and from there made a triumphant entry into London.

From 1st August to 18th September, when George I disembarked at Greenwich, Shrewsbury, as principal Regent, was virtually in charge of the kingdom. He immediately issued a proclamation offering a reward of £5,000 to anyone arresting the Pretender in the event of his landing. He then relinquished the

Treasurership, but accepted the less arduous posts of Groom of the Stole and Keeper of the Privy Purse.

At fifty-four the new King, who spoke no English, was not an attractive figure. He arrived with a suite of ninety persons, which included two exceptionally hideous mistresses, two dwarfs and two Turkish slaves. His wife, Sophia Dorothea of Celle, had been a prisoner for the last twenty years, on the grounds of her adultery (given out as desertion) with Philip of Königsmarck, whose murder had preceded her arrest and deportation to the Castle of Ahlden. The Prince of Wales (later George II), following his father, had decided to champion his mother, with the result that he and the King were not on speaking terms. George I made no secret of his dislike of English ways, or of his contempt for his ministers. He had no illusions; he knew perfectly well that he had been received merely to prevent the accession of the Pretender. Shrewsbury, conversing with him in French or Latin, exercised all his tact and suavity of manner; but he was hamstrung, socially, by his wife, who succeeded in being chosen Lady of the Bed-chamber to the Princess of Wales. Her efforts to entertain George I made him laugh; she became what would now be described as a comic turn in the royal circle, which was dull enough; Shrewsbury appeared to accept this situation. He had decided to serve for one more year, and then retire.

This plan did not please his wife, whose position at Court was now assured; she prevented his resignation by telling the King that he had no more faithful servant than her husband, and forced Shrewsbury to remain in office. According to Dartmouth, she 'kept her authority over him by the same means she had obtained it'. As these means are not described, the mystery originally created by Shrewsbury's coded entries in his travel diary prevails again. It cannot be solved by Dartmouth's failure to understand the Duke's policy of moderation. Dartmouth thought, as others did, that the murder of his father and brother had permanently weakened Shrewsbury's resolution. Meanwhile the Whigs, having put down the Jacobites through the national acceptance of George I, 'drove on too fast', according to Shrewsbury. As he continued his efforts to bring about a coalition and consolidate the peace, they described him as 'amphibious', and threatened him with impeachment if he did not retire, which he did in the summer of 1715. This did not prevent his being accused of supporting the Pretender's invasion of Scotland in the winter of that year. The rebellion of the 'Fifteen' lasted five months, and was defeated with some difficulty, temporarily uniting the rival parties. Then, once more, Shrewsbury was approached by Jacobite agents, who optimistically reported him as 'a real friend' to their cause; they seem to have mistaken his non-committal courtesy for acquiescence; and his refusal to denounce them to the Government encouraged their hope that he would change sides.

When the King left England to visit Hanover in 1716, the Shrewsburys were in constant attendance on the Prince and Princess of Wales, who had allied themselves with the Tories. So the Whigs accused the Duke of encouraging the Prince to seize the regency of the kingdom. Squibs were circulated referring to him as 'Polyphemus', or 'Ireland's Eye', and Lady Mary Wortley Montague published her *Roxana*, in which the Duchess appeared as 'Coquetilla, whose deluding airs, Corrupts our virgins, still our youth ensnares'—a clumsy libel no one took very seriously.

In these, the last two years of his life, the story of Shrewsbury's ancestor, the sixth Earl, seems to have been repeated. Bacon had described the Elizabethan nobleman as 'great and glorious'; yet, he added, 'there is a greater than he, which is my Lady Shrewsbury.' The Duke, thankful to retire, and ready to indulge his wife, still spoke, every now and then, in the Lords. In 1717 he was reported to have been involved in the activities of Gyllenborg, the Swedish Ambassador, who was arrested for secretly negotiating with the Pretender on behalf of the English Jacobites. Investigation revealed that Shrewsbury, who was now seriously ill, had had 'no intimacy' with those attempting to raise money for another invasion.

In January 1718 Shrewsbury moved into his house at Isleworth, where he was attended by his old friend, Sir Thomas Millington, and several other physicians. 'If he dies,' wrote a Jacobite agent, one of the many who had approached him in vain, 'the best head and the politest gentleman in England falls.' 'He has ever been the favourite of the nation,' added Swift. Now, the 'crazy corpse' of which the Duke had so often complained entered on its last journey; calmly, he prepared to abandon the struggle. The doctors said that he would recover. One who had not been called in reported on the others with professional acidity, subjoining the inevitable comment on Italian practices. 'I should have thought the prescriptions he has had surer than any draughts his lady ever mingled in her own country,' he wrote.

The Duke's servants, who were devoted to him, were full of hope. So was the Duchess; for as a widow, she would sink into obscurity—and that was not to be considered. Shrewsbury knew better. He made his will, and continued, between bouts of asthma, to receive a few friends, one of whom was a cousin, William Talbot, Bishop of Salisbury. On 31st January, realizing that the end was near, he summoned all his servants. Headed by the Groom of the Chambers, some thirty persons entered his room, and stood at the foot of the great bed. Many were in tears.

Shrewsbury was determined that those who had worked for him so faithfully should not be unduly shocked by his death, and also that they should bear witness to his beliefs. 'Let my physicians say what they will,' he now told them, 'I am sure I must die soon. I desire, if death should carry me off suddenly, that you will do my memory that justice to declare—as I do— that I die in the Communion of the Church of England, of which I have been above thirty years an unworthy member.' They were then dismissed, and the Duke arranged to receive the Sacraments from Bishop Talbot; characteristically, he remembered to ask the local clergyman, Dr Chark, to assist his cousin.

So everything was settled. Next day, 1st February, when the Duchess and Sir Thomas Millington were with him, he appeared to be on the mend. At about three in the afternoon they were summoned to dinner; neither wished to leave him. 'Go to dinner,' he said, 'and come and chat with me when you have done.' They obeyed, and his bodyservant was left in charge. Halfway through the meal they were sent for—too late. The Duke was dead. He had just reached his fifty-ninth year.

A fortnight later, Shrewsbury's brother-in-law—whom he had avoided and perhaps financed—stabbed his valet through the heart in the street, was arrested, sent to Newgate and condemned to be hanged. The Duchess did not attempt to save him; but she was deeply distressed that a Paleotti should suffer the death of a common criminal, and begged George I to allow him to be beheaded. The King had no opinion of Italians, however noble, and refused to interfere. Paleotti was then hanged at Tyburn. This scandal deprived the Duchess of her place at Court.

While those who had known him best recalled the King of Hearts as 'a great man, with a sweetness of behaviour . . . and nothing of the stiffness of a statesman, yet the capacity and knowledge of a piercing wit, of a very charming countenance, and the most generally beloved of the ladies', no one cared to frequent poor Coquetilla; for it was not now advisable—or even correct—to call on her. She remained well provided for, yet isolated, in the family house in Warwick Street, till her death in 1727.

Ironically, the Church Shrewsbury had abjured in youth now claimed her own. As he had no male heir, his dukedom and marquessate expired with him. The earldom and its sub-sidiary titles came to a cousin, Gilbert Talbot—a Roman Catholic priest. When he died, his brother George became fourteenth Earl of Shrewsbury, inheriting the estate, with the houses—that in Isleworth, Eyford in Gloucestershire, Heythrop in Oxfordshire, the hunting-box at Newmarket, Alton Castle and Grafton Park. All these mansions have now disappeared.

Epilogue

The story that begins with Queen Elizabeth sending Shaftesbury's grandfather to the Fleet prison for peculation, and ends
with George I refusing to allow Shrewsbury's brother-in-law
to be beheaded, might be described as a single narrative; as it
were a slender thread twisting in and out of a vast and intricate
tapestry. Because these studies have been confined to the personal
aspect, the treatment of great events recalls Montesquieu's
account of reading history without, he says, 'paying the least
attention' to the background of war, revolution and political
intrigue. He was only interested, he explains, 'in the long
succession of passion and fantasy that human nature provides'.
Naturally, the careers and opinions of the personages here
presented were influenced, and sometimes subjugated by, the
process of national affairs. Yet their characters may be con-
templated separately, as they move within that process. All
four stand out from the times in which they lived. None is
typical.

Bibliography

(Except where otherwise stated, the date refers to publication of the first edition).

Anthony Ashley Cooper, 1st Earl of Shaftesbury

AILESBURY, LORD, *Memoirs* (Roxburghe Club, 1890).

ASHLEY, MAURICE, *Life in Stuart England* (1964). *Charles II, the man and the statesman* (1971).

BROWNING, ANDREW, *Thomas Osborne, Earl of Danby & Duke of Leeds* (1913).

BRYANT, ARTHUR, *Charles II* (1931).

BURNET, GILBERT, *History of my own Time* (2nd ed., 1833)

Calendar of State Papers, Domestic Series 1640–1683.

CHENEVIX TRENCH, C., *The Western Rising* (1969).

CHRISTIE, W. D., *Life of 1st Earl of Shaftesbury* (1871).

CLARENDON, EDWARD HYDE, 1ST EARL OF, *History of the Rebellion & Civil Wars in England, 1641–60* (1707).

CRANSTON, MAURICE, *John Locke* (1957).

D'OYLEY, ELIZABETH, *James, Duke of Monmouth* (1938).

DRYDEN, JOHN, Collected Works.

EVELYN, JOHN, *Diary*.

FOXCROFT, H. C., *Life and Letters of Halifax* (1898).

GREY, ANCHITELL, *Debates of the House of Commons 1667 1694*, 10 vols. (1769).

HALEY, K. H. D., *The first Earl of Shaftesbury* (Oxford, 1968).

HUTCHINSON, LUCY, *Memoirs of Colonel Hutchinson &c.* (1806).

KENYON, J. P., *The Popish Plot* (1972). *The Stuarts: studies in English Kingship* (1958). *Robert Spencer, Earl of Sutherland* (1958).

LOCKE, JOHN, Collected Works.

NORTH, ROGER, *Examen* (1740).

OGG, DAVID, *England in the Reign of Charles II* (1952).

PEPYS, SAMUEL, *Diary*.

STRINGER, T., *Memoir* (see Christie) (1946).

TRAILL, H. D., *Shaftesbury* (1886).

TREVELYAN, G. M., *England under the Stuarts* (1904).

TURNER, F. C., *James II* (1948).

WEDGWOOD, C. V., *The Great Rebellion* Vol. 2. *The King's War 1641–47* (1958).

Sir William Temple

ASHLEY, MAURICE, *Charles II, the man and the statesman* (1971).

BAXTER, S. B., *William III* (1966).

BURNET, GILBERT, *History of my own Time and Supplement* (2nd ed., 1833).

CECIL, DAVID, *Two Quiet Lives* (1948).

EVELYN, JOHN, *Diary*.

GREW, M. E., *William Bentinck & William III* (1924).

HALEY, K. H. D., *William of Orange and the English Opposition, 1672–74* (1953).

LONGE, J. G. (ed.), *Martha Lady Giffard, her life and correspondence* (1911).

MOORE SMITH, G. C. (ed.), *The early essays & romances, with life &c of Sir William Temple by Lady Giffard* (1930).

MURRY, J. M., *Swift* (British Council: Writers & their Work, 1955).

OGG, DAVID, *England in the Reign of Charles II* (1952). *England in the Reigns of James II & William III* (1955).

OSBORNE, DOROTHY, LADY TEMPLE, *Letters to Sir W. Temple, 1652–4* (Everyman ed., 1914).

ROBB, N. A., *William of Orange: a personal portrait* (1966).

SAINT-SIMON, DUC DE, *Mémoires* (Pleiade ed., 1951).

SWIFT, JONATHAN, *Journal to Stella*.

TEMPLE, SIR WILLIAM, *Works*. 4 vols. (1770).

WOODBRIDGE, H. E., *Sir William Temple* (New York, 1940).

ZEE, H. & B. VAN DER, *William and Mary* (1973).

Sir John Reresby

ACTON, HAROLD, *The Last Medici* (1932).

ANON., *The Refin'd Courtier* (1678).

ASHLEY, MAURICE, *Charles II, the man and the statesman* (1971).

CHAPMAN, HESTER, *Great Villiers* (1949).

COLLISON-MORLEY, LACY, *Italy after the Renaissance: decadence &c. in 17th cent.* (1930).

HAMILTON, ANTHONY, *Memoirs of the Comte de Gramont* (trans. P. Quennell, 1930).

KENYON, J. P., *The Popish Plot* (1972).

MACAULAY, G. B., *History of England* (1763–83).

OGG, DAVID, *England in the Reigns of James II & William III* (1955).

RERESBY, JOHN, *Memoirs* (ed. A. Browning, Glasgow, 1936).

ROBB, N. A., *William of Orange: a personal portrait* (Vol. II) (1966).

TURNER, F. C., *James II* (1948).

ZEE, H. & B. VAN DER, *William and Mary* (1973).

ASHLEY, MAURICE, *Life in Stuart England* (1964).

BUCCLEUCH MSS, Vols. I & II.

BURNET, GILBERT, *History of my own Time* (2nd ed., 1833).

CHAPMAN, HESTER, *Mary II* (1953). *Great Villiers* (1949).

CHURCHILL, SARAH, 1ST DUCHESS OF MARLBOROUGH, *Memoirs* (ed. W. King, 1930).

CLARKE, J. S., *Life of James II* (1816).

COLLINS, ARTHUR, *The Peerage of England* (Vol. IV) (5th ed., 1779).

COXE, A., Shrewsbury MSS (1806).

GREEN, P., *Queen Anne* (1970).

HAMILTON, ANTHONY, *Memoirs of the Comte de Gramont* (trans. P. Quennell, 1930).

KENYON, J. P., *The Stuarts: studies in English Kingship* (1958).

MACAULAY, G. B., *History of England* (1763–83).

OGG, DAVID, *England in the Reigns of James II & William III* (1955).

ROBB, N. A., *William of Orange: a personal portrait* (Vol. II) (1966).

SAINT-SIMON, DUC DE, *Mémoires* (Pleiade ed., 1951).

SWIFT, JONATHAN, *Journal to Stella*

TREVELYAN, G. M., *England under the Stuarts* (1904). *England under Queen Anne* 3 vols. 1930–4.

TURBERVILLE AND NICHOLSON, *Charles Talbot, Duke of Shrewsbury* (1930).

ZEE, H. & B. VAN DER, *William and Mary* (1973).

Index

Shrewsbury Charles—*Cont.*
and marriage, 270–3; return to England, 274; refusal to take office, 276; in Harley group, 277, 280; Lord Chamberlain, 279, 280; peace proposals to France, 280, 281, 282; Lord-Lieutenant of Ireland, 282–3; principal Regent after Anne's death, 283; retirement, 284–5; illness and death, 285–6
Shrewsbury, Gilbert, thirteenth Earl of, 287
Shrewsbury, George, fourteenth Earl of, 287
Sidney, Algernon, 59, 71, 77, 137, 149–150
Sidney, Lady Dorothy, 86
Sidney, Henry, 134, 136, 140, 150, 171, 242, 246
Somerset, Charles Seymour, sixth Duke of, 206, 233
Southampton, Thomas Wriothesley, fourth Earl of, 25, 32, 36, 37
Southwell, Sir Robert, 143
Spencer, Sir Thomas, 158
Spiller, Sir Harry, 20
Stafford, William Howard, Viscount, 59
Strafford, Lady, 280
Strangways, Sir John, 21–2, 32
Stringer, Thomas, 42, 46, 47, 50, 57, 80
Sturminster Newton, 22
Sunderland, Henry Spencer, first Earl of, 86
Sunderland, Robert Spencer, second Earl of, 129, 130, 132, 207
Swift, Jonathan, 186, 255, 275, 280, 281, 285; as Temple's secretary, 142, 143–6; ordained in Ireland, 146; return to Temple's service, 148–9, 150; obituary of Temple, 150
Swift, Thomas, 145, 146
Sydenham, Dr Thomas, 40
Sylvius, Sir Gabriel, 118

Talbot, Sir John (uncle of Shrewsbury), 226–7, 229, 230, 232, 233, 234, 235, 273
Talbot, John (brother of Shrewsbury), 224, 239
Talbot, William, Bishop of Salisbury, 286
Taunton, 22, 195
Temple, Diana, 101, 110, 127–8, 129, 143

Temple, James, 85
Temple, Sir John (father of Sir William), 85, 86, 88, 90, 92, 94, 96, 97, 98, 99, 129
Temple, Mary Hammond, Lady (mother), 85
Temple, John (brother), 85
Temple, John (son), 99, 100, 101, 110, 127, 139; diplomatic career, 136, 140; marriage, 137, 138; suicide, 140–1, 150
Temple, Mrs John, 137, 138, 140, 141
Temple, Martha—*see* Giffard, Lady
Temple, Martha Jane, 149
Temple, Sir William: ancestry and birth, 85; education, 86; meets Dorothy Osborne, 87; mutual love, 88; letters and meetings, 88, 89–91, 92–7; opposition to marriage, 90, 91, 92, 93–94; tastes and interests, 95–6; translations and essays, 95, 99, 110, 146, 147; marriage, 97; birth of son and loss of five other children, 99, 100, 101, 128; in Ireland, 99; life at Sheen, 100; unsuccessful mission to Münster, 100–101; envoy at Brussels, 101; friendship with William of Orange, 103–4, 114, 115, 128, 145; achieves Triple Alliance, 103, 107; admiration for Dutch Republic, 104–5; Ambassador at Hague, 106–8; frustration, 106–7; retirement at Sheen, 109–10; judgements on literature and arts, 109, 149–150; studies, 110; ambitions for son, 110, 127, 136, 140; again Ambassador at Hague, 112–23, 128; peace efforts, 112–13, 116, 118, 119, 120, 124, 125; negotiates marriage of William and Mary, 118–19, 121, 122–3; refuses Secretaryship of State, 121, 125, 129, 140, 145; disgust at corrupt policies, 121, 125–6; alleged dullness and priggishness, 126–7; anecdotal vein, 127; as family man, 127–30, 136, 137, 138–9; plan for new Privy Council, 129–30; hostility to Shaftesbury, 130–131, 132; fears French domination, 131, 132; tolerance towards Catholicism, 131, 132; and problem of succession, 131, 133; diminished influence, 133–4; dismissed from Council, 134; withdrawal from politics, 134–5, 136; writes memoirs, 136, 137–8, 142; retirement at Moor Park,